MICROSOFT POWER PLATFORM DEVELOPER

MASTER THE EXAM (PL-400): 10 PRACTICE TESTS, 500 RIGOROUS EXAM QUESTIONS, SOLID FOUNDATIONS, GAIN WEALTH OF INSIGHTS, EXPERT EXPLANATIONS AND ONE ULTIMATE GOAL

ANAND M
AMEENA PUBLICATIONS

Copyright © 2024 ANAND M
All rights reserved.
ISBN: 9798323289257

DEDICATION

To the Visionaries in My Professional Odyssey

This book is dedicated to the mentors and leaders who guided me through triumph and adversity in my professional universe. Your guidance has illuminated the path to success and taught me to seize opportunities and surmount obstacles. Thank you for imparting the advice to those who taught me the value of strategic thinking and the significance of innovation to transform obstacles into stepping stones. Your visionary leadership has inspired my creativity and motivated me to forge new paths.

Thank you for sharing the best and worst of your experiences with me, kind and severe employers. As I present this book to the world, I am aware that you have been my inspiration. All of your roles as mentors, advisors, and even occasional adversaries have helped me become a better professional and storyteller.

This dedication is a tribute to your impact on my journey, a narrative woven with threads of gratitude, introspection, and profound gratitude for the lessons you've inscribed into my story.

With deep gratitude and enduring respect,
Anand M

FROM TECH TO LIFE SKILLS – MY EBOOKS COLLECTION

Dive into my rich collection of eBooks, curated meticulously across diverse and essential domains.

Pro Tips and Tricks Series: Empower yourself with life-enhancing skills and professional essentials with our well-crafted guides.

Hot IT Certifications and Tech Series: Stay ahead in the tech game. Whether you're eyeing certifications in AWS, PMP, or prompt engineering, harnessing the power of ChatGPT with tools like Excel, PowerPoint, Word, and more!, we've got you covered!

Essential Life Skills: Embark on a journey within. From yoga to holistic well-being, Master the art of culinary, baking, and more delve deep and rediscover yourself.

Stay Updated & Engaged

For an entire world of my knowledge, tips, and treasures, follow me on Amazon

https://www.amazon.com/author/anandm

Your Feedback Matters!

Your support, feedback, and ratings are the wind beneath my wings. It drives me to curate content that brings immense value to every aspect of life. Please take a moment to share your thoughts and rate the books. Together, let's keep the flame of knowledge burning bright!

Best Regards,

ANAND M

INTRODUCTION

Embark on your journey to mastering the **Microsoft Power Platform Developer exam (PL-400)** with "Master the Exam: Microsoft Power Platform Developer". This essential guide is designed for both seasoned Power Platform professionals and novices alike, transforming your exam preparation into a profound learning experience. It features 10 meticulously designed practice tests containing 500 rigorous exam questions, each crafted to deepen your understanding and expertise in Power Platform development.

Achieving the Microsoft Power Platform Developer certification marks a significant milestone in your career. It signifies comprehensive knowledge and adeptness in Microsoft's Power Platform capabilities. This book is an indispensable resource for anyone aspiring to excel in this dynamic field. It guides you through the complexities of Power Platform development, ensuring your preparation extends beyond just passing the exam to gaining a wealth of insights into practical applications.
In the ever-evolving realm of business applications and automation, the Microsoft Power Platform Developer credential is a testament to your expertise and skills in this cutting-edge area. Highly esteemed in the industry, this certification opens doors to numerous career opportunities and advancements.

As you delve into this book, here are the key details about the Microsoft Power Platform Developer exam:
Level: Associate
Length: The exam is 180 minutes long, offering ample time to demonstrate your Power Platform development acumen.
Cost: The exam fee is detailed on the official Microsoft website.
Format: The exam comprises various question types, testing both your practical abilities and theoretical knowledge in developing solutions using the Power Platform.
Delivery Method: The exam is available at authorized testing centers or as an online proctored exam, providing flexibility and convenience.

Each question in this book is accompanied by expert explanations, clarifying intricate topics and providing valuable insights. Our aim is to navigate you through the Power Platform development landscape, ensuring a well-rounded and comprehensive preparation.

This book is more than just a study guide; it's a companion on your path to Power Platform Developer certification. Whether your goal is to become a developer, a consultant, or to enhance your technical skills within the Power Platform ecosystem, this guide is the cornerstone of your journey to success. Embark on this enriching journey with "Microsoft Power Platform Developer: Master the Exam (PL-400)". Arm yourself with the knowledge, insights, and strategies essential for success in achieving your Microsoft Power Platform Developer certification. Let this book be your guide, lighting your path to excellence in Power Platform development.

ADVANTAGES OF CERTIFICATION

As you embark on the journey to earn the Microsoft Power Platform Developer certification, it's essential to appreciate the multitude of benefits that this prestigious credential brings. This certification is more than a demonstration of your development expertise; it's a key to numerous professional advantages:

Elevated Professional Recognition: In the rapidly evolving fields of business automation and application development, Microsoft Power Platform holds a significant position. Earning the Power Platform Developer certification distinguishes you as an expert in custom business solutions, automation, and app development within the Microsoft ecosystem. It validates your skills in utilizing Power Platform components like Power Apps, Power Automate, and Power BI, thereby enhancing your professional credibility in the tech community.

Career Advancement Opportunities: This certification is a powerful endorsement of your development capabilities. It's a stepping stone for career growth, often leading to more senior roles and better opportunities in the spheres of business application development, automation solutions, and system integration.

Financial Rewards: Achieving specialized certifications like this one is frequently linked to an increase in salary potential. Professionals with the Power Platform Developer certification are often rewarded with higher pay, reflecting the value of their expertise and the investment made in their professional development.

Competitive Edge in the Job Market: In the competitive domain of IT and business solution development, holding the Power Platform Developer certification sets you apart. It aligns you with specialized roles that match your expertise and career goals, making you a sought-after candidate for prestigious positions within organizations seeking to innovate and improve their business processes.

Comprehensive Understanding and Hands-On Expertise: This certification goes beyond theoretical knowledge, placing a strong emphasis on practical, hands-on experience with the Power Platform's tools and services. As a certified Power Platform Developer, you demonstrate not just knowledge, but also proficiency in designing, implementing, and maintaining solutions that optimize business processes and drive success.

In conclusion, the Microsoft Power Platform Developer certification is not just a mere accolade; it's a significant milestone in your career path. It equips you with the skills, knowledge, and connections needed to confidently navigate the complex and dynamic landscape of business application development and automation.

CONTENTS

PRACTICE TEST 1 - QUESTIONS ONLY 8
PRACTICE TEST 1 - ANSWERS ONLY 22
PRACTICE TEST 2 - QUESTIONS ONLY 38
PRACTICE TEST 2 - ANSWERS ONLY 51
PRACTICE TEST 3 - QUESTIONS ONLY 68
PRACTICE TEST 3 - ANSWERS ONLY 81
PRACTICE TEST 4 - QUESTIONS ONLY 98
PRACTICE TEST 4 - ANSWERS ONLY 112
PRACTICE TEST 5 - QUESTIONS ONLY 129
PRACTICE TEST 5 - ANSWERS ONLY 143
PRACTICE TEST 6 - QUESTIONS ONLY 160
PRACTICE TEST 6 - ANSWERS ONLY 174
PRACTICE TEST 7 - QUESTIONS ONLY 190
PRACTICE TEST 7 - ANSWERS ONLY 204
PRACTICE TEST 8 - QUESTIONS ONLY 221
PRACTICE TEST 8 - ANSWERS ONLY 235
PRACTICE TEST 9 - QUESTIONS ONLY 252
PRACTICE TEST 9 - ANSWERS ONLY 265
PRACTICE TEST 10 - QUESTIONS ONLY 282
PRACTICE TEST 10 - ANSWERS ONLY 296
ABOUT THE AUTHOR.. 314

PRACTICE TEST 1 - QUESTIONS ONLY

QUESTION 1

A company is implementing a Power Platform solution for their customer relationship management (CRM) system. They require a monitoring solution that can provide real-time insights into system performance and identify potential issues before they impact users. Additionally, the solution needs to integrate seamlessly with existing Azure resources. Which Azure service is primarily used for collecting, analyzing, and acting on telemetry data from Azure resources in real time?

A) Azure Monitor
B) Log Analytics
C) Azure Application Insights
D) Azure Diagnostics
E) Azure Metrics

QUESTION 2

A manufacturing company is planning to deploy a Power Platform solution to streamline its inventory management process. They need to identify scenarios where out-of-the-box solutions can meet their requirements effectively. Which scenario is best suited for leveraging out-of-the-box functionality?

A) Implementing basic CRUD operations for inventory items
B) Creating complex workflow automation for inventory alerts
C) Integrating with legacy ERP systems for real-time inventory updates
D) Customizing user interface components for advanced reporting
E) Building custom connectors for specialized inventory devices

QUESTION 3

You need to configure an Azure Function triggered by a timer to run a data synchronization task every 5 minutes from 8 AM to 8 PM daily in Microsoft Dataverse. What schedule expression should you use?

A) 0 */5 8-20 * * *
B) */5 8-20 * * *
C) 0 0/5 8-20 * * *
D) 5 8-20 * * *
E) 0 8-20/5 * * *

QUESTION 4

A multinational corporation is deploying a Power Platform solution to manage their global sales operations. They need to implement robust Data Loss Prevention (DLP) policies to prevent sensitive information from being leaked unintentionally.
Which actions should they include in their DLP policies to address this requirement? Select TWO.

A) Monitor and restrict the sharing of customer contact information outside the organization.
B) Allow unrestricted access to financial data within the organization.
C) Enable encryption for all email communications containing proprietary data.

D) Implement role-based access controls for sensitive customer records.
E) Automatically block the export of customer records to Excel files.

QUESTION 5

Given a requirement to optimize a Dataverse plugin for performance, identify the correct code snippet that implements caching within a C# plugin.

A) IOrganizationService service = new OrganizationService(context);

B) service.EnableProxyTypes();

C) IPluginExecutionContext context = (IPluginExecutionContext)serviceProvider.GetService(typeof(IPluginExecutionContext));

D) var serviceFactory = (IOrganizationServiceFactory)serviceProvider.GetService(typeof(IOrganizationServiceFactory)); var service = serviceFactory.CreateOrganizationService(context.UserId); service.CacheMode = OrganizationServiceCacheMode.Enabled;

E) Entity entity = (Entity)context.InputParameters["Target"];

QUESTION 6

You are creating a canvas app for a library management system using Microsoft Dataverse. You need to ensure that only available books are shown in a drop-down list. What PowerFx expression should you apply to the Items property of the drop-down list?

A) Filter('Books', Status = 'Available')
B) Collect('Available Books', Books)
C) Lookup('Books', Status = 'Available')
D) 'Books'
E) Filter('Books', Status.Value = 'Available')

QUESTION 7

A large multinational corporation is restructuring its Dataverse security roles to align with its evolving business processes and regulatory requirements. They need to define role-based access control strategies that ensure efficient data governance and compliance with industry standards.
Which considerations should they include when defining role-based access control strategies? Select THREE.

A) Implement least privilege principle to restrict access based on users' specific job responsibilities.

B) Utilize role hierarchies to simplify role assignment and management across the organization.

C) Define role templates to standardize access permissions for different functional roles within the organization.

D) Enable auditing and logging to track user activities and changes to security roles for accountability.

E) Implement dynamic role assignment based on user attributes and contextual information for fine-grained access control.

QUESTION 8

A multinational corporation is restructuring its business units within Microsoft Dataverse to align with its new organizational hierarchy. They need to understand the structure and purpose of business units to ensure a smooth transition and efficient data management.
What is the structure and purpose of business units in Microsoft Dataverse?

A) Business units represent logical containers for users, teams, and resources, facilitating access control and data segmentation based on organizational hierarchies.

B) Business units define geographical regions for data localization and compliance with regional regulations and data residency requirements.

C) Business units establish data silos for isolating sensitive information and preventing unauthorized access across different departments or functional areas.

D) Business units enable integration with external systems and third-party applications through standardized APIs and data exchange protocols.

E) Business units support role-based access control (RBAC) to assign granular permissions and privileges to users, ensuring data security and governance.

QUESTION 9

You are developing a solution for a company that requires complex data validations in Microsoft Dataverse. One of the requirements is to ensure that a field cannot be blank upon record creation. However, during testing, users can save records without filling in this required field. Which of the following could be potential reasons for this issue? Select the correct answers that apply.

A) The field's "Required" property is not set to "Yes" in the Dataverse table schema.

B) There is a JavaScript function overriding the default behavior of the field's required validation.

C) The user's security role does not have the necessary privileges to enforce field requirements.

D) The Dataverse environment is in a "sandbox" mode, allowing for bypassing of required field validations.

E) The field's data type is not compatible with the "Required" property settings.

QUESTION 10

You are tasked with enhancing a customer relationship management (CRM) system using Microsoft Dataverse. Your objective is to implement a security model that restricts access to sensitive customer data. Which of the following code snippets correctly configures a new security role using PowerFx?

A) Set(UserRole, NewRole({Name: "Sensitive Data Access", Permissions: {Read: 'All', Write: 'None'}}))

B) Patch(SecurityRoles, Defaults(SecurityRoles), {Title: "Sensitive Data Access", Permissions: JSON({Read: 'None', Write: 'All'})})

C) UserRole.Add("Sensitive Data Access", JSON({Read: 'All', Write: 'None'}))

D) New SecurityRole { Name = "Sensitive Data Access", ReadPermission = PermissionLevels.All,

WritePermission = PermissionLevels.None }

E) Patch(SecurityRoles, New SecurityRole {Name: "Sensitive Data Access", ReadPermission: 'All', WritePermission: 'None'})

QUESTION 11

A multinational corporation is implementing a customer relationship management (CRM) system using Microsoft Dataverse. They need to establish relationships between various entities to ensure seamless data interaction. Additionally, they want to enforce referential integrity to maintain data consistency. Which action aligns with enforcing referential integrity in Dataverse relationships?

A) Enable cascade delete for parent-child relationships
B) Configure Many-to-Many relationships for data normalization
C) Implement rollup fields for aggregated data calculations
D) Utilize connection roles for entity association
E) Set up alternate keys for unique identifiers

QUESTION 12

Your organization has a complex Microsoft Power Platform environment with multiple interconnected solutions deployed. Recently, a new requirement emerged to introduce enhancements to one of the existing solutions without disrupting the functionality of other solutions. However, you need to ensure that the deployed changes do not overwrite customizations made by users in the environment. What action should you take to meet these requirements effectively?

A) Create
B) Update
C) Upgrade
D) Patch

QUESTION 13

A multinational corporation is implementing a new Microsoft Power Platform solution to streamline its global operations. They need to import and export solutions between different environments efficiently. What are the recommended procedures for importing and exporting solutions in Microsoft Dataverse?

A) Use Power Platform Admin Center for manual import/export
B) Utilize Power Platform Build Tools for automated import/export
C) Develop custom PowerShell scripts for solution transfer
D) Leverage third-party tools for cross-environment solution transfer
E) Perform manual solution export from source environment and import into target environment

QUESTION 14

A large organization is planning to develop a model-driven app using Microsoft Power Platform to streamline their customer relationship management processes. What are the essential steps to create a model-driven app in Power Apps? Select the correct answers that apply.

A) Define entities and relationships in Dataverse

B) Configure form views and dashboards for user interaction
C) Implement business logic using Power Automate flows
D) Customize the app interface with responsive design elements
E) Deploy the app to various environments for testing and production

QUESTION 15

You are customizing a form in a model-driven app for a healthcare organization's patient management system. The app aims to optimize data entry efficiency and ensure regulatory compliance. What are two actions that you can perform by using a business rule in this scenario? Select the correct answers that apply.

A) Access external data.
B) Enable or disable a column based on patient status.
C) Show or hide a column based on user role.
D) Run the rule on demand.

QUESTION 16

A large retail company is developing a Power App to manage inventory across multiple stores. They want to enhance the app's functionality by integrating custom JavaScript code. What are potential benefits of integrating JavaScript into the Power App? Select the correct answers that apply.

A) Access to browser APIs for advanced functionality
B) Seamless integration with external databases and APIs
C) Improved performance through client-side processing
D) Enhanced security features for user authentication
E) Simplified data visualization using third-party libraries

QUESTION 17

A retail company wants to develop a Power App to automate their inventory management process. They need to write advanced Power Fx formulas to calculate inventory turnover ratios and identify slow-moving items. Which scenario represents a use case for complex Power Fx formulas in this context? Select the correct answers that apply.

A) Calculating the ratio of sales to average inventory for each product
B) Identifying products with a turnover ratio below a certain threshold for reordering
C) Extracting historical sales data from external sources for trend analysis
D) Calculating the total value of inventory based on current market prices
E) Generating reports on inventory turnover trends over time

QUESTION 18

You are developing a model-driven app for a sales team's lead management system. The app requires executing custom code when a user selects a button on the ribbon. However, only specific users with administrative privileges should be able to run this code. What should you use to achieve this requirement?

A) Custom API
B) Custom process action
C) Classic workflow
D) Business rule

QUESTION 19

A large retail chain is experiencing performance issues with their Power Apps-based inventory management system. Which tool or feature should the development team primarily use to troubleshoot and diagnose the root cause of the problem?

A) Azure Monitor
B) Log Analytics
C) Power Apps Monitor
D) Performance Metrics Dashboard
E) Application Insights

QUESTION 20

Design a Canvas app where data must be pre-loaded upon application start to enhance user experience. Which PowerFx script effectively achieves this?

A) LoadData('ProductInfo', 'SELECT * FROM Products', true)
B) ClearCollect(ProductCache, Products)
C) Collect(ProductCache, LookUp(Products, true))
D) Set(ProductCache, Filter(Products, IsActive = true))
E) ClearCollect(ProductCache, Filter(Products, IsActive = true))

QUESTION 21

You are developing a canvas app for a project management system. The app requires implementing a custom visual to display project timelines. However, you need to ensure that the visual is highly interactive and responsive. Which approach should you use? Select the correct answers that apply.

A) Client scripting
B) Power Apps component framework code component
C) Web API
D) Liquid template

QUESTION 22

A Power Apps developer needs to enhance a custom form with dynamic behavior based on user interactions. Which of the following represents a common use case for JavaScript with the Client API in this scenario?

A) Validate form input before submission
B) Trigger notifications for specific field changes
C) Populate form fields with data from external APIs
D) Implement conditional visibility for form sections

E) Calculate and display real-time analytics within the form

QUESTION 23

A Power Apps developer is tasked with creating client scripts to interact with Dataverse Web API for a custom canvas app. Which of the following represents a correct step-by-step approach to creating scripts using Dataverse Web API?

A) Obtain client credentials from Azure Active Directory
B) Authenticate with Dataverse Web API using OAuth 2.0
C) Retrieve an access token using client credentials grant flow
D) Make HTTP requests to Dataverse Web API endpoints
E) Handle authentication errors and refresh access tokens as needed

QUESTION 24

Your organization is implementing a project management solution using Microsoft Dataverse. You need to integrate an external project tracking system, which exposes a RESTful Web API, to synchronize project data within the solution. Considering the integration requirements, which three options should you utilize to ensure an effective integration solution? Select the correct answers that apply.

A) Azure function
B) Custom connector
C) Custom API
D) HTTP request
E) Business rule

QUESTION 25

You are tasked with initializing a new PCF (Power Apps Component Framework) component for a model-driven app. Which TypeScript snippet correctly sets up the component to interact with the Dataverse?

A) public init(context: ComponentFramework.Context<IInputs>): void { this.context = context; }
B) constructor(private context: ComponentFramework.Context<IInputs>) {}
C) initializeComponent(context: ComponentFramework.Context<IInputs>) { this._context = context; }
D) function init(context: ComponentFramework.Context<IInputs>) { this.context = context; }
E) init(context: ComponentFramework.Context<IInputs>) => { this.context = context; }

QUESTION 26

A Power Apps developer is tasked with implementing a custom interface for a PCF component. Which interface is commonly used for data input and validation in Power Apps?

A) IInputParameter
B) IContext
C) IEntityForm
D) IDataSet
E) IStandardControlProps

QUESTION 27

Your organization is developing a canvas app for managing customer feedback. You need to implement a feature that allows users to submit feedback forms with attachments. Which integration option should you choose to achieve this requirement? Select the correct answers that apply.

A) Custom API
B) Power Automate flow
C) Azure Logic Apps
D) Power Apps custom control

QUESTION 28

A Power Apps developer is tasked with retrieving data from an external API and displaying it within a PCF component. Which method allows the developer to make authenticated requests to the Web API from the PCF component?

A) OAuth 2.0 authorization
B) Basic authentication
C) API key authentication
D) Client certificate authentication
E) Windows authentication

QUESTION 29

A company is implementing a complex business process in their Power Apps environment and needs to understand the stages of the plug-in execution pipeline for customization. Which of the following accurately describes the stages of the plug-in execution pipeline?

A) Pre-validation, Pre-operation, Post-operation, Post-validation
B) Pre-validation, Pre-operation, Main operation, Post-operation, Post-validation
C) Pre-operation, Main operation, Post-operation, Pre-validation, Post-validation
D) Pre-validation, Main operation, Post-operation, Pre-operation, Post-validation
E) Pre-operation, Main operation, Pre-validation, Post-validation, Post-operation

QUESTION 30

Your organization is migrating data from an external SQL Server database to Microsoft Dataverse tables using Azure Data Factory pipelines. As part of the migration process, you need to ensure that data integrity is maintained, and any errors encountered during the migration are captured for review and resolution. What are two recommended strategies to achieve this goal? Select the correct answers that apply.

A) Implement row-level error handling in Azure Data Factory pipelines to capture and log records with data integrity violations.

B) Utilize SQL Server Integration Services (SSIS) to perform data validation checks before transferring data to Dataverse tables.

C) Enable Change Tracking on the SQL Server database to track modifications and ensure synchronization with Dataverse tables.

D) Configure Azure Data Factory pipelines to retry failed data transfer operations with exponential backoff and jitter.

QUESTION 31

A development team is implementing plug-ins in their Power Platform solution and needs to understand the overview of the Organization service. Which statement best describes the Organization service in plug-ins?

A) It provides direct access to the database tables for performing CRUD operations.
B) The service allows plug-ins to interact with Microsoft Dataverse using a set of APIs.
C) It is a web service that enables integration with external systems and services.
D) The service facilitates user authentication and authorization within plug-ins.
E) It offers real-time monitoring and logging capabilities for plug-in executions.

QUESTION 32

A team of Power Platform developers needs to configure a Custom API message in Dataverse. Which step is essential for configuring a Custom API?

A) Defining the authentication method.
B) Creating a new custom connector.
C) Generating an API key for authorization.
D) Specifying the request and response schema.
E) Selecting the target environment for deployment.

QUESTION 33

You are configuring a canvas app to display order details retrieved from Microsoft Dataverse. The order records contain a lookup field to the "Products" entity. You need to ensure that the canvas app displays the name of the associated product for each order. What attribute should you include in your canvas app to display the product's name?

A) _product_name
B) _productid_name
C) _product_name_value
D) _productid_value

QUESTION 34

A company is developing a Power Platform solution that integrates with multiple external systems through REST APIs. The security team has highlighted the importance of implementing robust security protocols for these APIs. Which security protocol is commonly used to secure REST APIs?

A) Basic Authentication
B) Digest Authentication
C) OAuth 2.0
D) JWT Authentication
E) NTLM Authentication

QUESTION 35

How can you import and utilize an OpenAPI definition to create custom connectors in Power Platform?

A) PowerAppsAdminCenter > Data > Custom Connectors > Import OpenAPI
B) PowerAutomate > Data > Gateways > Add OpenAPI Specification
C) PowerApps > Custom Connectors > New Custom Connector > Import an OpenAPI file
D) PowerApps > Data > Entities > Import OpenAPI Definition
E) PowerApps > Connectors > Create new connector > Import from OpenAPI

QUESTION 36

A JavaScript routine needs to query multiple records from a dataset in Microsoft Power Platform for reporting purposes. What is the most suitable HTTP method to use for this Web API call?

A) GET
B) POST
C) PUT
D) DELETE
E) PATCH

QUESTION 37

A company is developing a Power Platform solution that requires interacting with Dataverse entities using the Web API. Which HTTP methods are commonly used for CRUD operations via the Web API?

A) GET, POST, PATCH, DELETE
B) PUT, DELETE, PATCH, OPTIONS
C) GET, POST, PUT, PATCH
D) POST, PUT, DELETE, OPTIONS
E) GET, PUT, DELETE, OPTIONS

QUESTION 38

A company is developing a Power Platform solution that integrates with external APIs, occasionally encountering rate limits and API throttling. Which of the following best describes the purpose of defining and configuring retry policies in this scenario?

A) To bypass rate limits by retrying failed requests immediately
B) To avoid exceeding API usage quotas by adjusting request frequency
C) To minimize network latency by retrying requests with exponential backoff
D) To enforce a maximum retry count and interval for failed requests
E) To prioritize certain types of requests over others based on urgency

QUESTION 39

For a utility company automating bill adjustments, how should a Power Automate cloud flow be set up to handle scenarios where the billing API times out? Select the correct answers that apply.

A) Add a retry mechanism

B) Implement a "run after" condition for timeouts
C) Send an email alert for each API call
D) Log the timeout in a database
E) Notify the billing department upon timeout

QUESTION 40

A healthcare provider uses Azure Functions to process patient data from multiple sources in real-time. The function must trigger whenever new data arrives in the Azure Event Hub. The task is to write a function that optimizes the processing of these data streams while ensuring compliance with HIPAA security requirements.

A) JavaScript: context.bindings.inputData = eventHubMessage;

B) C#: public static void Run([EventHubTrigger("samples-workitems", Connection = "EventHubConnectionAppSetting")] string myEventHubMessage, ILogger log)

C) TypeScript: const eventProcessor = EventProcessorClient(EventHubConsumerClient.defaultConsumerGroupName, client, processEvents, processError, options);

D) JSON: { "bindings": [{ "type": "eventHubTrigger", "name": "eventData", "connection": "EventHubConnection", "direction": "in"}] }

E) C#: public static void ProcessData([EventHubTrigger("data-stream", Connection = "AzureEventHubConnection")] string inputData, ILogger log)

QUESTION 41

A company is implementing a Power Platform solution to automate invoice approval processes. Which step is essential in creating and configuring a cloud flow for this scenario?

A) Defining triggers based on user input
B) Specifying conditional logic for approval routing
C) Configuring data connections for accessing invoice data
D) Implementing error handling mechanisms for failed approvals
E) Setting up notifications for stakeholders

QUESTION 42

A Power Automate flow should trigger when a document added to a SharePoint library requires immediate legal review because its "Sensitive" field is set to true. What expressions should you use? Select the correct answers that apply.

A) @equals(triggerBody()?['Sensitive'], true)
B) @not(empty(triggerBody()?['Sensitive']))
C) @contains(triggerBody()?['Title'], 'Urgent')
D) @greater(triggerBody()?['Sensitive'], 0)
E) @and(equals(triggerBody()?['Sensitive'], true), contains(triggerBody()?['Title'], 'Legal'))

QUESTION 43

A multinational corporation is developing a Power Platform solution to manage sensitive customer data, including API keys and database connection strings. They need to ensure that this information is securely stored and accessed within their cloud flows. What technique should they utilize to integrate Azure Key Vault for managing secrets effectively?

A) Storing secrets directly within flow configurations
B) Utilizing custom encryption algorithms for secret storage
C) Implementing Azure Key Vault connectors within flows
D) Encoding secrets using base64 encoding before storage
E) Utilizing SharePoint lists for secret management

QUESTION 44

A multinational logistics company is streamlining its shipment tracking process using the Power Platform. They want to incorporate cloud flow steps into their existing business process flows to automate status updates and notifications for customers. What is a key consideration for integrating cloud flow steps into business process flows in this scenario?

A) Ensuring compatibility with legacy systems for seamless data exchange
B) Customizing flow steps to handle specific business logic and requirements
C) Minimizing latency by optimizing data transfer between flows and processes
D) Implementing comprehensive error handling mechanisms for fault tolerance
E) Utilizing dynamic expressions to dynamically configure flow actions

QUESTION 45

For integrating a custom connector in Power Platform with a document management system that requires document-specific tokens for authentication, which authentication type should you configure?

A) OAuth 2.0
B) API key
C) Dynamic token
D) Single sign-on
E) Password based

QUESTION 46

A multinational corporation is developing a Power Platform solution to streamline its supply chain management. They need to publish Dataverse events using the IServiceEndpointNotificationService to trigger downstream processes in real-time. What are the key steps involved in publishing an event using IServiceEndpointNotificationService?

A) Registering a service endpoint with Azure Event Grid and configuring event subscriptions

B) Implementing custom code to define event triggers and handlers for IServiceEndpointNotificationService

C) Configuring event publishing settings in Power Automate to invoke IServiceEndpointNotificationService

D) Generating an event schema and defining event properties for IServiceEndpointNotificationService

E) Deploying a custom plugin to the Dataverse environment to enable event publication through IServiceEndpointNotificationService

QUESTION 47

A retail company is developing a Power Platform solution to streamline inventory management across multiple stores. They need to register different types of service endpoints to integrate with their inventory tracking system and notify store managers about low stock levels. What are the essential steps to register different types of service endpoints for this scenario? Select the correct answers that apply.

A) Registering a webhook endpoint for real-time notifications
B) Configuring an Azure Service Bus endpoint for reliable message delivery
C) Setting up an Azure Event Hub for high-throughput event ingestion
D) Creating a custom HTTP endpoint for external system integration
E) Configuring OAuth authentication for secure endpoint access

QUESTION 48

When retrieving data from a specific Microsoft Dataverse entity using Web API and you need to include related entity data, what query option should you use?

A) $expand
B) $select
C) $filter
D) $lookup
E) $include

QUESTION 49

A retail company is developing a Power Platform solution to manage product inventory across multiple warehouses. They need to ensure data integrity and enforce uniqueness for product codes. How can they achieve this using alternate keys in Dataverse? Select the correct answers that apply.

A) Defining an alternate key on the product entity with the product code attribute as the unique identifier.

B) Creating a custom validation rule in Power Apps to check for duplicate product codes before saving records.

C) Utilizing JavaScript functions to enforce uniqueness constraints for product codes on the client-side.
D) Implementing a plugin or custom workflow in Dataverse to validate product codes and prevent duplicates.

E) Setting up a scheduled Power Automate flow to check for duplicate product codes and notify administrators.

QUESTION 50

A healthcare organization is integrating patient data from various sources into Microsoft Dataverse for comprehensive patient management. They encounter challenges due to the complexity of the data sets, including different data formats and structures. Which technique would be most effective for integrating such complex data sets?

A) Implementing custom data connectors for each data source to handle data transformation.
B) Using Azure Data Factory to orchestrate ETL processes and automate data integration workflows.
C) Developing custom scripts in Microsoft Power Automate to manipulate and synchronize data.
D) Leveraging Azure Logic Apps to trigger data integration tasks based on predefined conditions.
E) Utilizing Microsoft Power Query to standardize and clean the data before importing it into Dataverse.

PRACTICE TEST 1 - ANSWERS ONLY

QUESTION 1

Answer - [A) Azure Monitor]

A) Azure Monitor - Azure Monitor is the correct answer as it is specifically designed for collecting, analyzing, and acting on telemetry data from Azure resources in real time, aligning with the scenario requirements.

B) Log Analytics - Log Analytics focuses more on log management rather than real-time telemetry data analysis.

C) Azure Application Insights - While Application Insights is useful for application performance monitoring, it does not primarily focus on real-time telemetry data from Azure resources.

D) Azure Diagnostics - Azure Diagnostics provides diagnostic data from Azure resources but may not offer real-time insights and analysis.

E) Azure Metrics - Azure Metrics provides basic monitoring data but may not offer the detailed telemetry analysis required in real time.

QUESTION 2

Answer - [A) Implementing basic CRUD operations for inventory items]

A) Implementing basic CRUD operations for inventory items - Basic Create, Read, Update, and Delete (CRUD) operations are well-supported by out-of-the-box features in Power Platform, making it suitable for this scenario.

B) Creating complex workflow automation for inventory alerts - Complex workflow automation may require custom development beyond out-of-the-box capabilities.

C) Integrating with legacy ERP systems for real-time inventory updates - Integration with legacy systems often necessitates custom development to meet specific requirements.

D) Customizing user interface components for advanced reporting - Advanced customization of UI components typically requires custom development.

E) Building custom connectors for specialized inventory devices - Building custom connectors is a form of custom development and not considered out-of-the-box functionality.

QUESTION 3

Answer - A) 0 */5 8-20 * * *

A) Correct. Triggers every 5 minutes from 8 AM to 8 PM.
B) Incorrect. This expression lacks the precise minute setting required.
C) Incorrect. Incorrect format for specifying minutes.
D) Incorrect. This expression is formatted incorrectly and does not specify a range.
E) Incorrect. Incorrect use of the slash for minute intervals in the cron expression.

QUESTION 4

Answer - A and E) Monitor and restrict the sharing of customer contact information outside the organization. Automatically block the export of customer records to Excel files.

A) - Correct. Monitoring and restricting the sharing of customer contact information outside the organization aligns with the objective of preventing sensitive information leakage.

B) - Incorrect. Allowing unrestricted access to financial data contradicts the goal of implementing DLP policies.

C) - Incorrect. While encryption enhances security, it may not directly address the specific requirement of preventing unintentional data leaks.

D) - Incorrect. Role-based access controls are important but may not directly prevent sensitive information leakage outside the organization.

E) - Correct. Automatically blocking the export of customer records to Excel files helps enforce data protection measures against unauthorized data transfer.

QUESTION 5

Answer - D

Option A - Incorrect. This line initializes the service but does not implement caching.
Option B - Incorrect. This method enables early bound types, not caching.
Option C - Incorrect. Retrieves the execution context but doesn't enable caching.
Option D - Correct. This snippet correctly initializes the Organization service with caching enabled, optimizing performance.
Option E - Incorrect. Retrieves an entity from the context but doesn't relate to performance optimization.

QUESTION 6

Answer - A) Filter('Books', Status = 'Available')

A) Correct. Filters the Books data source to only include those with a status of 'Available'.
B) Incorrect. Collect creates a new collection but does not filter the items for the drop-down list.
C) Incorrect. Lookup is used to find a single record, not to filter a list.
D) Incorrect. This would include all books, regardless of availability.
E) Incorrect. The syntax for accessing the Status field should not include .Value in this context.

QUESTION 7

Answer - A, C, and E) Implement least privilege principle to restrict access based on users' specific job responsibilities. Define role templates to standardize access permissions for different functional roles within the organization. Implement dynamic role assignment based on user attributes and contextual information for fine-grained access control.

A) - Correct. Implementing the least privilege principle ensures that users have access only to the resources necessary for their specific job responsibilities, enhancing data security and minimizing the risk of unauthorized access.

B) - Incorrect. Role hierarchies may complicate role assignment and management, especially in large organizations, and may not align with the principle of least privilege.

C) - Correct. Defining role templates helps standardize access permissions for different functional roles, streamlining role assignment and ensuring consistency across the organization.

D) - Incorrect. While auditing and logging are important for accountability, they are not directly related to defining role-based access control strategies.

E) - Correct. Implementing dynamic role assignment based on user attributes enables fine-grained access control and adapts access permissions based on changing user contexts, enhancing security and flexibility.

QUESTION 8

Answer - A) Business units represent logical containers for users, teams, and resources, facilitating access control and data segmentation based on organizational hierarchies.

A) - Correct. Business units in Microsoft Dataverse serve as logical containers that help organize users, teams, and resources, enabling efficient access control and data segmentation aligned with organizational hierarchies.

B) - Incorrect. While business units may impact data localization, their primary purpose is to organize users and resources, not define geographical regions for compliance purposes.

C) - Incorrect. While business units may contribute to data segmentation, their primary purpose is not to establish data silos but to facilitate organizational hierarchy and access control.

D) - Incorrect. While business units may support integration, their primary purpose is not to enable integration with external systems but to organize internal resources.

E) - Incorrect. While business units may support RBAC, their primary purpose is not to enforce access control mechanisms but to organize users and resources within Dataverse.

QUESTION 9

Answer - [C] and [E].

A) The "Required" property being unset would prevent the field from being mandatory.

B) JavaScript functions typically enhance, rather than override, default behaviors.

D) "Sandbox" mode primarily affects testing environments, not validation rules.

C) Without the necessary privileges, users cannot be enforced to fill in required fields.

E) Incompatible data types may lead to issues with validation settings.

QUESTION 10

Answer - B

Option A - Incorrect: The syntax does not match PowerFx standards for defining roles.

Option B - Correct: This syntax correctly uses PowerFx to patch a new security role into the

SecurityRoles table.

Option C - Incorrect: This uses an undefined method and incorrect syntax for JSON object definition.

Option D - Incorrect: This appears to be C# syntax which is not applicable in PowerFx context.

Option E - Incorrect: This mixes PowerFx and C# syntax improperly.

QUESTION 11

Answer - [A] Enable cascade delete for parent-child relationships

Option A is correct as enabling cascade delete ensures that when a parent record is deleted, related child records are also deleted, maintaining referential integrity.

Option B is incorrect as Many-to-Many relationships are not directly related to enforcing referential integrity but rather to establishing associations between records.

Option C is incorrect as rollup fields are used for data aggregation, not for enforcing referential integrity.

Option D is incorrect as connection roles are used to define relationships between records, not to enforce referential integrity.

Option E is incorrect as alternate keys are used for identifying unique records, not for enforcing referential integrity.

QUESTION 12

Answer - [D] Patch.

A) Creating a new solution wouldn't prevent overwriting existing customizations and might introduce unnecessary complexity.
B) Updating a solution could potentially overwrite user customizations and impact other interconnected solutions.
C) Upgrading a solution may also lead to overwriting existing customizations and could cause disruptions in other solutions.
D) Patching allows for deploying specific changes without affecting existing customizations or disrupting other solutions.

QUESTION 13

Answer - [B] Utilize Power Platform Build Tools for automated import/export

Option B is correct as utilizing Power Platform Build Tools allows for automated import/export processes, enabling efficient solution transfer between environments while maintaining integrity and consistency.

Option A, C, D, and E may involve manual efforts or third-party dependencies, which could introduce complexities and potential errors during solution transfer.

QUESTION 14

Answer - [A, B, D] Define entities and relationships in Dataverse, Configure form views and dashboards for user interaction, Customize the app interface with responsive design elements

Options A, B, and D are correct as they represent essential steps in creating a model-driven app in Power Apps, including defining data structure, configuring user interfaces, and customizing app design.

Options C and E are incorrect as they do not directly relate to the initial creation process of the model-driven app.

QUESTION 15

Answer - [B] and [C].

A) Business rules cannot directly access external data.

B) Business rules can enable or disable a column dynamically based on patient status, facilitating efficient data entry and compliance with regulations.

C) Business rules can show or hide a column based on user role, ensuring that sensitive information is accessible only to authorized personnel, thereby enhancing data security and compliance.

QUESTION 16

Answer - [A, B, C] Access to browser APIs for advanced functionality, Seamless integration with external databases and APIs, Improved performance through client-side processing

Options A, B, and C are correct as they represent potential benefits of integrating JavaScript into a Power App, including access to browser APIs, seamless integration with external resources, and improved performance through client-side processing.

Options D and E are incorrect because while JavaScript can enhance security and data visualization, these are not direct benefits of integrating JavaScript into a Power App.

QUESTION 17

Answer - [A, B, C, E] Calculating the ratio of sales to average inventory for each product, Identifying products with a turnover ratio below a certain threshold for reordering, Extracting historical sales data from external sources for trend analysis, Generating reports on inventory turnover trends over time

Options A, B, C, and E represent scenarios where complex Power Fx formulas are required to perform calculations, analysis, and reporting related to inventory management.

Option D involves straightforward arithmetic operations and does not necessitate complex formulas.

QUESTION 18

Answer - [B] Custom process action.

A) Custom APIs are typically used for integrating external systems or services with the Power Platform but do not provide user-specific execution control.
B) Custom process actions allow developers to define custom actions that can be executed by specific users, making them suitable for restricting code execution to specific users with administrative privileges. This ensures that only authorized personnel can access and execute the custom code,

maintaining data integrity and security within the lead management system.

C) Classic workflows are automation processes but do not offer the capability to control code execution based on user roles or privileges.

D) Business rules are used for implementing simple business logic within the app's user interface but do not involve executing custom code on the ribbon.

QUESTION 19

Answer - [A] Azure Monitor

Azure Monitor is specifically designed for monitoring and diagnosing performance issues in Azure services, including Power Apps-based solutions. It provides comprehensive insights into the health and performance of applications, making it the ideal choice for troubleshooting performance problems.

QUESTION 20

Answer - E

Option A - Incorrect: Incorrect syntax for LoadData function.

Option B - Incorrect: ClearCollect without a filter does not pre-load data efficiently.

Option C - Incorrect: Incorrect usage of LookUp to collect data.

Option D - Incorrect: Set does not collect multiple records.

Option E - Correct: Correctly pre-loads active products into a collection for faster access.

QUESTION 21

Answer - [B] Power Apps component framework code component.

A) Client scripting is suitable for adding interactivity to controls but may not offer the necessary customization for complex visuals like project timelines.

B) Power Apps component framework code components provide the flexibility and interactivity needed for creating custom visuals, making them ideal for implementing project timelines in a canvas app.

C) Web API is used for data integration and retrieval, not for creating custom visuals within the canvas app.

D) Liquid templates are primarily used for rendering dynamic content, not for creating custom visuals.

QUESTION 22

Answer - [D] Implement conditional visibility for form sections

A) Validate form input before submission - While JavaScript can be used for form validation, the question specifically asks for dynamic behavior based on user interactions, not form submission.

B) Trigger notifications for specific field changes - This could be a valid use case, but it's not as common as implementing conditional visibility for form sections.

C) Populate form fields with data from external APIs - While this is a common use case for JavaScript with the Client API, it doesn't directly relate to dynamic behavior based on user interactions within the form.

D) Implement conditional visibility for form sections - This is a common use case where JavaScript can dynamically show or hide form sections based on user interactions, making it the correct answer.

E) Calculate and display real-time analytics within the form - While JavaScript can perform calculations and display data, this use case doesn't specifically address dynamic behavior based on user interactions within the form.

QUESTION 23

Answer - [B] Authenticate with Dataverse Web API using OAuth 2.0

A) Obtain client credentials from Azure Active Directory - This step precedes authentication but is not directly related to creating client scripts for interacting with the Dataverse Web API.

B) Authenticate with Dataverse Web API using OAuth 2.0 - This is the correct initial step to authenticate and obtain access to the Dataverse Web API.

C) Retrieve an access token using client credentials grant flow - While obtaining an access token is necessary, it typically follows authentication rather than preceding it.

D) Make HTTP requests to Dataverse Web API endpoints - Making HTTP requests comes after authentication and obtaining an access token.

E) Handle authentication errors and refresh access tokens as needed - This step is important for managing authentication but typically occurs after the initial authentication process.

QUESTION 24

Answer - [B] Custom connector
[C] Custom API
[D] HTTP request.

B) Custom connectors provide a streamlined approach to integrate Microsoft Dataverse with external systems like the project tracking system's RESTful Web API, facilitating seamless synchronization of project data within the solution.

C) Custom APIs offer tailored integration solutions, enabling direct communication between Microsoft Dataverse and the RESTful Web API of the external project tracking system, ensuring data consistency and reliability in the project management solution.

D) HTTP requests can facilitate real-time data exchange and communication between the project management solution in Microsoft Dataverse and the RESTful Web API of the external project tracking system, supporting seamless integration and synchronization of project data.

QUESTION 25

Answer - A

Option A - Correct: Proper syntax for initializing context in a PCF component.

Option B - Incorrect: Constructor is not used for initialization in PCF components.

Option C - Incorrect: Method name and syntax do not follow the PCF conventions.

Option D - Incorrect: Incorrect function declaration for TypeScript in PCF.

Option E - Incorrect: Arrow function syntax is not valid for the init method in PCF components.

QUESTION 26

Answer - [C] IEntityForm.

A) IInputParameter - This interface is used to retrieve input parameters passed to the component but is not directly related to data input and validation.

B) IContext - The IContext interface provides contextual information but is not specifically designed for data input and validation.

C) IEntityForm - IEntityForm is commonly used for data input and validation within Power Apps components, making it the correct choice.

D) IDataSet - This interface represents a dataset but is not primarily focused on data input and validation.

E) IStandardControlProps - While used for standard control properties, this interface is not specifically tailored for data input and validation.

QUESTION 27

Answer - [B] Power Automate flow.

B) Power Automate flow provides workflow automation capabilities, including the ability to handle form submissions with attachments. By configuring a flow triggered by the submission action, users can seamlessly attach files to their feedback forms within the canvas app.

Option A) Custom API: Custom APIs are used for integrating external systems with the Power Platform but are not designed for handling form submissions with attachments within canvas apps.

Option C) Azure Logic Apps: Azure Logic Apps are suitable for orchestrating complex workflows and integrations but may be overly complex for simple form submissions with attachments.

Option D) Power Apps custom control: Custom controls in canvas apps are used for visualizing and interacting with data but do not inherently support form submissions with attachments.

QUESTION 28

Answer - [A] OAuth 2.0 authorization

A) OAuth 2.0 authorization - OAuth 2.0 provides a secure and widely-used method for authenticating requests to Web APIs, making it suitable for PCF components.

B) Basic authentication - Basic authentication requires sending credentials with each request, which may not be suitable for client-side PCF components due to security concerns.

C) API key authentication - API key authentication is simpler but less secure compared to OAuth 2.0, often used for public APIs rather than PCF components.

D) Client certificate authentication - Client certificate authentication is more complex and typically used for server-to-server communication rather than client-side components.

E) Windows authentication - Windows authentication is specific to Windows-based systems and may not be applicable in all scenarios, especially for client-side components like PCF.

QUESTION 29

Answer - [B] Pre-validation, Pre-operation, Main operation, Post-operation, Post-validation

A) Pre-validation, Pre-operation, Post-operation, Post-validation - Incorrect order of stages.

B) Pre-validation, Pre-operation, Main operation, Post-operation, Post-validation - Correct order of stages.

C) Pre-operation, Main operation, Post-operation, Pre-validation, Post-validation - Incorrect order of stages.

D) Pre-validation, Main operation, Post-operation, Pre-operation, Post-validation - Incorrect order of stages.

E) Pre-operation, Main operation, Pre-validation, Post-validation, Post-operation - Incorrect order of stages.

QUESTION 30

Answer - [A] Implement row-level error handling in Azure Data Factory pipelines to capture and log records with data integrity violations.
Answer - [D] Configure Azure Data Factory pipelines to retry failed data transfer operations with exponential backoff and jitter.

A) Implementing row-level error handling in Azure Data Factory pipelines allows you to capture and log records that encounter data integrity violations during the migration process. By identifying and logging problematic records, you can review them later for resolution while ensuring the integrity of the overall migration.

D) Configuring Azure Data Factory pipelines to retry failed data transfer operations with exponential backoff and jitter helps improve the resilience of the migration process. By automatically retrying failed operations with increasing delays, you can increase the likelihood of successful data transfers and minimize the impact of transient errors.

Option B) Utilize SQL Server Integration Services (SSIS): While SSIS may offer data validation capabilities, it may introduce additional complexity and dependencies in the migration workflow, potentially affecting performance and scalability.

Option C) Enable Change Tracking: While change tracking may facilitate synchronization between SQL Server and Dataverse, it does not inherently address data integrity or error handling requirements during the migration process.

QUESTION 31

Answer - [B] The service allows plug-ins to interact with Microsoft Dataverse using a set of APIs.

A) It provides direct access to the database tables for performing CRUD operations - Incorrect, direct database access is not recommended within plug-ins.

B) The service allows plug-ins to interact with Microsoft Dataverse using a set of APIs - Correct, the Organization service provides APIs for interacting with Dataverse entities within plug-ins.

C) It is a web service that enables integration with external systems and services - This describes a web API, not the Organization service.

D) The service facilitates user authentication and authorization within plug-ins - Authentication and authorization are handled separately from the Organization service.

E) It offers real-time monitoring and logging capabilities for plug-in executions - Monitoring and logging are not primary functions of the Organization service.

QUESTION 32

Answer - [D] Specifying the request and response schema.

A) Defining the authentication method - While important, this step comes after specifying the request and response schema.

B) Creating a new custom connector - Custom connectors are used for external services, not for configuring Custom API messages in Dataverse.

C) Generating an API key for authorization - Authorization methods are configured after defining the request and response schema.

D) Specifying the request and response schema - Correct, specifying the schema is essential for defining how data is sent to and received from the Custom API.

E) Selecting the target environment for deployment - Environment selection is part of the deployment process and not specific to configuring Custom APIs.

QUESTION 33

Answer - [A] _product_name

A) In this context, the _product_name attribute likely contains the display name of the associated product record. When configuring a canvas app to display related information, you should include the _product_name attribute to ensure that the product's name is displayed correctly for each order.

Option B) _productid_name - Incorrect: This attribute may contain the GUID of the associated product record, not the product's name.

Option C) _product_name_value - Incorrect: This attribute combination is unlikely to exist and may not provide the product's name.

Option D) _productid_value - Incorrect: This attribute combination is unlikely to exist and may not provide the product's name.

QUESTION 34

Answer - [C] OAuth 2.0

A) Basic Authentication - While simple, Basic Authentication is less secure compared to other methods like OAuth 2.0.

B) Digest Authentication - Similar to Basic Authentication, Digest Authentication is less commonly used in modern REST API security.

C) OAuth 2.0 - Correct, OAuth 2.0 is a widely adopted protocol for securing REST APIs, providing secure access without exposing user credentials.

D) JWT Authentication - JWT is often used in conjunction with OAuth 2.0 for token-based authentication, but OAuth 2.0 is the overarching protocol.

E) NTLM Authentication - NTLM is a Windows-based authentication protocol and is not typically used for securing REST APIs.

QUESTION 35

Answer - C

Option A - Incorrect: Custom Connectors are not managed in the PowerApps Admin Center.

Option B - Incorrect: Gateways do not handle OpenAPI specifications.

Option C - Correct: Direct method for importing an OpenAPI file into PowerApps for custom connector creation.

Option D - Incorrect: Entities section does not handle API imports.

Option E - Incorrect: "Connectors" menu does not have an "Import from OpenAPI" option.

QUESTION 36

Answer - A) GET

A) GET - Correct. Ideal for retrieving data, especially for reports where data is only read and not modified.
B) POST - Incorrect. Used mainly for creating data.
C) PUT - Incorrect. Used for updating entire records.
D) DELETE - Incorrect. Used for deleting records.
E) PATCH - Incorrect. Used for partial updates.

QUESTION 37

Answer - [A] GET, POST, PATCH, DELETE

A) GET, POST, PATCH, DELETE - Correct, these HTTP methods are commonly used for CRUD operations: GET (retrieve data), POST (create new data), PATCH (update existing data), DELETE (delete data).

B) PUT, DELETE, PATCH, OPTIONS - PUT is less commonly used for updates in the Web API, and OPTIONS is used for retrieving supported HTTP methods, not CRUD operations.

C) GET, POST, PUT, PATCH - PUT is less commonly used for updates, and PATCH is typically preferred for partial updates.

D) POST, PUT, DELETE, OPTIONS - PUT is less commonly used for updates, and OPTIONS is used for retrieving supported HTTP methods, not CRUD operations.

E) GET, PUT, DELETE, OPTIONS - PUT is less commonly used for updates, and OPTIONS is used for retrieving supported HTTP methods, not CRUD operations.

QUESTION 38

Answer - [D] To enforce a maximum retry count and interval for failed requests

A) To bypass rate limits by retrying failed requests immediately - This approach could exacerbate rate-limiting issues and lead to more frequent throttling.

B) To avoid exceeding API usage quotas by adjusting request frequency - While adjusting request frequency may help manage API usage, it does not specifically address retry policies.

C) To minimize network latency by retrying requests with exponential backoff - While exponential backoff can improve resilience, retry policies encompass more than just backoff strategies.

D) To enforce a maximum retry count and interval for failed requests - Correct, defining retry policies allows developers to control how many times failed requests are retried and the interval between retries, helping manage API limitations.

E) To prioritize certain types of requests over others based on urgency - While request prioritization is important, it is not the primary purpose of defining retry policies.

QUESTION 39

Answer - A), B), and E)

A) Correct. Essential for attempting to reconnect and complete the operation.

B) Correct. Specific handling for timeouts improves robustness of the flow.

C) Incorrect. This would result in excessive notifications, not specific to handling timeouts.

D) Incorrect. While logging is useful for diagnostics, it does not actively resolve the timeout issue.

E) Correct. Ensures that the billing department is aware and can take necessary actions.

QUESTION 40

Answer - E)

A) Incorrect - This JavaScript snippet lacks the correct Event Hub trigger setup.

B) Incorrect - The function lacks specifics to handle real-time data streams effectively, also missing compliance setup.

C) Incorrect - This TypeScript snippet doesn't set up an Azure Function but initiates an EventProcessorClient incorrectly.

D) Incorrect - JSON configuration lacks event hub name and does not directly influence function code.

E) Correct - This C# function setup correctly specifies the event hub trigger and uses proper logging, compliant with HIPAA through secure logging practices and appropriate data handling within the Azure infrastructure.

QUESTION 41

Answer - [C] Configuring data connections for accessing invoice data

A) Defining triggers based on user input - Triggers are important but may not directly relate to accessing invoice data, which is crucial for invoice approval processes.

B) Specifying conditional logic for approval routing - Conditional logic is important for routing approvals but does not address the initial step of accessing invoice data.

C) Configuring data connections for accessing invoice data - Correct, configuring data connections allows the cloud flow to retrieve invoice data from relevant sources, enabling automation of approval processes.

D) Implementing error handling mechanisms for failed approvals - Error handling is important but does not directly relate to the initial setup of accessing invoice data.

E) Setting up notifications for stakeholders - Notifications are useful but are not the primary focus in the initial configuration of accessing invoice data.

QUESTION 42

Answer - A) and E)

A) Correct. Specifically checks if the 'Sensitive' field is set to true, indicating immediate legal review is needed.

B) Incorrect. Only ensures the field is not empty, does not specify its value.

C) Incorrect. The presence of 'Urgent' in the title doesn't relate to the sensitivity condition.

D) Incorrect. Incorrect use of the 'greater' function on a boolean.

E) Correct. Combines necessary conditions for triggering on legal documents.

QUESTION 43

Answer - [C] Implementing Azure Key Vault connectors within flows

A) Storing secrets directly within flow configurations - Storing secrets directly in flow configurations poses a security risk and does not leverage Azure Key Vault's secure storage capabilities.

B) Utilizing custom encryption algorithms for secret storage - Custom encryption may not provide the same level of security and management features as Azure Key Vault.

C) Implementing Azure Key Vault connectors within flows - Correct, Azure Key Vault connectors allow Power Platform users to securely access and manage secrets stored in Azure Key Vault directly from their cloud flows, ensuring a high level of security and compliance.

D) Encoding secrets using base64 encoding before storage - Base64 encoding does not provide encryption and may expose secrets to unauthorized access.

E) Utilizing SharePoint lists for secret management - SharePoint lists are not designed for secure storage of sensitive information like Azure Key Vault.

QUESTION 44

Answer - [B] Customizing flow steps to handle specific business logic and requirements

A) Ensuring compatibility with legacy systems for seamless data exchange - While compatibility is important, the key consideration is customizing flow steps to meet specific business requirements.

B) Customizing flow steps to handle specific business logic and requirements - Correct, integrating cloud flow steps requires customization to align with the unique business processes and requirements of the logistics company.

C) Minimizing latency by optimizing data transfer between flows and processes - While latency optimization is valuable, it may not be the primary consideration for integrating flow steps into business processes.

D) Implementing comprehensive error handling mechanisms for fault tolerance - Error handling is essential but may not be the key consideration for initial integration planning.

E) Utilizing dynamic expressions to dynamically configure flow actions - Dynamic expressions can enhance flexibility but may not be the primary focus when integrating flow steps into business processes.

QUESTION 45

Answer - C) Dynamic token

A) Incorrect. OAuth 2.0 typically uses static tokens for user sessions, not document-specific.
B) Incorrect. API keys are not typically document-specific.
C) Correct. Dynamic token authentication dynamically assigns tokens, suitable for document-specific access.
D) Incorrect. Single sign-on is for user authentication across systems.
E) Incorrect. Password-based is not suitable for document-specific access.

QUESTION 46

Answer - [B] Implementing custom code to define event triggers and handlers for IServiceEndpointNotificationService

A) Registering a service endpoint with Azure Event Grid and configuring event subscriptions - While Azure Event Grid can be used for event-driven architectures, it's not directly related to publishing events using IServiceEndpointNotificationService.

B) Implementing custom code to define event triggers and handlers for IServiceEndpointNotificationService - Correct, IServiceEndpointNotificationService requires custom code implementation to define event triggers and handlers for event publication.

C) Configuring event publishing settings in Power Automate to invoke IServiceEndpointNotificationService - Power Automate is not typically used to directly invoke IServiceEndpointNotificationService for event publishing.

D) Generating an event schema and defining event properties for IServiceEndpointNotificationService - Event schema and properties may be part of the implementation but do not directly address the steps for publishing events.

E) Deploying a custom plugin to the Dataverse environment to enable event publication through IServiceEndpointNotificationService - Custom plugins may be used but are not specific to enabling event publication through IServiceEndpointNotificationService.

QUESTION 47

Answer - [A, B, C, D, E] Registering a webhook endpoint for real-time notifications, Configuring an Azure Service Bus endpoint for reliable message delivery, Setting up an Azure Event Hub for high-throughput event ingestion, Creating a custom HTTP endpoint for external system integration, Configuring OAuth authentication for secure endpoint access

A) Registering a webhook endpoint for real-time notifications - Webhooks are commonly used for real-time event notifications.

B) Configuring an Azure Service Bus endpoint for reliable message delivery - Service Bus provides reliable message queuing for guaranteed delivery.

C) Setting up an Azure Event Hub for high-throughput event ingestion - Event Hub is suitable for high-throughput event ingestion scenarios.

D) Creating a custom HTTP endpoint for external system integration - Custom HTTP endpoints allow integration with external systems via RESTful APIs.

E) Configuring OAuth authentication for secure endpoint access - OAuth authentication enhances security by providing secure access control to endpoints.

QUESTION 48

Answer - A) $expand

A) Correct. $expand is used to include related records in the response.
B) Incorrect. $select is used to specify which fields to retrieve, not for related data.
C) Incorrect. $filter is used to restrict the returned data based on conditions.
D) Incorrect. $lookup is not a valid OData query option.
E) Incorrect. $include is not a valid query option in the Microsoft Dataverse Web API.

QUESTION 49

Answer - [A, D] Defining an alternate key on the product entity with the product code attribute as the unique identifier, Implementing a plugin or custom workflow in Dataverse to validate product codes and prevent duplicates.

A) Defining an alternate key on the product entity with the product code attribute as the unique identifier. - This is the correct approach to enforce uniqueness for product codes using alternate keys in

Dataverse.

B) Creating a custom validation rule in Power Apps to check for duplicate product codes before saving records. - While this approach can catch duplicates at the client-side, it's not as robust as enforcing uniqueness at the database level using alternate keys.

C) Utilizing JavaScript functions to enforce uniqueness constraints for product codes on the client-side. - Client-side validation using JavaScript does not provide the same level of data integrity as enforcing uniqueness with alternate keys in Dataverse.

D) Implementing a plugin or custom workflow in Dataverse to validate product codes and prevent duplicates. - This approach allows for server-side validation and enforcement of uniqueness, aligning with best practices for managing alternate keys.

E) Setting up a scheduled Power Automate flow to check for duplicate product codes and notify administrators. - While this approach can notify administrators of duplicates, it does not prevent them from being created in the first place.

QUESTION 50

Answer - [B] Using Azure Data Factory to orchestrate ETL processes and automate data integration workflows.

A) Implementing custom data connectors for each data source to handle data transformation. - While custom data connectors can be useful, managing multiple connectors for different data sources can be complex and may not efficiently address the challenges of integrating diverse data sets.

B) Using Azure Data Factory to orchestrate ETL processes and automate data integration workflows. - Azure Data Factory is specifically designed for orchestrating complex ETL processes and automating data integration tasks across diverse data sources, making it the most effective choice for handling complex data sets.

C) Developing custom scripts in Microsoft Power Automate to manipulate and synchronize data. - While custom scripts can provide flexibility, they may not offer the scalability and efficiency required for handling large volumes of complex data.

D) Leveraging Azure Logic Apps to trigger data integration tasks based on predefined conditions. - Azure Logic Apps are suitable for workflow automation but may not provide the comprehensive ETL capabilities needed for complex data integration scenarios.

E) Utilizing Microsoft Power Query to standardize and clean the data before importing it into Dataverse. - Power Query is primarily used for data preparation and cleansing, but it may not be sufficient for addressing the challenges posed by complex data structures and formats in integration scenarios.

PRACTICE TEST 2 - QUESTIONS ONLY

QUESTION 1

A financial services firm is deploying a Power Platform solution for their enterprise resource planning (ERP) system. They require a monitoring solution that can provide detailed insights into system performance, including raw log data from various components of the solution. It's essential for them to have access to comprehensive data for effective troubleshooting. Which type of data is crucial for diagnosing issues and troubleshooting in Power Platform solutions?

A) Aggregated performance data
B) Raw log data
C) Application errors
D) Infrastructure health
E) Business intelligence reports

QUESTION 2

A retail company is considering options for implementing a customer relationship management (CRM) solution using Power Platform. They want to understand the difference between customization and configuration in this context. Which statement best describes the distinction between customization and configuration?

A) Customization involves modifying existing features, while configuration involves adding new functionality.
B) Customization involves tailoring the system to meet specific needs, while configuration involves adjusting settings within existing capabilities.
C) Customization focuses on user interface changes, while configuration focuses on backend processes.
D) Customization requires coding, while configuration can be done through a graphical interface.
E) Customization is performed by developers, while configuration is performed by administrators.

QUESTION 3

An organization uses an Azure Function to process end-of-day reports every weekday at 6 PM in Microsoft Dataverse. Which cron expression should you use to schedule this function?

A) 0 18 * * 1-5
B) 0 18 1-5 * *
C) 0 0 18 * * 1-5
D) 0 18 * * MON-FRI
E) 18 0 * * 1-5

QUESTION 4

A healthcare organization is configuring security roles within their Power Platform environment to ensure appropriate access control for different user groups. They need to establish security roles that align with the principle of least privilege.
Which actions should they take when configuring security roles to adhere to this principle? Select TWO.

A) Grant all users full access to sensitive patient records.
B) Limit access to administrative functions to a dedicated administrative user role.
C) Assign read-only permissions to all users for financial reports.
D) Allow all users to create and delete records across all entities.
E) Restrict access to personally identifiable information (PII) to authorized personnel only.

QUESTION 5

In a Power Apps canvas app, you need to ensure that the gallery only shows items from the "Orders" table where the status is "Pending". Which PowerFx expression should you use?

A) Filter('Orders', Status.Value = 'Pending')
B) Filter(Orders, 'Status' = "Pending")
C) Filter('Orders', Status = 'Pending')
D) 'Orders'.Filter(Status = 'Pending')
E) Collect('PendingOrders', Filter(Orders, Status = 'Pending'))

QUESTION 6

In a canvas app for a HR system, you need to display only active employees in a combobox from the Employee table in Dataverse. Which PowerFx expression is appropriate for the Items property?

A) Filter('Employee', Status = 'Active')
B) 'Employee'
C) Distinct('Employee', Status)
D) Filter('Employee', IsActive = true)
E) Collect('Active Employees', Filter(Employee, IsActive = true))

QUESTION 7

A technology company is creating custom roles in Dataverse to tailor access permissions to specific business requirements and user roles. They need to ensure effective management and maintenance of these custom roles to support ongoing operations.
Which practices should they adopt when creating and managing custom roles in Dataverse? Select THREE.

A) Document role definitions, permissions, and responsibilities to maintain clarity and consistency in role management.
B) Regularly review and update role assignments to reflect changes in organizational structure and business processes.
C) Implement version control for role configurations to track changes and roll back to previous versions if necessary.
D) Delegate role management tasks to business stakeholders to distribute responsibility and improve agility in role administration.
E) Establish role approval workflows to enforce governance and ensure compliance with security policies.

QUESTION 8

A software development team is tasked with setting up business units in Microsoft Dataverse for a client's project. They need to ensure the proper procedures are followed to configure business units effectively and meet the client's business requirements.

What are the setup procedures for configuring business units in Microsoft Dataverse? Select THREE.

A) Define business unit hierarchies by creating parent-child relationships to reflect the organizational structure and reporting lines.

B) Assign security roles and privileges to business units to control access to data and resources based on organizational roles and responsibilities.

C) Configure business unit settings such as time zone, currency, and language preferences to align with regional and organizational requirements.

D) Establish business unit ownership for records and data entities to enforce data ownership and accountability within the organization.

E) Implement business unit quotas and limits to manage resource utilization and scalability for each organizational unit.

QUESTION 9

You are tasked with configuring business process flows (BPFs) in Microsoft Dataverse for an organization's sales process. However, users report that they cannot see the BPFs in the expected entity forms. What could be potential reasons for this issue? Select the correct answers that apply.

A) The BPFs are not activated for the target entity.
B) Users do not have the necessary security privileges to access BPFs.
C) The entity forms are not updated to include the BPF control.
D) The BPFs are configured with incorrect stage transitions.
E) The organization's license does not include access to BPF functionalities.

QUESTION 10

In a project focusing on data integration within Microsoft Power Platform, you need to write a script that retrieves data from an external SQL database and displays it in a Power Apps app using PowerFx. Which script is correctly written to perform this task?

A) Collect(ExternalData, LookUp('[dbo].[Customers]', "Country = 'USA'"))
B) ClearCollect(ExternalData, SQL('SELECT * FROM Customers WHERE Country = "USA'"))
C) ClearCollect(ExternalData, EvaluateSQL("SELECT * FROM Customers WHERE Country = 'USA'"))
D) ClearCollect(ExternalData, GetSQLData("SELECT * FROM Customers WHERE Country = 'USA'"))
E) AddColumns('[dbo].[Customers]', "Country = 'USA'", "CustomerData")

QUESTION 11

A software development company is building a project management application using Microsoft Power Platform. They need to configure relationships between the "Project" and "Task" entities in Microsoft Dataverse. Additionally, they want to ensure that tasks are automatically associated with the corresponding project when created. Which type of relationship should be configured between the "Project" and "Task" entities to achieve automatic association?

A) Many-to-One
B) One-to-Many
C) Many-to-Many
D) Self-Referential
E) Hierarchy

QUESTION 12

Your organization has developed a comprehensive custom application on the Microsoft Power Platform to streamline business processes. Now, there is a requirement to roll out a major update to enhance the application's capabilities. However, you want to ensure that the existing data and configurations are preserved during the update process to avoid any disruptions to ongoing operations. Which action should you choose to achieve this goal while minimizing risks?

A) Create
B) Update
C) Upgrade
D) Patch

QUESTION 13

A software development company is transferring a Power Platform solution from a development environment to a production environment. They need to understand the implications of solution transfer between environments to ensure a smooth deployment process. What implications should the company consider when transferring solutions between environments in Microsoft Dataverse? Select the correct answers that apply.

A) Version compatibility between environments
B) Data loss during solution export/import
C) Customizations specific to source environment
D) Licensing requirements for solution components
E) Network latency during solution transfer

QUESTION 14

When configuring a model-driven app in Power Apps, developers need to consider various factors to ensure optimal performance and functionality. What are some key considerations in app configuration? Select the correct answers that apply.

A) Optimize entity relationships for efficient data retrieval
B) Minimize the use of complex business rules to enhance performance
C) Implement role-based security to control user access
D) Utilize client-side scripting to enhance user experience
E) Regularly monitor app usage and performance metrics

QUESTION 15

Your task is to enhance the user interface of a model-driven app for a retail company's inventory management system. The goal is to streamline inventory tracking and improve user productivity. What are two key actions that you can perform using a business rule in this context? Select the correct answers that apply.

A) Access external data.
B) Enable or disable a column based on inventory levels.
C) Show or hide a column based on user role.
D) Run the rule on demand.

QUESTION 16

When using JavaScript to configure commands and buttons in Power Apps, developers need to consider security implications. Which security considerations are relevant when using JavaScript in Power Apps? Select the correct answers that apply.

A) Prevention of cross-site scripting (XSS) attacks
B) Secure handling of sensitive data and credentials
C) Protection against injection attacks, such as SQL injection
D) Ensuring compliance with data protection regulations
E) Encryption of data transmitted between client and server

QUESTION 17

A healthcare organization is building a Power App to track patient appointments and optimize scheduling based on historical data. They need to ensure optimal performance of Power Fx formulas to handle large datasets efficiently. What techniques can they employ to optimize the performance of Power Fx formulas in this scenario? Select the correct answers that apply.

A) Minimizing the use of nested functions and calculations to reduce processing overhead
B) Leveraging delegation to offload data processing to the data source where possible
C) Implementing selective loading techniques to fetch only necessary data for calculations
D) Using variable caching to store intermediate results and reduce formula complexity
E) Splitting complex calculations into smaller, manageable steps to improve formula readability

QUESTION 18

You are building a model-driven app for a project management system. The app requires executing specialized code when a user clicks on a button in the app's ribbon. However, this functionality should be restricted to project managers only. Which option should you choose to meet this requirement?

A) Custom API
B) Custom process action
C) Classic workflow
D) Business rule

QUESTION 19

A software development company is encountering slow loading times and unresponsive behavior in their model-driven app. What is a common issue that could contribute to poor app performance in this scenario? Select the correct answers that apply.

A) Overly complex data queries
B) Inadequate network bandwidth
C) Excessive use of client-side scripting
D) Lack of proper error handling mechanisms
E) Insufficient server resources

QUESTION 20

Implement query delegation in a large dataset within a Canvas app to improve performance. What is the correct PowerFx formula to ensure delegation?

A) Filter(LargeData, StartsWith(Title, TextInput1.Text))
B) Collect(LocalCache, Filter(LargeData, Title = TextInput1.Text))
C) ClearCollect(LocalCache, Search(LargeData, TextInput1.Text, 'Title'))
D) ClearCollect(LocalCache, Filter(LargeData, Title.Contains(TextInput1.Text)))
E) Filter(LargeData, Title.StartsWith(TextInput1.Text))

QUESTION 21

You are building a canvas app for an inventory management system. The app requires incorporating a custom visual to display real-time inventory levels. However, you want to ensure that the visual is easily customizable and reusable across different screens within the app. Which approach should you choose?

A) Client scripting
B) Power Apps component framework code component
C) Web API
D) Liquid template

QUESTION 22

A Power Apps developer is writing JavaScript code to interact with the Client API object model. Which of the following best practices should the developer follow to ensure code reliability and maintainability?

A) Use asynchronous functions for long-running operations
B) Minimize the use of global variables to avoid namespace pollution
C) Include comments to explain complex logic and functionality
D) Utilize try-catch blocks for error handling
E) Optimize code for performance by minimizing function calls

QUESTION 23

A Power Apps developer is integrating Dataverse Web API into a canvas app to retrieve data from custom entities. Which of the following authentication and authorization practices should the developer follow when interacting with Dataverse Web API?

A) Use OAuth 1.0 for authentication to ensure compatibility with older browsers
B) Store client credentials directly within the canvas app for simplicity
C) Implement user-based authentication to enforce granular access control
D) Utilize OAuth 2.0 with client credentials grant flow for service-to-service authentication
E) Allow anonymous access to Dataverse Web API endpoints for broad accessibility

QUESTION 24

Your organization is deploying a customer service solution using Microsoft Dataverse. You need to integrate an external customer support system, which exposes a RESTful Web API, to enable ticket creation and updates within the solution. Considering the integration requirements, which three options should you employ to ensure a seamless integration solution? Select the correct answers that apply.

A) Azure function
B) Custom connector
C) Custom API
D) HTTP request
E) Business rule

QUESTION 25

To enhance a model-driven app, you need to configure a PCF component's manifest file. What is the correct XML configuration for a field that binds to a text attribute?

A) `<property name="textField" type="SingleLine.Text" usage="bound" />`
B) `<control-property name="textField" type="String" bind="true" />`
C) `<data-set name="textField" type="SingleLine.Text" binding="true" />`
D) `<property name="textField" type="SingleLine.Text" bound="true" />`
E) `<field name="textField" type="String" bound="true" />`

QUESTION 26

A Power Apps developer needs to customize the behavior of a PCF component interface. Which approach allows for the implementation of custom logic and event handling?

A) Implementing the IDataSet interface.
B) Extending the IStandardControlProps interface.
C) Utilizing the IContext interface for context-based operations.
D) Creating event listeners directly within the HTML template.
E) Implementing the OnChange event handler for data manipulation.

QUESTION 27

Your organization is developing a canvas app for expense reporting. You need to ensure that users can capture receipts using their device's camera and attach them to expense reports within the app. Which development option should you choose to implement this feature?

A) Power Apps custom control
B) Custom connector

C) Azure Blob Storage
D) Power Automate flow

QUESTION 28

In a scenario where a Power Apps developer needs to handle errors when making Web API calls from a PCF component, which approach should the developer follow to ensure robust error handling?

A) Implement try-catch blocks within the PCF component code.
B) Use HTTP status codes to interpret errors returned by the Web API.
C) Utilize Azure Application Insights for real-time error monitoring.
D) Log errors to the browser console for debugging purposes.
E) Retry failed API requests with exponential backoff.

QUESTION 29

A development team is discussing the role of the plug-in execution pipeline in executing business logic within their Power Platform solution. Which statement best describes the role of the pipeline?

A) The pipeline validates user input before executing business logic.
B) It defines the sequence in which plug-ins are executed during record processing.
C) The pipeline orchestrates the execution of asynchronous workflows triggered by data changes.
D) It handles error handling and recovery during plug-in execution.
E) The pipeline manages the transactional consistency of data operations within a single transaction.

QUESTION 30

Your organization is migrating data from an existing SharePoint Online document library to Dataverse tables using Power Automate flows. During the migration, you encounter errors related to file format mismatches and unsupported metadata fields, leading to failed data transfers. What are two potential strategies to address these errors and ensure the successful completion of the migration? Select the correct answers that apply.

A) Utilize Power Automate expressions to dynamically convert unsupported file formats to compatible formats before transferring data to Dataverse tables.
B) Restrict the migration scope to exclude files with unsupported metadata fields until the issues are resolved or metadata mappings are updated.
C) Enable metadata validation settings in the SharePoint Online document library to enforce compliance with Dataverse table requirements before initiating the migration.
D) Implement conditional logic in Power Automate flows to skip files with unsupported formats or metadata fields and continue with the migration process.

QUESTION 31

A Power Platform developer is tasked with performing CRUD operations within plug-ins using the Organization service. Which operations can be performed using the Organization service?

A) Create, Read, Update, Delete, Execute
B) Insert, Retrieve, Modify, Remove, Execute

C) Add, Get, Change, Drop, Invoke
D) New, Fetch, Edit, Remove, Execute
E) Generate, Retrieve, Alter, Discard, Invoke

QUESTION 32

A Power Platform developer is defining input and output parameters for a Custom API message in Dataverse. What is an important consideration when defining input and output parameters?

A) Using a fixed schema for all input parameters.
B) Ensuring compatibility with third-party systems for output parameters.
C) Limiting the number of input parameters to improve performance.
D) Specifying parameter data types and validation rules.
E) Sharing input parameters across multiple Custom API messages.

QUESTION 33

You are building a model-driven app for managing customer relationships. The app includes a custom entity named "Interactions" with a lookup field to the "Contacts" entity. Users should be able to view the name of the associated contact when viewing interaction records. What attribute should you specify in your model-driven app to display the contact's name?

A) _contact_name
B) _contactid_name
C) _contact_name_value
D) _contactid_value

QUESTION 34

In a Power Platform solution, the development team needs to implement OAuth authentication for an external REST API. Which step is essential in implementing OAuth authentication?

A) Generating a client secret for the application.
B) Registering the application with the OAuth provider.
C) Storing user credentials in plaintext within the application code.
D) Using HTTP Basic Authentication for token exchange.
E) Exposing sensitive tokens in client-side JavaScript code.

QUESTION 35

What is the best approach to handle version control and updates for APIs imported into Power Platform from GitHub?

A) Link the GitHub repository to PowerApps and set up webhooks for auto-updates.
B) Manually update the API definitions in PowerApps whenever the GitHub repo changes.
C) Use Power Automate to check for changes in GitHub and apply updates in PowerApps.
D) Configure Azure DevOps CI/CD pipelines to push updates from GitHub to PowerApps.
E) Implement a script in Azure Functions to fetch and update API definitions periodically.

QUESTION 36

If a custom JavaScript action needs to reset a user's password via a Web API in Microsoft Power Platform, which HTTP method would be most appropriate?

A) POST
B) GET
C) PUT
D) PATCH
E) OPTIONS

QUESTION 37

In implementing authentication practices for accessing the Dataverse Web API, which method provides secure access while avoiding the need to store user credentials within the Power Platform solution?

A) OAuth 2.0 client credentials flow
B) Basic authentication with encrypted credentials
C) API key authentication with IP whitelisting
D) SAML-based single sign-on (SSO)
E) User-managed access tokens

QUESTION 38

When handling API rate limits in a Power Platform solution, what is a recommended best practice for resilient API calls?

A) Implementing long-running transactions to minimize API calls
B) Using multiple API keys to distribute requests across different quotas
C) Caching API responses to reduce the frequency of requests
D) Implementing circuit breaker patterns to detect and handle API failures
E) Increasing request payload sizes to minimize the number of requests

QUESTION 39

A non-profit organization uses a cloud flow to manage donor records and needs to integrate an external CRM API. What configuration ensures data integrity if the API fails? Select the correct answers that apply.

A) Configure automatic retries
B) Use dual-write to a backup system
C) Send notification to IT support
D) Redirect the flow to a fallback API
E) Use conditional paths based on API success

QUESTION 40

An e-commerce company wants to schedule a daily Azure Function to update inventory and pricing data from their SQL database to their CDS (Dataverse). The solution must consider error handling and scalability in case of high volume data days such as Black Friday.

A) SQL: SELECT * FROM Products;
B) C#: public static void Run([TimerTrigger("0 30 4 * * *")] TimerInfo myTimer, ILogger log)
C) JavaScript: setInterval(async () => { await updateDatabase(); }, 86400000);
D) PowerFx: UpdateData(DataSourceInfo('Products', DataSourceInfo.LastUpdated))
E) TypeScript: @TimerTrigger("0 */1440 * * *") export function scheduledWork(context: { log: (msg: string) => void; }) { context.log("Updating inventory"); }

QUESTION 41

In a Power Platform solution, developers are integrating a cloud flow with a Power Apps canvas app to automate data collection processes. What is a key consideration for seamless integration between the cloud flow and Power Apps?

A) Utilizing Power Automate connectors for direct app integration
B) Implementing custom authentication mechanisms for enhanced security
C) Ensuring data consistency by synchronizing data schemas between components
D) Leveraging context variables to pass data between the flow and app
E) Embedding flow logic directly within the Power Apps canvas

QUESTION 42

In a SharePoint integrated Power Automate flow, trigger only if a newly added document is marked as "Final" in the 'DocumentStatus' field and it belongs to the 'Finance' department folder. Which expressions are correct? Select the correct answers that apply.

A) @equals(triggerBody()?['DocumentStatus'], 'Final')
B) @contains(triggerBody()?['DepartmentFolder'], 'Finance')
C) @and(equals(triggerBody()?['DocumentStatus'], 'Final'), contains(triggerBody()?['DepartmentFolder'], 'Finance'))
D) @not(equals(triggerBody()?['DocumentStatus'], 'Draft'))
E) @startsWith(triggerBody()?['DepartmentFolder'], 'Fin')

QUESTION 43

A software development company is building a Power Platform solution that integrates with various Azure services. They need to grant secure access to these services without exposing credentials in plain text within their applications. What approach should they take to configure service principals via Microsoft Entra for secure access?

A) Hard-coding service principal credentials within the application code
B) Granting all permissions to service principals for maximum flexibility
C) Using managed identities for Azure resources to authenticate service principals
D) Sharing service principal credentials via email for team collaboration
E) Creating separate service principals for each application function

QUESTION 44

A technology consulting firm is assisting a healthcare organization in implementing Power Platform solutions for patient management. They need to add a cloud flow step to an existing business process flow for automated appointment reminders to patients. What impact does adding a cloud flow step have on business process execution in this scenario?

A) Streamlining workflow execution by reducing manual intervention and delays
B) Enhancing scalability by enabling asynchronous processing of workflow steps
C) Improving data accuracy and integrity through automated data validation and verification
D) Increasing complexity and maintenance overhead due to additional integration points
E) Optimizing resource utilization by leveraging cloud-based processing capabilities

QUESTION 45

You need to create a Power Platform custom connector to interact with a legacy system that only supports basic authentication. What type of authentication is most appropriate?

A) Password based
B) OAuth 2.0
C) API key
D) Certificate based
E) Single sign-on

QUESTION 46

A retail company is developing a Power Platform solution to automate inventory management processes. They need to configure the necessary requirements to publish Dataverse events using IServiceEndpointNotificationService effectively. What are the essential configuration requirements for publishing events using IServiceEndpointNotificationService?

A) Enabling webhook endpoints in the Dataverse environment and securing them with OAuth 2.0 authentication
B) Defining event mappings to map Dataverse entity changes to corresponding events for publication
C) Granting appropriate permissions to service accounts for invoking IServiceEndpointNotificationService
D) Configuring Azure Service Bus queues for reliable event delivery and message persistence
E) Setting up Azure Application Insights to monitor event publication performance and errors

QUESTION 47

A transportation logistics company is developing a Power Platform solution to track vehicle movements and optimize delivery routes. They are evaluating different types of service endpoints for their scenario. Which of the following accurately compares the capabilities and use cases of different service endpoints?

A) Webhooks provide real-time event notifications, while Azure Event Hub offers high throughput event ingestion.
B) Azure Service Bus ensures reliable message delivery, while Azure Event Hub supports event-driven architectures.
C) Custom HTTP endpoints allow synchronous communication, while Azure Service Bus enables asynchronous messaging.
D) Webhooks are suitable for one-way communication, while Azure Service Bus supports bidirectional

messaging.
 E) Azure Event Hub is ideal for low-latency scenarios, while Custom HTTP endpoints offer flexibility in endpoint configuration.

QUESTION 48

You are updating a Microsoft Dataverse record via the Web API and need to ensure that your update doesn't overwrite a more recent update made by another user. What should you include in your request?

A) If-Match header
 B) If-None-Match header
 C) $filter query
 D) ConcurrencyBehavior header
 E) If-Unmodified-Since header

QUESTION 49

A manufacturing company is experiencing performance issues in their Power Platform solution due to a large volume of records and frequent data lookups. They want to optimize database performance by using alternate keys in Dataverse. What impact does using alternate keys have on database performance? Select the correct answers that apply.

A) Improved query performance for record retrieval operations due to indexed alternate keys.
 B) Increased storage utilization for maintaining alternate key indexes in the database.
 C) Reduced latency for data insertion and update operations with enforced uniqueness constraints.
 D) Enhanced scalability by distributing data across multiple alternate key partitions.
 E) Minimized network overhead for data synchronization with alternate key-based replication.

QUESTION 50

A manufacturing company is implementing ETL processes in the Power Platform to synchronize production data between its ERP system and Microsoft Dataverse. Which statement best describes the role of ETL processes in this scenario?

A) ETL processes facilitate real-time data synchronization between systems to ensure data consistency.
 B) ETL processes automate the extraction, transformation, and loading of data between disparate systems.
 C) ETL processes enable direct querying of remote data sources without data duplication.
 D) ETL processes enforce data security and compliance standards during data integration tasks.
 E) ETL processes handle user authentication and access control for data exchange between systems.

PRACTICE TEST 2 - ANSWERS ONLY

QUESTION 1

Answer - [B) Raw log data]

B) Raw log data - Raw log data, including logs generated by applications and services, is essential for diagnosing issues and troubleshooting as it provides detailed insights into system behavior.

A) Aggregated performance data - Aggregated performance data may provide high-level insights but may not offer the granularity needed for effective troubleshooting.

C) Application errors - While application errors are important, they may not provide the comprehensive data required for troubleshooting various issues.

D) Infrastructure health - Monitoring infrastructure health is valuable but may not directly provide insights into application-level issues.

E) Business intelligence reports - Business intelligence reports focus more on data analysis rather than raw log data required for troubleshooting.

QUESTION 2

Answer - [B) Customization involves tailoring the system to meet specific needs, while configuration involves adjusting settings within existing capabilities.]

A) Customization involves modifying existing features, while configuration involves adding new functionality - This statement inaccurately suggests that configuration adds new functionality, which is typically associated with customization.

B) Customization involves tailoring the system to meet specific needs, while configuration involves adjusting settings within existing capabilities - This statement correctly distinguishes between customization (making specific adjustments to meet unique requirements) and configuration (adjusting settings within the existing system).

C) Customization focuses on user interface changes, while configuration focuses on backend processes - While this may sometimes be the case, it does not encompass the full scope of customization and configuration.

D) Customization requires coding, while configuration can be done through a graphical interface - While customization often involves coding, configuration can also be performed through graphical interfaces such as Power Platform's interface.

E) Customization is performed by developers, while configuration is performed by administrators - While developers may handle customization tasks, administrators can also perform configuration tasks.

QUESTION 3

Answer - A) 0 18 * * 1-5

A) Correct. Runs at 6 PM on weekdays.
B) Incorrect. This places the day-of-month incorrectly.

C) Incorrect. Misformatted with incorrect placement of hour.
D) Incorrect. Though logically correct, cron expressions don't use day name abbreviations in Azure Functions.
E) Incorrect. Misplaced hour and minute fields in the cron expression.

QUESTION 4

Answer - B and E) Limit access to administrative functions to a dedicated administrative user role. Restrict access to personally identifiable information (PII) to authorized personnel only.

A) - Incorrect. Granting all users full access to sensitive patient records violates the principle of least privilege.

B) - Correct. Limiting access to administrative functions to a dedicated administrative user role ensures that only authorized personnel have access to sensitive operations, adhering to the principle of least privilege.

C) - Incorrect. Assigning read-only permissions to all users for financial reports may not align with the principle of least privilege if some users do not require access to financial data.

D) - Incorrect. Allowing all users to create and delete records across all entities contradicts the principle of least privilege by granting excessive permissions.

E) - Correct. Restricting access to personally identifiable information (PII) to authorized personnel only helps enforce data privacy and security, aligning with the principle of least privilege.

QUESTION 5

Answer - C) Filter('Orders', Status = 'Pending')

A) Incorrect. Incorrect syntax for status field comparison.

B) Incorrect. Incorrect syntax and use of quotation marks.

C) Correct. Correctly uses Filter to display only orders with a status of "Pending".

D) Incorrect. Incorrect method and syntax for applying filter.

E) Incorrect. Collect is not necessary for filtering and is used incorrectly.

QUESTION 6

Answer - D) Filter('Employee', IsActive = true)

A) Incorrect. Assumes there is a field named Status, which is not specified as being correct.
B) Incorrect. This would list all employees.
C) Incorrect. Distinct is used to remove duplicates, not filter by status.
D) Correct. Assumes IsActive is the correct field indicating active status and filters accordingly.
E) Incorrect. Collect is used incorrectly and the syntax is also incorrect.

QUESTION 7

Answer - A, B, and E) Document role definitions, permissions, and responsibilities to maintain clarity and consistency in role management. Regularly review and update role assignments to reflect changes in organizational structure and business processes. Establish role approval workflows to enforce governance and ensure compliance with security policies.

A) - Correct. Documenting role definitions, permissions, and responsibilities helps maintain clarity and consistency in role management, ensuring that roles align with business requirements and security policies.

B) - Correct. Regularly reviewing and updating role assignments ensures that access permissions remain aligned with changes in organizational structure and business processes, reducing the risk of unauthorized access.

C) - Incorrect. While version control can be useful for tracking changes, it may not be necessary for role configurations in all scenarios and could add unnecessary complexity to role management.

D) - Incorrect. Delegating role management tasks to business stakeholders may increase the risk of misconfiguration and inconsistent role assignments, especially if stakeholders lack expertise in security best practices.

E) - Correct. Establishing role approval workflows helps enforce governance and compliance with security policies by requiring authorization for role changes, enhancing security and accountability.

QUESTION 8

Answer - A, B, and C) Define business unit hierarchies by creating parent-child relationships to reflect the organizational structure and reporting lines. Assign security roles and privileges to business units to control access to data and resources based on organizational roles and responsibilities. Configure business unit settings such as time zone, currency, and language preferences to align with regional and organizational requirements.

A) - Correct. Defining business unit hierarchies through parent-child relationships helps reflect the organizational structure and reporting lines within Microsoft Dataverse, facilitating effective data management and access control.

B) - Correct. Assigning security roles and privileges to business units enables granular control over data access and resource usage based on organizational roles and responsibilities, ensuring compliance and data security.

C) - Correct. Configuring business unit settings such as time zone, currency, and language preferences ensures alignment with regional and organizational requirements, enhancing user experience and data consistency across the organization.

D) - Incorrect. While establishing business unit ownership is important, it is not a setup procedure specifically related to configuring business units within Microsoft Dataverse.

E) - Incorrect. Implementing business unit quotas and limits may be relevant for resource management but is not a standard setup procedure for configuring business units in Dataverse.

QUESTION 9

Answer - [A], [C], and [E].

B) Security privileges would prevent interaction, not visibility, of BPFs.

D) Incorrect stage transitions would affect BPF functionality, not visibility.

A) BPFs need to be activated to be visible and functional.

C) Without the BPF control on forms, users cannot interact with BPFs.

E) Licensing issues may restrict access to certain features.

QUESTION 10

Answer - B

Option A - Incorrect: The syntax for LookUp does not correctly apply to SQL queries.

Option B - Correct: This PowerFx code correctly uses ClearCollect to retrieve data from an SQL database with the appropriate query.

Option C - Incorrect: EvaluateSQL is not a recognized function in PowerFx.

Option D - Incorrect: GetSQLData is not a recognized function in PowerFx.

Option E - Incorrect: AddColumns is used incorrectly and does not fetch data from SQL.

QUESTION 11

Answer - [B] One-to-Many

Option B is correct as a One-to-Many relationship allows multiple tasks (many) to be associated with a single project (one), enabling automatic association of tasks with their corresponding projects.

Option A is incorrect as Many-to-One would imply multiple projects associated with a single task, which does not align with the requirement.

Option C is incorrect as Many-to-Many relationships are used for scenarios where multiple records can be associated with each other, not for automatic association between entities.

Option D is incorrect as Self-Referential relationships involve entities being related to themselves, which is not applicable in this scenario.

Option E is incorrect as Hierarchy relationships represent parent-child relationships within the same entity, not between different entities like "Project" and "Task".

QUESTION 12

Answer - [C] Upgrade.

A) Creating a new solution would start from scratch, potentially leading to data loss and configuration discrepancies.
B) Updating a solution might overwrite existing configurations and could pose risks to data integrity.
C) Upgrading allows for deploying major updates while preserving existing data and configurations, minimizing risks of disruptions to ongoing operations.
D) Patching is typically used for minor fixes rather than major updates and may not be suitable for comprehensive enhancements.

QUESTION 13

Answer - [A, B, C] Version compatibility between environments, Data loss during solution export/import, Customizations specific to source environment

Options A, B, and C are correct as version compatibility, data loss, and customizations specific to the source environment are critical considerations when transferring solutions between environments, ensuring compatibility, data integrity, and functionality consistency.

Options D and E may also be factors to consider but are less directly related to the implications of solution transfer.

QUESTION 14

Answer - [A, B, C, E] Optimize entity relationships for efficient data retrieval, Minimize the use of complex business rules to enhance performance, Implement role-based security to control user access, Regularly monitor app usage and performance metrics

Options A, B, C, and E are correct as they represent key considerations in configuring a model-driven app in Power Apps, focusing on data optimization, performance, security, and monitoring.

Option D, while potentially beneficial, is less directly related to app configuration and more to enhancing user experience.

QUESTION 15

Answer - [B] and [C].

A) Business rules cannot directly access external data.

B) Business rules can enable or disable a column dynamically based on inventory levels, allowing users to focus on relevant information and improving productivity in inventory management tasks.

C) Business rules can show or hide a column based on user role, ensuring that employees have access to the necessary information for their roles, thereby optimizing user experience and efficiency.

QUESTION 16

Answer - [A, B, C] Prevention of cross-site scripting (XSS) attacks, Secure handling of sensitive data and credentials, Protection against injection attacks, such as SQL injection

Options A, B, and C are correct as they represent security considerations when using JavaScript in Power Apps, including preventing XSS attacks, handling sensitive data securely, and protecting against injection attacks.

Options D and E, while important, are not directly related to JavaScript usage in Power Apps.

QUESTION 17

Answer - [A, B, C, D] Minimizing the use of nested functions and calculations to reduce processing overhead, Leveraging delegation to offload data processing to the data source where possible, Implementing selective loading techniques to fetch only necessary data for calculations, Using variable caching to store intermediate results and reduce formula complexity

Options A, B, C, and D are correct as they represent techniques for optimizing the performance of Power Fx formulas, including minimizing complexity, leveraging delegation, selective loading, and variable caching.

Option E, while beneficial for readability, may not directly impact formula performance.

QUESTION 18

Answer - [B] Custom process action.

A) Custom APIs are typically used for integrating external systems or services with the Power Platform but do not provide user-specific execution control.

B) Custom process actions enable developers to define custom actions that can be executed by specific users, making them suitable for restricting code execution to project managers. This ensures that only authorized personnel, such as project managers, have access to execute the specialized code, maintaining data confidentiality and integrity within the project management system.

C) Classic workflows are automation processes but do not offer the capability to control code execution based on user roles or privileges.

D) Business rules are used for implementing simple business logic within the app's user interface but do not involve executing custom code on the ribbon.

QUESTION 19

Answer - [A, B, C, D, E] Overly complex data queries, Inadequate network bandwidth, Excessive use of client-side scripting, Lack of proper error handling mechanisms, Insufficient server resources

Options A, B, C, D, and E represent common issues that could impact app performance, including data query complexity, network limitations, client-side scripting overhead, error handling deficiencies, and resource constraints.

QUESTION 20

Answer - A

Option A - Correct: Uses StartsWith, which supports delegation.

Option B - Incorrect: Equality in Filter may not delegate depending on the connector.

Option C - Incorrect: Search function does not delegate.

Option D - Incorrect: Contains does not support delegation.

Option E - Incorrect: Incorrect syntax for StartsWith usage.

QUESTION 21

Answer - [A] Client scripting.

A) Client scripting allows for customization and interactivity, making it suitable for creating reusable and

customizable custom visuals across different screens within the app.
B) While Power Apps component framework code components offer customization, they may not provide the level of reusability desired across various screens within the app.
C) Web API is used for data integration and retrieval, not for creating custom visuals within the canvas app.
D) Liquid templates are primarily used for rendering dynamic content, not for creating custom visuals.

QUESTION 22

Answer - [C] Include comments to explain complex logic and functionality

A) Use asynchronous functions for long-running operations - While using asynchronous functions is important for performance, it may not directly contribute to code reliability and maintainability.

B) Minimize the use of global variables to avoid namespace pollution - Minimizing the use of global variables is a good practice but doesn't specifically address code reliability and maintainability in the context of JavaScript code interacting with the Client API object model.

C) Include comments to explain complex logic and functionality - Including comments helps improve code readability and maintainability, especially when dealing with complex logic and functionality, making it the correct answer.

D) Utilize try-catch blocks for error handling - Error handling is important, but it's not as directly related to ensuring code reliability and maintainability as including comments for clarity.

E) Optimize code for performance by minimizing function calls - While optimizing code for performance is important, it's not the primary concern when ensuring code reliability and maintainability.

QUESTION 23

Answer - [D] Utilize OAuth 2.0 with client credentials grant flow for service-to-service authentication

A) Use OAuth 1.0 for authentication to ensure compatibility with older browsers - OAuth 1.0 is outdated and less secure compared to OAuth 2.0, and it's not specifically recommended for use with Dataverse Web API.

B) Store client credentials directly within the canvas app for simplicity - Storing credentials within the app introduces security risks and is generally not recommended.

C) Implement user-based authentication to enforce granular access control - While user-based authentication may be appropriate for some scenarios, service-to-service authentication with OAuth 2.0 is typically used for Dataverse Web API integration.

D) Utilize OAuth 2.0 with client credentials grant flow for service-to-service authentication - This is the recommended approach for authenticating service-to-service interactions with Dataverse Web API, making it the correct answer.

E) Allow anonymous access to Dataverse Web API endpoints for broad accessibility - Allowing anonymous access may compromise data security and is generally not advisable for production environments.

QUESTION 24

Answer - [A] Azure function
 [B] Custom connector
 [D] HTTP request.

A) Azure functions can execute custom logic to facilitate real-time communication between Microsoft Dataverse and the RESTful Web API of the external customer support system, enabling ticket creation and updates within the customer service solution.

B) Custom connectors offer a standardized integration approach, enabling efficient connectivity between Microsoft Dataverse and the RESTful Web API of the external customer support system, ensuring seamless ticket management within the solution.

D) HTTP requests can facilitate data exchange and communication between the customer service solution in Microsoft Dataverse and the RESTful Web API of the external customer support system, supporting seamless integration and ticket management.

QUESTION 25

Answer - A

Option A - Correct: Correct XML element for defining a bound text property in a PCF manifest file.

Option B - Incorrect: control-property is not a valid tag in PCF manifest.

Option C - Incorrect: data-set is used for collections, not single fields.

Option D - Incorrect: The attribute should be usage="bound", not bound="true".

Option E - Incorrect: field is not a valid tag for PCF manifest properties.

QUESTION 26

Answer - [D] Creating event listeners directly within the HTML template.

A) Implementing the IDataSet interface - While the IDataSet interface handles data binding, it does not directly enable custom logic or event handling.

B) Extending the IStandardControlProps interface - Extending interfaces allows for additional properties but does not inherently enable custom logic or event handling.

C) Utilizing the IContext interface for context-based operations - The IContext interface provides contextual information but is not primarily focused on custom logic or event handling.

D) Creating event listeners directly within the HTML template - This approach allows for the direct implementation of custom logic and event handling within the component's UI, making it the correct choice.

E) Implementing the OnChange event handler for data manipulation - While OnChange events are useful for data manipulation, they are not directly related to customizing interface behavior.

QUESTION 27

Answer - [A] Power Apps custom control.

A) Power Apps custom controls can be used to integrate device features like the camera directly into canvas apps, allowing users to capture receipts and attach them to expense reports within the app interface. This provides a seamless and user-friendly experience for expense reporting.

Option B) Custom connector: Custom connectors are used for integrating external data sources with the Power Platform but do not directly support device features like the camera for capturing receipts.
Option C) Azure Blob Storage: Azure Blob Storage is a cloud storage solution, which can be used to store files including receipts, but it requires additional integration and is not directly integrated into the app interface.
Option D) Power Automate flow: While Power Automate flow can be used to automate processes including receipt capture, it does not provide the same level of user interaction and integration as a custom control within the canvas app interface.

QUESTION 28

Answer - [B] Use HTTP status codes to interpret errors returned by the Web API.

A) Implement try-catch blocks within the PCF component code - While try-catch blocks can capture errors, HTTP status codes provide more specific information about API request outcomes.

B) Use HTTP status codes to interpret errors returned by the Web API - HTTP status codes convey detailed information about request success or failure, aiding in error handling within PCF components.

C) Utilize Azure Application Insights for real-time error monitoring - Application Insights is valuable for monitoring, but HTTP status codes are more directly relevant to error interpretation.

D) Log errors to the browser console for debugging purposes - Logging to the console is useful for debugging but may not provide comprehensive error handling for production environments.

E) Retry failed API requests with exponential backoff - While retrying requests is a valid strategy, it may not address the core issue of error interpretation within the PCF component.

QUESTION 29

Answer - [B] It defines the sequence in which plug-ins are executed during record processing.

A) The pipeline validates user input before executing business logic - Pre-validation stage handles input validation, not the entire pipeline.

B) It defines the sequence in which plug-ins are executed during record processing - Correct, the plug-in execution pipeline determines the order of plug-in execution.

C) The pipeline orchestrates the execution of asynchronous workflows triggered by data changes - This is the role of asynchronous processing, not the plug-in pipeline.

D) It handles error handling and recovery during plug-in execution - Error handling is part of the pipeline, but not its primary role.

E) The pipeline manages the transactional consistency of data operations within a single transaction -

Transaction support is part of the pipeline but not its primary role.

QUESTION 30

Answer - [A] Utilize Power Automate expressions to dynamically convert unsupported file formats to compatible formats before transferring data to Dataverse tables.

Answer - [D] Implement conditional logic in Power Automate flows to skip files with unsupported formats or metadata fields and continue with the migration process.

A) Utilizing Power Automate expressions allows you to dynamically convert unsupported file formats to compatible formats before transferring data to Dataverse tables. By performing format conversion within the migration workflow, you can ensure that all files meet the required format specifications, minimizing the risk of migration errors.

D) Implementing conditional logic in Power Automate flows enables you to skip files with unsupported formats or metadata fields during the migration process. By bypassing problematic files and continuing with the migration, you can ensure the overall progress of the migration while addressing specific error scenarios.

Option B) Restrict migration scope: While excluding problematic files may mitigate errors, it may also delay the migration process and require additional effort to resolve metadata issues before proceeding.

Option C) Enable metadata validation settings: While metadata validation may enforce compliance, it may not directly address format mismatches or unsupported metadata fields encountered during the migration process.

QUESTION 31

Answer - [A] Create, Read, Update, Delete, Execute

A) Create, Read, Update, Delete, Execute - Correct, these are the standard CRUD operations supported by the Organization service.

B) Insert, Retrieve, Modify, Remove, Execute - Some terms are close but not the standard operations.

C) Add, Get, Change, Drop, Invoke - These terms do not align with standard CRUD operations.

D) New, Fetch, Edit, Remove, Execute - "New" and "Fetch" are not standard CRUD operations.

E) Generate, Retrieve, Alter, Discard, Invoke - "Generate" and "Alter" are not standard CRUD operations.

QUESTION 32

Answer - [D] Specifying parameter data types and validation rules.

A) Using a fixed schema for all input parameters - Flexibility in input parameter schemas may be necessary to accommodate various data structures.

B) Ensuring compatibility with third-party systems for output parameters - Output parameters should be designed based on the requirements of the consuming applications, not third-party systems.

C) Limiting the number of input parameters to improve performance - The number of parameters should be based on functional requirements, not performance considerations.

D) Specifying parameter data types and validation rules - Correct, defining data types and validation rules ensures data integrity and compatibility with consuming applications.

E) Sharing input parameters across multiple Custom API messages - While feasible, it may lead to dependencies and potential conflicts between different Custom API messages.

QUESTION 33

Answer - [A] _contact_name

A) In the context of model-driven apps and related entities, the _contact_name attribute contains the display name of the associated contact record. When configuring a model-driven app to display related information, you should specify the _contact_name attribute to ensure that the contact's name is displayed correctly for each interaction record.

Option B) _contactid_name - Incorrect: This attribute may contain the GUID of the associated contact record, not the contact's name.
Option C) _contact_name_value - Incorrect: This attribute combination is unlikely to exist and may not provide the contact's name.
Option D) _contactid_value - Incorrect: This attribute combination is unlikely to exist and may not provide the contact's name.

QUESTION 34

Answer - [B] Registering the application with the OAuth provider.

A) Generating a client secret for the application - While necessary, this step comes after registering the application with the OAuth provider.

B) Registering the application with the OAuth provider - Correct, registering the application establishes trust between the application and the OAuth provider, enabling secure authentication and token exchange.

C) Storing user credentials in plaintext within the application code - Storing credentials in plaintext is a security risk and should be avoided.

D) Using HTTP Basic Authentication for token exchange - OAuth authentication does not involve exchanging tokens via HTTP Basic Authentication.

E) Exposing sensitive tokens in client-side JavaScript code - Exposing tokens in client-side code poses a security risk as they can be easily intercepted.

QUESTION 35

Answer - D

Option A - Incorrect: PowerApps does not support direct linking with GitHub for APIs.

Option B - Inefficient: Manually updating is not scalable or reliable.

Option C - Incorrect: Overly complex and not directly supported for API management.

Option D - Correct: Utilizing Azure DevOps for CI/CD pipelines is an efficient way to manage and automate updates from GitHub.

Option E - Possible but not directly integrated into Power Platform tools.

QUESTION 36

Answer - A) POST

A) POST - Correct. Suitable for actions that change the state or require secure data transmission.
B) GET - Incorrect. Not secure for sensitive actions like password changes.
C) PUT - Incorrect. Generally used for replacing resources.
D) PATCH - Incorrect. For partial updates.
E) OPTIONS - Incorrect. Describes communication options for the target resource.

QUESTION 37

Answer - [A] OAuth 2.0 client credentials flow

A) OAuth 2.0 client credentials flow - Correct, this method allows secure access to the Web API without storing user credentials by obtaining access tokens using client credentials.

B) Basic authentication with encrypted credentials - Basic authentication involves storing credentials, which is less secure and not recommended for accessing the Web API.

C) API key authentication with IP whitelisting - While API key authentication is simple, it may not provide the necessary security, and IP whitelisting alone may not be sufficient.

D) SAML-based single sign-on (SSO) - SAML-based SSO is more suitable for user authentication and may not be applicable for machine-to-machine communication with the Web API.

E) User-managed access tokens - User-managed access tokens require storing user credentials and are less suitable for machine-to-machine communication without user interaction.

QUESTION 38

Answer - [D] Implementing circuit breaker patterns to detect and handle API failures

A) Implementing long-running transactions to minimize API calls - Long-running transactions may increase the risk of hitting rate limits and are not a recommended approach for handling API rate limits.

B) Using multiple API keys to distribute requests across different quotas - While multiple API keys can help distribute load, it may not directly address API rate limit issues.

C) Caching API responses to reduce the frequency of requests - Caching can improve performance but may not prevent rate limit violations or handle API failures.

D) Implementing circuit breaker patterns to detect and handle API failures - Correct, circuit breaker patterns help detect and respond to API failures, preventing unnecessary retries and reducing the impact of failures on the system.

E) Increasing request payload sizes to minimize the number of requests - Increasing payload sizes may not always be feasible or effective in reducing the number of requests.

QUESTION 39

Answer - A), B), C), and D)

A) Correct. Helps maintain data flow continuity by attempting to resend data.

B) Correct. Ensures data is not lost by writing to an alternative storage during API failure.

C) Correct. Allows quick technical response to API failures.

D) Correct. Provides an alternative path for data handling when primary API is down.

E) Incorrect. Conditional paths help manage flow but don't necessarily ensure data integrity.

QUESTION 40

Answer - B)

A) Incorrect - Direct SQL query is too simplistic and doesn't schedule tasks or manage errors/scalability.

B) Correct - This C# TimerTrigger is correctly set up to trigger daily and includes an ILogger for error handling and logging.

C) Incorrect - JavaScript's setInterval is unsuitable for Azure Functions and does not provide the necessary scalability or error handling.

D) Incorrect - PowerFx is used within Power Apps and cannot schedule Azure Functions.

E) Incorrect - The TypeScript example has a syntax error in the cron expression and does not compile in Azure Functions for scheduling tasks.

QUESTION 41

Answer - [D] Leveraging context variables to pass data between the flow and app

A) Utilizing Power Automate connectors for direct app integration - While connectors are important, they may not directly facilitate seamless integration by themselves.

B) Implementing custom authentication mechanisms for enhanced security - Authentication is important but may not directly relate to integration between the cloud flow and Power Apps.

C) Ensuring data consistency by synchronizing data schemas between components - Data consistency is important but may not directly address the need for passing data between the flow and app.

D) Leveraging context variables to pass data between the flow and app - Correct, context variables allow seamless data exchange between the cloud flow and Power Apps, facilitating integration and automation.

E) Embedding flow logic directly within the Power Apps canvas - Embedding flow logic within the app may not ensure flexibility and separation of concerns in the solution architecture.

QUESTION 42

Answer - A), B), and C)

A) Correct. Checks if the status is exactly 'Final'.

B) Correct. Verifies document is in the 'Finance' department folder.

C) Correct. Combines both conditions necessary for the specific department and status.

D) Incorrect. Checking for not being a 'Draft' does not ensure it is 'Final'.

E) Incorrect. Starts with may not accurately pinpoint the 'Finance' folder.

QUESTION 43

Answer - [C] Using managed identities for Azure resources to authenticate service principals

A) Hard-coding service principal credentials within the application code - Hard-coding credentials exposes them to unauthorized access and is not recommended for security reasons.

B) Granting all permissions to service principals for maximum flexibility - Granting excessive permissions increases the risk of security breaches and violates the principle of least privilege.

C) Using managed identities for Azure resources to authenticate service principals - Correct, managed identities provide an Azure Active Directory identity for the service principal, eliminating the need to store credentials in the application code or configuration files.

D) Sharing service principal credentials via email for team collaboration - Sharing credentials via email is insecure and violates security best practices.

E) Creating separate service principals for each application function - While creating separate service principals can enhance security, using managed identities is a more streamlined and secure approach.

QUESTION 44

Answer - [D] Increasing complexity and maintenance overhead due to additional integration points

A) Streamlining workflow execution by reducing manual intervention and delays - While adding cloud flow steps can streamline execution, it may not be the only impact and could introduce other considerations such as increased complexity.

B) Enhancing scalability by enabling asynchronous processing of workflow steps - Asynchronous processing can improve scalability, but it may not be the primary impact of adding a cloud flow step.

C) Improving data accuracy and integrity through automated data validation and verification - While automation can enhance data quality, it may not be the primary impact of adding a cloud flow step.

D) Increasing complexity and maintenance overhead due to additional integration points - Correct, adding cloud flow steps introduces additional integration points and can increase complexity and maintenance overhead for the business process flow.

E) Optimizing resource utilization by leveraging cloud-based processing capabilities - While cloud-based processing can optimize resource utilization, it may not be the primary impact of adding a cloud flow step.

QUESTION 45

Answer - A) Password based

A) Correct. Basic authentication typically involves password-based credentials.
B) Incorrect. OAuth 2.0 is too advanced for legacy systems.
C) Incorrect. API key is not equivalent to basic authentication.
D) Incorrect. Certificate-based authentication is more secure and not typical for legacy systems.
E) Incorrect. SSO is not applicable for basic authentication in legacy systems.

QUESTION 46

Answer - [C] Granting appropriate permissions to service accounts for invoking IServiceEndpointNotificationService

A) Enabling webhook endpoints in the Dataverse environment and securing them with OAuth 2.0 authentication - While security is important, this choice does not directly address the configuration requirements for IServiceEndpointNotificationService.

B) Defining event mappings to map Dataverse entity changes to corresponding events for publication - Event mappings may be part of the configuration but do not specifically relate to IServiceEndpointNotificationService setup.

C) Granting appropriate permissions to service accounts for invoking IServiceEndpointNotificationService - Correct, configuring permissions for service accounts to invoke IServiceEndpointNotificationService is essential for event publication.

D) Configuring Azure Service Bus queues for reliable event delivery and message persistence - Azure Service Bus queues are not directly related to publishing events using IServiceEndpointNotificationService.

E) Setting up Azure Application Insights to monitor event publication performance and errors - While monitoring is important, it's not a configuration requirement for publishing events using IServiceEndpointNotificationService.

QUESTION 47

Answer - [A] Webhooks provide real-time event notifications, while Azure Event Hub offers high throughput event ingestion.

A) Webhooks provide real-time event notifications, while Azure Event Hub offers high throughput event ingestion - This comparison accurately describes the capabilities and use cases of webhooks and Azure Event Hub. Webhooks are designed for real-time notifications, while Event Hub excels in handling high volumes of events.

B) Azure Service Bus ensures reliable message delivery, while Azure Event Hub supports event-driven architectures - While both statements are true, they do not compare the capabilities of different service endpoints.

C) Custom HTTP endpoints allow synchronous communication, while Azure Service Bus enables asynchronous messaging - This comparison is inaccurate as Azure Service Bus can support both synchronous and asynchronous messaging.

D) Webhooks are suitable for one-way communication, while Azure Service Bus supports bidirectional messaging - While webhooks are typically used for one-way communication, Azure Service Bus can also support bidirectional messaging.

E) Azure Event Hub is ideal for low-latency scenarios, while Custom HTTP endpoints offer flexibility in endpoint configuration - This comparison does not accurately reflect the capabilities and use cases of different service endpoints.

QUESTION 48

Answer - A) If-Match header

A) Correct. The If-Match header is used for optimistic concurrency, ensuring updates are made only if the record hasn't changed since last fetched.
B) Incorrect. If-None-Match is used to make conditional requests based on the absence of a record.
C) Incorrect. $filter is for filtering data, not managing concurrency.
D) Incorrect. ConcurrencyBehavior is not a valid header in Dataverse.
E) Incorrect. If-Unmodified-Since is not used in Dataverse API.

QUESTION 49

Answer - [A, B, C] Improved query performance for record retrieval operations due to indexed alternate keys, Increased storage utilization for maintaining alternate key indexes in the database, Reduced latency for data insertion and update operations with enforced uniqueness constraints.

A) Improved query performance for record retrieval operations due to indexed alternate keys. - Indexed alternate keys can significantly improve query performance by providing fast access paths to data, especially for lookup operations.

B) Increased storage utilization for maintaining alternate key indexes in the database. - While indexed alternate keys improve query performance, they require additional storage space to maintain index structures, impacting overall storage utilization.

C) Reduced latency for data insertion and update operations with enforced uniqueness constraints. - Enforcing uniqueness with alternate keys can help prevent duplicate records, reducing the latency associated with data validation during insertion and update operations.

D) Enhanced scalability by distributing data across multiple alternate key partitions. - Alternate keys do not inherently distribute data across partitions; their primary purpose is to enforce uniqueness constraints and improve query performance.

E) Minimized network overhead for data synchronization with alternate key-based replication. - Alternate keys do not directly impact network overhead for data synchronization; their focus is on data integrity and query performance within the database.

QUESTION 50

Answer - [B] ETL processes automate the extraction, transformation, and loading of data between disparate systems.

A) ETL processes facilitate real-time data synchronization between systems to ensure data consistency. - While ETL processes can contribute to data consistency, they are not necessarily real-time and focus more on batch-oriented data integration tasks.

B) ETL processes automate the extraction, transformation, and loading of data between disparate systems. - This statement accurately describes the role of ETL processes, which involve extracting data from source systems, transforming it into the desired format, and loading it into the target system.

C) ETL processes enable direct querying of remote data sources without data duplication. - ETL processes involve data movement and transformation rather than direct querying, and they typically result in data duplication in the target system.

D) ETL processes enforce data security and compliance standards during data integration tasks. - While ETL processes can contribute to data security and compliance, their primary focus is on data movement and transformation rather than enforcement of security standards.

E) ETL processes handle user authentication and access control for data exchange between systems. - Authentication and access control are typically handled separately from ETL processes, focusing more on securing data access rather than data movement itself.

PRACTICE TEST 3 - QUESTIONS ONLY

QUESTION 1

An e-commerce platform is expanding its operations and scaling up its Power Platform solutions to accommodate increased user traffic. They need a monitoring solution that not only analyzes historical data but also predicts potential issues based on past trends, enabling them to take proactive measures to ensure system stability and performance. Which feature of monitoring and diagnostics provides proactive insights by forecasting potential issues based on historical data and trends?

A) Real-time monitoring
B) Historical data analysis
C) Predictive analytics
D) Custom dashboards
E) Third-party integrations

QUESTION 2

An insurance company is evaluating the default functionality of a Power Platform solution for claims processing. They need to understand the limitations of the default features to assess the need for customization. What is a limitation of default functionality in Power Platform that may necessitate customization for claims processing?

A) Inability to handle complex business logic
B) Limited data storage capacity
C) Lack of support for external integrations
D) Difficulty in customizing user interface components
E) Absence of role-based access control

QUESTION 3

You are tasked with setting up a timer-triggered Azure Function to initiate a weekly database cleanup every Sunday at 3 AM in Microsoft Dataverse. What is the correct cron expression?

A) 0 3 * * SUN
B) 0 3 * * 0
C) 0 3 * * 7
D) 0 0 3 * * 0
E) 0 0 3 * * SUN

QUESTION 4

A large corporation is structuring teams and business units within their Power Platform environment to facilitate efficient collaboration and data management. They need to ensure that the setup reflects the organization's hierarchical structure and reporting relationships.
Which actions should they take when configuring teams and business units to achieve this objective? Select THREE.

A) Create separate business units for each department within the organization.

B) Designate team leaders as managers within their respective business units.
C) Define hierarchical relationships between business units to represent reporting structures.
D) Establish security roles based on team memberships to control access to sensitive data.
E) Implement role-based access controls to restrict access to specific business units based on job roles.

QUESTION 5

How would you implement a TypeScript function to handle and parse a JSON response from a Dataverse Web API query to retrieve contact records?

A) function parseContacts(response: any): void { console.log('Contacts: ', response.value); }

B) function getContacts(): void { fetch('https://your-org.api.crm.dynamics.com/api/data/v9.1/contacts').then(response => response.json()).then(data => console.log(data)); }

C) let contacts = JSON.parse(response); for (let contact of contacts) { console.log(contact.name); }

D) interface Contact { contactId: string; firstName: string; lastName: string; } async function fetchContacts(): Promise<Contact[]> { const response = await fetch('https://your-org.api.crm.dynamics.com/api/data/v9.1/contacts'); const data: Contact[] = await response.json(); return data; }

E) document.getElementById('contacts').innerHTML = response;

QUESTION 6

To support a role-based access scenario in a canvas app, you need to filter a list to show items only from the user's department. The app uses Dataverse and the user's department is stored in a variable userDept. What PowerFx should be used?

A) Filter('Items', Department = userDept)
B) Lookup('Items', Department = userDept)
C) 'Items'
D) Filter('Items', Department.Value = userDept)
E) Collect('UserDeptItems', Filter(Items, Department = userDept))

QUESTION 7

A financial institution is considering the use of security roles and teams in Dataverse to manage access control for its customer relationship management (CRM) system. They need to understand the differences between security roles and teams to make informed decisions about their implementation strategy.
How do security roles differ from teams in Dataverse in terms of access control? Select THREE.

A) Security roles define access permissions based on user privileges, whereas teams define access permissions based on user membership in organizational units.

B) Security roles are static and apply to individual users, whereas teams are dynamic and apply to groups of users with similar roles or responsibilities.

C) Security roles are hierarchical and can be inherited by subordinate roles, whereas teams are flat structures with no inherent hierarchy.

D) Security roles grant access to data and functionality, whereas teams provide a mechanism for sharing records and collaborating with other users.

E) Security roles are enforced at the system level, whereas teams are enforced at the record level, allowing for fine-grained access control.

QUESTION 8

A large enterprise is evaluating the impact of configuring business units in Microsoft Dataverse on data visibility and access control. They need to understand how business units affect data access and visibility across different organizational units and user roles.
How does configuring business units in Microsoft Dataverse impact data visibility?

A) Business units restrict data visibility to records owned by users within the same organizational unit, limiting access to data across business unit boundaries.

B) Business units enable data sharing and collaboration across organizational boundaries by providing a unified view of records and resources within the entire Dataverse environment.

C) Business units enhance data visibility by allowing users to access and view records owned by any user within the same business unit, regardless of their roles or permissions.

D) Business units enforce strict data segregation and isolation, preventing users from accessing records or resources outside their assigned business unit.

E) Business units facilitate data visibility by establishing role-based access control (RBAC) policies that govern data access and visibility based on user roles and responsibilities.

QUESTION 9

You are developing a solution using Microsoft Dataverse that involves creating a custom workflow process. However, upon testing, the workflow does not trigger as expected. What could be potential reasons for this issue? Select the correct answers that apply.

A) The workflow scope is set to "User" instead of "Organization."
B) The workflow's trigger condition is not met based on the specified criteria.
C) The workflow's asynchronous processing is disabled in the environment settings.
D) The workflow logic contains a syntax error, preventing execution.
E) The workflow's execution time exceeds the maximum allowed duration.

QUESTION 10

As part of configuring Microsoft Dataverse, you are to set up a table that logs user access and changes. Which of the following TypeScript snippets would correctly implement an event handler for logging changes on the 'Contacts' table?

A) Dataverse.tables.contacts.onChange(logChange)
B) Contacts.addEventListener("change", logChange);
C) Xrm.Page.data.entity.addOnChange(logChange);
D) entity.on('contacts.change', logChange);

E) Contacts.onChange.execute(logChange);

QUESTION 11

A healthcare organization is implementing a patient management system using Microsoft Dataverse. They need to configure relationships between the "Patient" and "Appointment" entities to track patient appointments. Additionally, they want to ensure that when a patient record is deleted, associated appointment records are retained for historical purposes. Which relationship behavior should be configured for the "Patient-Appointment" relationship to meet this requirement?

A) Restrict delete
B) Cascade All
C) Remove Link
D) Parental
E) Referential

QUESTION 12

You are responsible for managing a Microsoft Power Platform environment where several critical solutions are deployed to support various business processes. One of the solutions requires minor adjustments to address emerging business needs without impacting the functionality of other solutions. What approach should you take to make these adjustments efficiently while maintaining system stability?

A) Create
B) Update
C) Upgrade
D) Patch

QUESTION 13

A development team is tasked with ensuring the integrity of solutions during import and export processes in Microsoft Dataverse. What are the best practices for ensuring integrity during solution transfer? Select the correct answers that apply.

A) Perform thorough testing in the target environment after solution import
B) Use solution validation tools to check for errors before export
C) Implement version control to track changes in solutions
D) Document all customizations and configurations included in the solution
E) Disable all components before exporting the solution

QUESTION 14

Integrating a model-driven app with other Power Platform components can enhance its functionality and extend its capabilities. How can a model-driven app be integrated with other Power Platform components? Select the correct answers that apply.

A) Trigger Power Automate flows based on app events
B) Embed Canvas Apps within model-driven app forms

C) Utilize Dataverse connectors to access external data sources
D) Integrate Power Virtual Agents for chatbot interactions
E) Establish API connections with third-party services for data exchange

QUESTION 15

You are designing a model-driven app for a financial institution's loan processing system. The app aims to streamline loan application processing and ensure data accuracy. What are two functionalities that you can achieve by using a business rule in this scenario? Select the correct answers that apply.

A) Access external data.
B) Enable or disable a column based on application status.
C) Show or hide a column based on user role.
D) Run the rule on demand.

QUESTION 16

Performance is a critical factor when configuring commands and buttons using JavaScript in Power Apps. What are key performance considerations that developers should keep in mind? Select the correct answers that apply.

A) Minimize the use of synchronous operations to avoid blocking UI responsiveness
B) Optimize script loading by reducing external dependencies
C) Implement lazy loading for non-essential scripts to improve initial app load times
D) Utilize browser caching to store frequently accessed scripts locally
E) Batch script executions to reduce the number of round trips to the server

QUESTION 17

A transportation company is developing a Power App to track vehicle maintenance schedules and alert mechanics when service is due. During testing, they encounter issues with formula behavior and need to debug them efficiently. What approaches can they use to debug Power Fx formulas effectively? Select the correct answers that apply.

A) Utilizing the Formula Auditing feature in Power Apps to trace formula execution steps
B) Inserting temporary logging statements within formulas to capture intermediate values
C) Splitting complex formulas into smaller parts and testing each component individually
D) Using the Error() function to handle exceptions and identify error-prone sections of code
E) Collaborating with other developers to review formula logic and identify potential issues

QUESTION 18

You are tasked with developing a model-driven app for an inventory management system. The app requires executing custom code when a user selects a button on the ribbon, but this functionality should only be available to users with inventory manager roles. What option should you select to meet this requirement?

A) Custom API
B) Custom process action

C) Classic workflow
D) Business rule

QUESTION 19

A development team is tasked with debugging a canvas app that is not functioning as expected. Which debugging technique involves stepping through app logic line by line to identify errors or unexpected behavior?

A) Breakpoint debugging
B) Logging and tracing
C) Unit testing
D) Error code analysis
E) Performance profiling

QUESTION 20

You are developing a model-driven app and need to implement JavaScript for dynamic UI adjustments based on data changes. What is the correct script to subscribe to data changes on a form?

A) Xrm.Page.data.entity.addOnChange('field', myFunction)
B) Xrm.Page.getAttribute('field').addOnChange(myFunction)
C) document.getElementById('field').addEventListener('change', myFunction)
D) Xrm.Data.entity.attributes.get('field').addOnChange(myFunction)
E) formContext.getAttribute('field').addOnChange(myFunction)

QUESTION 21

You are tasked with developing a canvas app for a sales dashboard. The app requires integrating a custom visual to represent sales performance data graphically. However, you need the visual to be easily scalable and maintainable as the app grows in complexity. Which approach should you employ?

A) Client scripting
B) Power Apps component framework code component
C) Web API
D) Liquid template

QUESTION 22

A Power Apps developer is troubleshooting a JavaScript function that is not executing as expected. Which of the following debugging tips should the developer consider to identify and resolve the issue effectively?

A) Use console.log() statements to output debug information
B) Step through the code using breakpoints in the browser developer tools
C) Review browser console errors for syntax or runtime issues
D) Utilize the Client API trace log for detailed function execution logs
E) Enable verbose logging in the Power Apps environment settings

QUESTION 23

A Power Apps developer is exploring common use cases for integrating client scripts with Dataverse Web API. Which of the following scenarios represents a typical use case for leveraging Dataverse Web API in client scripting?

A) Retrieving user authentication tokens for SSO implementation
B) Querying Dataverse data to populate form fields dynamically
C) Sending bulk email notifications to users from a canvas app
D) Encrypting sensitive data before storage in Dataverse
E) Performing database migrations between Dataverse environments

QUESTION 24

Your organization is developing a vendor management solution using Microsoft Dataverse. You need to integrate an external vendor management system, which exposes a RESTful Web API, to synchronize vendor information within the solution. Considering the integration requirements, which three options should you leverage to create an effective integration solution? Select the correct answers that apply.

A) Azure function
B) Custom connector
C) Custom API
D) HTTP request
E) Business rule

QUESTION 25

What is the best practice for handling dependencies in a PCF component initialization script?

A) import { Xrm } from 'xrm';
B) import * as Xrm from '@microsoft/xrm';
C) require(['xrm'], function(Xrm) { this.Xrm = Xrm; });
D) import { Xrm } from '@types/xrm';
E) import Xrm from '@microsoft/powerapps-sdk';

QUESTION 26

A Power Apps developer is adhering to best practices for robust implementations of PCF component interfaces. What is a recommended practice for ensuring compatibility and consistency across different Power Apps environments?

A) Embedding external JavaScript libraries for enhanced functionality.
B) Hardcoding configuration parameters within the component code.
C) Minimizing dependencies on specific Power Apps controls or features.
D) Using inline CSS styles for consistent visual presentation.
E) Leveraging undocumented Power Platform APIs for advanced interactions.

QUESTION 27

Your organization is developing a canvas app for managing project tasks. You need to implement a feature that sends push notifications to users when their assigned tasks are due. Which integration option should you choose to implement this feature? Select the correct answers that apply.

A) Power Apps custom control
B) Power Automate flow
C) Azure Notification Hubs
D) Custom API

QUESTION 28

When optimizing performance for Web API calls in PCF components, what is a recommended strategy to minimize latency and improve responsiveness?

A) Batch multiple API requests into a single call.
B) Increase the timeout duration for API requests.
C) Minify the PCF component script to reduce file size.
D) Implement server-side caching for frequently accessed data.
E) Pre-fetch data in advance to reduce on-demand API calls.

QUESTION 29

A Power Platform developer is configuring error handling within a plug-in execution pipeline to ensure robustness in their solution. Which mechanism is commonly used for error handling within the pipeline?

A) Try-catch blocks within the plug-in code
B) Rollback mechanism for database transactions
C) Logging of exception details to the platform's trace log
D) Queuing system for reprocessing failed plug-ins
E) Automatic retry mechanism for transient faults

QUESTION 30

Your organization is migrating data from an on-premises Oracle database to Microsoft Dataverse tables using a custom .NET application. During the migration, you encounter errors related to database connectivity issues and timeouts due to network latency. What are two recommended approaches to mitigate these errors and ensure the successful completion of the migration? Select the correct answers that apply.

A) Optimize database query performance by indexing frequently accessed tables and optimizing SQL queries to minimize data retrieval time.

B) Implement connection resiliency features in the .NET application, such as automatic reconnection logic and retry policies, to handle transient network failures gracefully.

C) Upgrade the on-premises Oracle database to a newer version with improved network connectivity and performance optimizations for data migration scenarios.

D) Configure network load balancers with improved bandwidth allocation and quality of service (QoS) settings to prioritize traffic between the Oracle database and Dataverse environment.

QUESTION 31

A team of Power Platform developers is discussing best practices for using the Organization service in plug-ins. What is a recommended best practice when utilizing the service in plug-ins?

A) Implementing complex business logic directly within plug-ins for better performance.
B) Performing extensive data validation and error handling within the plug-in code.
C) Minimizing the use of the Organization service to reduce dependencies on Microsoft Dataverse.
D) Utilizing early-bound classes instead of the Organization service for improved type safety.
E) Deploying plug-ins without sandboxing to maximize access to system resources.

QUESTION 32

When considering security practices for Custom APIs in Dataverse, what is a recommended approach?

A) Granting unrestricted access to all users.
B) Implementing role-based access control (RBAC).
C) Storing sensitive data directly within the API endpoints.
D) Using HTTP Basic authentication for simplicity.
E) Sharing API keys publicly for easy integration.

QUESTION 33

You are developing a custom connector in Power Automate to interact with an external API. The API returns data related to customer orders stored in Microsoft Dataverse. When retrieving order records, you need to include the name of the associated "Customers." What attribute should you include in your custom connector to retrieve the customer's name along with the order details?

A) _customer_name
B) _customerid
C) _customer_value
D) _customerid_name

QUESTION 34

A Power Platform solution needs to handle sensitive data, such as personally identifiable information (PII), in API requests and responses. What approach should be taken to ensure the security of sensitive data?

A) Encrypting all data in transit and at rest.
B) Storing sensitive data in plain text within API requests.
C) Using SSL/TLS for secure communication.
D) Logging sensitive data in clear text to facilitate troubleshooting.
E) Sharing sensitive data with third-party services without encryption.

QUESTION 35

When integrating Azure services APIs into Power Platform, what key configuration is necessary in the API definition for proper authentication and authorization?

A) Specify OAuth settings in the API definition to integrate with Azure Active Directory.
B) Include API keys directly in the API URL for each request.
C) Use basic authentication with username and password embedded in the API calls.
D) Configure the API to accept anonymous access for seamless integration.
E) Set up a virtual network in Azure to securely connect to Power Platform.

QUESTION 36

You need to design a JavaScript function to log user activities and send data to a backend server for analytics. Which HTTP method should be used to ensure data is added correctly?

A) GET
B) POST
C) PUT
D) PATCH
E) DELETE

QUESTION 37

When handling large data sets through the Dataverse Web API, what is a recommended approach to improve performance and efficiency?

A) Implementing pagination with appropriate page sizes.
B) Utilizing batch requests for simultaneous operations.
C) Increasing server-side timeouts for long-running queries.
D) Reducing data redundancy through denormalization.
E) Distributing data across multiple environments.

QUESTION 38

In a Power Platform solution, developers are tasked with monitoring and logging retries for API calls. Which of the following tools or services is most suitable for this purpose?

A) Azure Monitor
B) Power Automate
C) Power Apps Portal
D) Microsoft Dataverse
E) Azure DevOps

QUESTION 39

In a scenario where a Power Automate flow integrates with a logistics API to update shipment statuses, how can you ensure continuity of service during API maintenance? Select the correct answers that apply.

A) Schedule the flow to avoid known maintenance times
B) Use a backup API
C) Log all API downtime
D) Notify logistics managers of downtime
E) Implement a retry mechanism

QUESTION 40

A logistics company uses Azure Functions to handle shipping notifications sent via HTTP requests whenever a shipment status changes. The function should verify the authentication of the request before processing.

A) JavaScript: if (req.query.key == process.env.AUTH_KEY) { context.res = { body: "Authenticated" }; }

B) JSON: { "bindings": [{ "authLevel": "function", "type": "httpTrigger", "direction": "in" }] }

C) TypeScript: import { AzureFunction, Context, HttpRequest } from '@azure/functions'; export const httpTrigger: AzureFunction = async function (context: Context, req: HttpRequest): Promise<void> { if (req.headers['x-api-key'] === process.env.API_KEY) { context.res = { status: 200, body: 'Authorized' }; } else { context.res = { status: 401, body: 'Unauthorized' }; } }

D) C#: public static HttpResponseMessage Run(HttpRequestMessage req, TraceWriter log) { if (req.Headers.Authorization.Parameter == Environment.GetEnvironmentVariable("API_KEY")) { return req.CreateResponse(HttpStatusCode.OK, "Authorized"); } else { return req.CreateResponse(HttpStatusCode.Unauthorized, "Unauthorized"); } }

E) HTML: <p>API Key: <input type="text" id="apiKey"></p>

QUESTION 41

When managing flow logic in Power Automate cloud flows, what advanced technique can improve performance and maintainability?

A) Using nested conditionals for complex branching
B) Employing parallel branches for concurrent execution
C) Implementing recursive loops for iterative processing
D) Utilizing custom plugins for extending flow functionality
E) Centralizing common logic in separate child flows

QUESTION 42

Configure a Power Automate flow to trigger when documents in the "Reports" SharePoint library have been updated and are marked with a 'Reviewed' tag in their metadata. Which expressions should you use? Select the correct answers that apply.

A) @equals(triggerBody()?['Tags'], 'Reviewed')
B) @contains(triggerBody()?['LibraryName'], 'Reports')
C) @and(equals(triggerBody()?['Tags'], 'Reviewed'), contains(triggerBody()?['LibraryName'], 'Reports'))
D) @not(empty(triggerBody()?['Tags']))
E) @greater(triggerOutputs()?['VersionNumber'], 1)

QUESTION 43

A financial institution is deploying a Power Platform solution to automate regulatory compliance processes. They need to ensure that Azure Key Vault and Microsoft Entra are used in accordance with security and compliance best practices. What is a best practice for using Azure Key Vault and Entra in Power Platform development?

A) Sharing Azure Key Vault secrets across multiple applications
B) Storing sensitive information in plain text within Azure Key Vault
C) Limiting access to Azure Key Vault based on least privilege principles
D) Hard-coding Entra service principal credentials in application code
E) Allowing unrestricted access to Entra service principals

QUESTION 44

A manufacturing company is integrating Power Platform solutions into its production processes to improve efficiency. They want to configure and customize flow steps to ensure seamless data flow between manufacturing systems and business applications. What is a best practice for configuration and customization of flow steps in this scenario?

A) Implementing error handling logic using custom JavaScript code actions
B) Utilizing pre-built connectors and templates for rapid development and deployment
C) Embedding complex business logic directly within flow actions for performance optimization
D) Minimizing data transformation and manipulation to reduce processing overhead
E) Leveraging Power Automate Desktop for offline data processing and synchronization

QUESTION 45

A custom connector in Power Platform must access an analytics API that grants permissions based on application-level security requirements. Which authentication should you use?

A) Client credentials
B) OAuth 2.0
C) API key
D) Certificate based
E) Dynamic authentication

QUESTION 46

A technology startup is developing a Power Platform solution to manage customer support tickets efficiently. They want to explore common use cases for publishing Dataverse events using IServiceEndpointNotificationService. What are some common use cases for publishing events using IServiceEndpointNotificationService? Select the correct answers that apply.

A) Triggering external workflows or processes in response to Dataverse data changes
B) Notifying users or stakeholders about critical system events or updates in real-time
C) Integrating Dataverse with external systems and services asynchronously
D) Orchestrating complex business logic and approvals based on Dataverse events
E) Monitoring performance metrics and resource utilization in real-time

QUESTION 47

A financial services company is developing a Power Platform solution to process sensitive customer data and transactions. They are concerned about security practices when registering service endpoints to ensure compliance with regulatory requirements. What security practices should they consider for endpoint registration in this scenario? Select the correct answers that apply.

A) Implementing OAuth authentication for secure endpoint access
B) Encrypting data transmission between endpoints using SSL/TLS
C) Restricting endpoint access based on IP whitelisting
D) Enabling role-based access control (RBAC) for endpoint management
E) Regularly updating endpoint credentials and access tokens

QUESTION 48

To efficiently count the number of contacts in Microsoft Dataverse that have an email address specified, which query should you use in the Web API?

A) $count with $filter
B) $sum
C) $total
D) $calculate
E) $aggregate

QUESTION 49

A financial services company is looking to implement best practices for managing alternate keys in their Power Platform solution. What are some best practices they should consider? Select the correct answers that apply.

A) Regularly monitoring and maintaining alternate key indexes for optimal performance.
B) Documenting the purpose and usage of each alternate key for future reference and troubleshooting.
C) Avoiding excessive use of alternate keys to minimize database overhead and complexity.
D) Reviewing and updating alternate key configurations as business requirements evolve over time.
E) Implementing proper error handling mechanisms to manage exceptions related to alternate key violations.

QUESTION 50

A financial services firm is experiencing discrepancies and errors in financial data during the integration process between its accounting system and Dataverse. Which approach would be most effective for handling such data discrepancies and errors? Select the correct answers that apply.

A) Implementing data validation rules and error handling mechanisms in the ETL process to identify and correct errors.
B) Enforcing strict data governance policies to prevent data discrepancies at the source.
C) Increasing the frequency of data synchronization to minimize the impact of discrepancies.
D) Setting up alerts and notifications to notify administrators of data errors in real-time.
E) Conducting regular data audits and reconciliations to identify and resolve discrepancies proactively.

PRACTICE TEST 3 - ANSWERS ONLY

QUESTION 1

Answer - [C) Predictive analytics]

C) Predictive analytics - Predictive analytics can analyze historical data and trends to forecast potential issues, allowing proactive measures to be taken to ensure system stability and performance.

A) Real-time monitoring - Real-time monitoring provides immediate insights but may not offer predictive capabilities based on historical data.

B) Historical data analysis - While historical data analysis is important, it may not include predictive capabilities without specific predictive analytics tools.

D) Custom dashboards - Custom dashboards provide visualization of data but may not inherently include predictive analytics features.

E) Third-party integrations - Third-party integrations may enhance monitoring capabilities but may not specifically provide predictive analytics functionality.

QUESTION 2

Answer - [A) Inability to handle complex business logic]

A) Inability to handle complex business logic - Default functionality may not always support complex business logic, requiring customization to meet specific requirements.

B) Limited data storage capacity - Power Platform typically provides ample data storage capacity, so this is not a significant limitation.

C) Lack of support for external integrations - Power Platform is designed for integration with external systems, so this limitation is unlikely.

D) Difficulty in customizing user interface components - Customizing UI components is generally supported in Power Platform, so this is not a primary limitation.

E) Absence of role-based access control - Role-based access control is a fundamental feature in Power Platform and is unlikely to be absent.

QUESTION 3

Answer - B) 0 3 * * 0

A) Incorrect. Azure cron doesn't use day name abbreviations.
B) Correct. Executes every Sunday at 3 AM, with Sunday as 0.
C) Incorrect. Incorrect day value for Sunday.
D) Incorrect. Misplaced hour and minute, incorrect cron format.
E) Incorrect. Uses day name and misformatted time.

QUESTION 4

Answer - A, B, and C) Create separate business units for each department within the organization. Designate team leaders as managers within their respective business units. Define hierarchical relationships between business units to represent reporting structures.

A) - Correct. Creating separate business units for each department facilitates organizational structure alignment within the Power Platform environment.

B) - Correct. Designating team leaders as managers within their respective business units ensures clear reporting relationships and accountability.

C) - Correct. Defining hierarchical relationships between business units accurately represents reporting structures and ensures data management efficiency.

D) - Incorrect. Establishing security roles based on team memberships may not directly reflect organizational hierarchy and reporting relationships.

E) - Incorrect. While role-based access controls are important, they may not directly address the objective of structuring teams and business units to reflect organizational hierarchy.

QUESTION 5

Answer - D

Option A - Incorrect. This function logs the response but does not handle fetching or parsing from an API.

Option B - Incorrect. Correctly fetches and logs data but lacks type safety and parsing into a usable data structure.

Option C - Incorrect. Attempts to parse JSON but does not correctly fetch or structure the data from an API.

Option D - Correct. This option correctly fetches contact data from the Dataverse API and parses it into a strongly typed array of Contacts, demonstrating best practice for handling API responses in TypeScript.

Option E - Incorrect. Incorrectly attempts to display the raw response data in HTML.

QUESTION 6

Answer - A) Filter('Items', Department = userDept)

A) Correct. Correctly filters items where the department matches the user's department stored in userDept.
B) Incorrect. Lookup is used for finding a single record.
C) Incorrect. Would return all items.
D) Incorrect. Assumes Department is a complex type which is not specified.
E) Incorrect. Collect function is not necessary and the use of Filter inside Collect is redundant in this context.

QUESTION 7

Answer - A, B, and D) Security roles define access permissions based on user privileges, whereas teams define access permissions based on user membership in organizational units. Security roles are static and apply to individual users, whereas teams are dynamic and apply to groups of users with similar roles or responsibilities. Security roles grant access to data and functionality, whereas teams provide a mechanism for sharing records and collaborating with other users.

A) - Correct. Security roles define access permissions based on user privileges, specifying what users can do within the system, whereas teams determine access based on user membership in specific groups or units.

B) - Correct. Security roles are static and apply to individual users, whereas teams are dynamic and apply to groups of users with similar roles or responsibilities, adjusting access based on group membership.

C) - Incorrect. While security roles can be hierarchical, teams are not inherently hierarchical structures but rather groups of users with shared access permissions.

D) - Correct. Security roles grant access to data and functionality, determining what users can view and modify, while teams facilitate record sharing and collaboration among users with similar roles or responsibilities.

E) - Incorrect. Both security roles and teams can be enforced at either the system level or the record level, depending on the specific configuration and access control requirements.

QUESTION 8

Answer - A) Business units restrict data visibility to records owned by users within the same organizational unit, limiting access to data across business unit boundaries.

A) - Correct. Configuring business units in Microsoft Dataverse restricts data visibility to records owned by users within the same organizational unit, ensuring data isolation and access control across business unit boundaries.

B) - Incorrect. While business units may facilitate collaboration, their primary purpose is to segment data and control access within organizational units, not provide a unified view across the entire Dataverse environment.

C) - Incorrect. Business units do not necessarily allow users to access records owned by any user within the same unit; instead, they restrict data visibility based on ownership and access permissions.

D) - Incorrect. While business units may enforce data segregation, their primary purpose is not strict isolation but controlled access based on organizational hierarchies and permissions.

E) - Incorrect. While RBAC policies may be applied within business units, they are not the direct result of configuring business units but rather a separate access control mechanism.

QUESTION 9

Answer - [B] and [D].

A) Workflow scope affects who can trigger the workflow, not its execution.

C) Asynchronous processing settings wouldn't affect workflow triggering.

E) Execution time limits would terminate, not prevent, workflow execution.

B) If trigger conditions are not met, the workflow won't activate.

D) Syntax errors would halt workflow execution.

QUESTION 10

Answer - B

Option A - Incorrect: The syntax does not match any known methods in TypeScript for handling Dataverse events.

Option B - Correct: Adds an event listener to the Contacts table, correctly using JavaScript event handling syntax which is applicable in TypeScript.

Option C - Incorrect: Xrm.Page is used within form scripts, not for logging data table changes.

Option D - Incorrect: This syntax does not conform to any known TypeScript or JavaScript standards for Dataverse.

Option E - Incorrect: There is no execute method for onChange event in TypeScript.

QUESTION 11

Answer - [E] Referential

Option E is correct as configuring the relationship with the Referential behavior ensures that associated appointment records remain intact even if the patient record is deleted, meeting the requirement for retaining historical appointment data.

Option A, Restrict delete, would prevent the deletion of a patient record if associated appointments exist, which is not desired in this scenario.

Option B, Cascade All, would delete associated appointment records when a patient record is deleted, which does not align with the requirement to retain historical data.

Option C, Remove Link, would only remove the association between patient and appointment records, not retain appointment records upon patient deletion.

Option D, Parental, is not a valid relationship behavior in Microsoft Dataverse.

QUESTION 12

Answer - [B] Update.

A) Creating a new solution may introduce unnecessary complexity and could disrupt existing system stability.
B) Updating allows for making adjustments to an existing solution without affecting other solutions, ensuring system stability and minimizing risks.
C) Upgrading might involve significant changes and could impact system stability and interconnected solutions.
D) Patching is typically used for addressing specific issues or minor fixes and may not be suitable for making adjustments to a solution.

QUESTION 13

Answer - [A, B, C] Perform thorough testing in the target environment after solution import, Use solution validation tools to check for errors before export, Implement version control to track changes in solutions

Options A, B, and C are correct as performing thorough testing, using solution validation tools, and implementing version control are essential best practices for ensuring the integrity of solutions during import and export processes, minimizing errors and maintaining consistency.

Options D and E may also contribute to solution integrity but are not directly related to the import/export process.

QUESTION 14

Answer - [A, B, C, D, E] Trigger Power Automate flows based on app events, Embed Canvas Apps within model-driven app forms, Utilize Dataverse connectors to access external data sources, Integrate Power Virtual Agents for chatbot interactions, Establish API connections with third-party services for data exchange

Options A, B, C, D, and E are correct as they represent various methods of integrating a model-driven app with other Power Platform components, including automation, embedding, data access, chatbot integration, and API connections.

QUESTION 15

Answer - [B] and [C].

A) Business rules cannot directly access external data.

B) Business rules can enable or disable a column dynamically based on application status, facilitating streamlined loan processing and ensuring data accuracy.

C) Business rules can show or hide a column based on user role, ensuring that sensitive information is accessible only to authorized personnel, thereby enhancing data security and compliance with regulatory requirements.

QUESTION 16

Answer - [A, B, C, E] Minimize the use of synchronous operations to avoid blocking UI responsiveness, Optimize script loading by reducing external dependencies, Implement lazy loading for non-essential scripts to improve initial app load times, Batch script executions to reduce the number of round trips to the server

Options A, B, C, and E are correct as they represent key performance considerations when configuring commands and buttons using JavaScript in Power Apps, including avoiding UI blocking, reducing dependencies, lazy loading, and batch execution.

Option D, while potentially beneficial, is not directly related to JavaScript performance in Power Apps.

QUESTION 17

Answer - [A, B, C, D] Utilizing the Formula Auditing feature in Power Apps to trace formula execution steps, Inserting temporary logging statements within formulas to capture intermediate values, Splitting complex formulas into smaller parts and testing each component individually, Using the Error() function to handle exceptions and identify error-prone sections of code

Options A, B, C, and D are correct as they represent effective approaches to debug Power Fx formulas, including using Formula Auditing, logging, modularization, and error handling.

Option E, while helpful, may not directly facilitate the debugging process.

QUESTION 18

Answer - [B] Custom process action.

A) Custom APIs are typically used for integrating external systems or services with the Power Platform but do not provide user-specific execution control.

B) Custom process actions allow developers to define custom actions that can be executed by specific users, making them suitable for restricting code execution to users with inventory manager roles. This ensures that only authorized personnel, such as inventory managers, can execute the custom code, maintaining data security and accuracy within the inventory management system.

C) Classic workflows are automation processes but do not offer the capability to control code execution based on user roles or privileges.

D) Business rules are used for implementing simple business logic within the app's user interface but do not involve executing custom code on the ribbon.

QUESTION 19

Answer - [A] Breakpoint debugging

Breakpoint debugging allows developers to pause app execution at specific points (breakpoints) and inspect variable values and execution flow, making it an effective technique for identifying errors in app logic.

QUESTION 20

Answer - B

Option A - Incorrect: Obsolete method for accessing entity data.

Option B - Correct: Proper use of the modern client API for subscribing to field changes.

Option C - Incorrect: DOM manipulation is not recommended in model-driven apps.

Option D - Incorrect: Incorrect API path and method.

Option E - Correct but requires clarification that formContext must be defined.

QUESTION 21

Answer - [C] Web API.

A) Client scripting may offer customization but may not provide scalability and maintainability required for a growing app complexity.
B) Power Apps component framework code components offer customization but may not be the best choice for scalability and maintainability.
C) Web API allows for seamless integration of graphical representations from external sources, providing scalability and maintainability as the app grows.
D) Liquid templates are primarily used for rendering dynamic content, not for creating custom visuals.

QUESTION 22

Answer - [B] Step through the code using breakpoints in the browser developer tools

A) Use console.log() statements to output debug information - While console.log() statements can be helpful for debugging, they may not provide the same level of insight as stepping through the code with breakpoints.

B) Step through the code using breakpoints in the browser developer tools - This is a recommended debugging practice that allows developers to inspect variable values and the flow of execution, making it the correct answer.

C) Review browser console errors for syntax or runtime issues - Reviewing browser console errors is important, but it may not provide the same level of debugging capability as stepping through the code with breakpoints.

D) Utilize the Client API trace log for detailed function execution logs - While the Client API trace log can be useful, it may not provide real-time debugging capabilities like browser developer tools.

E) Enable verbose logging in the Power Apps environment settings - Enabling verbose logging can generate a lot of data, but it may not offer the same interactive debugging experience as stepping through the code with breakpoints.

QUESTION 23

Answer - [B] Querying Dataverse data to populate form fields dynamically

A) Retrieving user authentication tokens for SSO implementation - This task typically involves authentication mechanisms rather than directly querying Dataverse data.

B) Querying Dataverse data to populate form fields dynamically - This is a common use case for integrating client scripts with Dataverse Web API, making it the correct answer.

C) Sending bulk email notifications to users from a canvas app - Bulk email notifications may involve external services or custom logic but are not directly related to querying Dataverse data.

D) Encrypting sensitive data before storage in Dataverse - Data encryption is a security measure and doesn't necessarily involve querying Dataverse data.

E) Performing database migrations between Dataverse environments - Database migrations typically require administrative actions rather than client scripting with Dataverse Web API.

QUESTION 24

Answer - [A] Azure function
[C] Custom API
[E] Business rule.

A) Azure functions can execute custom logic to facilitate real-time communication between Microsoft Dataverse and the RESTful Web API of the external vendor management system, enabling seamless synchronization of vendor information within the solution.

C) Custom APIs provide tailored integration solutions, enabling direct communication between Microsoft Dataverse and the RESTful Web API of the external vendor management system, ensuring data consistency and reliability in the vendor management solution.

E) Business rules can enforce specific logic and conditions to regulate data synchronization between Microsoft Dataverse and the RESTful Web API of the external vendor management system, enhancing integration effectiveness.

QUESTION 25

Answer - B

Option A - Incorrect: Incorrect module specifier.

Option B - Correct: Correct import statement for using Xrm in a PCF component.

Option C - Incorrect: require is not the recommended import style in modern TypeScript.

Option D - Incorrect: @types/xrm is for type definitions, not actual implementations.

Option E - Incorrect: No such package @microsoft/powerapps-sdk; it misleads the module name.

QUESTION 26

Answer - [C] Minimizing dependencies on specific Power Apps controls or features.

A) Embedding external JavaScript libraries for enhanced functionality - While external libraries can provide additional functionality, they may introduce compatibility issues and should be used judiciously.

B) Hardcoding configuration parameters within the component code - Hardcoding configuration parameters limits flexibility and makes maintenance challenging, especially across environments.

C) Minimizing dependencies on specific Power Apps controls or features - By minimizing dependencies, components remain compatible and consistent across different Power Apps environments, enhancing flexibility and maintainability.

D) Using inline CSS styles for consistent visual presentation - Inline styles may lead to code duplication and are not recommended for maintaining consistent visual presentation.

E) Leveraging undocumented Power Platform APIs for advanced interactions - Relying on undocumented APIs is risky and may lead to compatibility issues and unexpected behavior.

QUESTION 27

Answer - [B] Power Automate flow.

B) Power Automate flow offers robust workflow automation capabilities, including the ability to trigger push notifications based on various conditions such as task due dates. By configuring a flow to send notifications when tasks are due, users can stay informed and proactive in managing their tasks within the canvas app.

Option A) Power Apps custom control: Custom controls in canvas apps are used for visualizing and interacting with data but do not inherently support push notifications.

Option C) Azure Notification Hubs: Azure Notification Hubs provide scalable push notification delivery to various platforms but require additional integration and are not directly integrated into canvas apps.

Option D) Custom API: Custom APIs are used for integrating external systems with the Power Platform but are not designed for sending push notifications directly within canvas apps.

QUESTION 28

Answer - [A] Batch multiple API requests into a single call.

A) Batch multiple API requests into a single call - Consolidating multiple requests reduces overhead and improves efficiency, especially for client-side PCF components.

B) Increase the timeout duration for API requests - While adjusting timeouts may address certain issues, it does not inherently improve performance.

C) Minify the PCF component script to reduce file size - Minification reduces file size but does not directly impact API call performance.

D) Implement server-side caching for frequently accessed data - Server-side caching can improve performance but may not be applicable to client-side PCF components.

E) Pre-fetch data in advance to reduce on-demand API calls - Pre-fetching data may improve perceived performance but does not address latency directly.

QUESTION 29

Answer - [C] Logging of exception details to the platform's trace log

A) Try-catch blocks within the plug-in code - While useful, this approach is more for specific code-level exceptions rather than pipeline-wide error handling.

B) Rollback mechanism for database transactions - This is part of transaction management but not specifically for error handling within the pipeline.

C) Logging of exception details to the platform's trace log - Correct, logging exceptions to the trace log helps in identifying and troubleshooting errors within the pipeline.

D) Queuing system for reprocessing failed plug-ins - Queuing is more for retrying failed operations rather than error handling per se.

E) Automatic retry mechanism for transient faults - Automatic retry mechanisms are beneficial but not specific to error handling within the pipeline.

QUESTION 30

Answer - [B] Implement connection resiliency features in the .NET application, such as automatic reconnection logic and retry policies, to handle transient network failures gracefully.

Answer - [D] Configure network load balancers with improved bandwidth allocation and quality of service (QoS) settings to prioritize traffic between the Oracle database and Dataverse environment.

B) Implementing connection resiliency features in the .NET application allows you to handle transient network failures gracefully by automatically reconnecting and retrying failed connections. By incorporating retry policies and reconnection logic, you can mitigate the impact of network latency and timeouts on the migration process, ensuring its successful completion.

D) Configuring network load balancers with improved bandwidth allocation and QoS settings helps prioritize traffic between the Oracle database and Dataverse environment, reducing the likelihood of connectivity issues and timeouts. By optimizing network performance, you can ensure smoother data migration and minimize the impact of network-related errors.

Option A) Optimize database query performance: While optimizing query performance may improve data retrieval speed, it may not directly address connectivity issues or network latency affecting the migration process.

Option C) Upgrade the Oracle database: While upgrading the database may offer performance improvements, it may not be feasible or practical during the migration process and may introduce additional complexities or dependencies.

QUESTION 31

Answer - [B] Performing extensive data validation and error handling within the plug-in code.

A) Implementing complex business logic directly within plug-ins for better performance - This can lead to maintenance challenges and is not recommended.

B) Performing extensive data validation and error handling within the plug-in code - Correct, thorough validation and error handling help ensure data integrity and robustness of plug-ins.

C) Minimizing the use of the Organization service to reduce dependencies on Microsoft Dataverse - This may limit functionality and is not necessarily a best practice.

D) Utilizing early-bound classes instead of the Organization service for improved type safety - Early-bound classes are not always feasible or necessary for every scenario.

E) Deploying plug-ins without sandboxing to maximize access to system resources - Sandboxing provides security and isolation benefits, so removing it is not a best practice.

QUESTION 32

Answer - [B] Implementing role-based access control (RBAC).

A) Granting unrestricted access to all users - This approach compromises security and violates least privilege principles.

B) Implementing role-based access control (RBAC) - Correct, RBAC allows granular control over who can access the Custom API based on their roles and permissions.

C) Storing sensitive data directly within the API endpoints - Storing sensitive data within API endpoints poses security risks and violates security best practices.

D) Using HTTP Basic authentication for simplicity - Basic authentication may be simple but lacks robust security features provided by more advanced authentication mechanisms.

E) Sharing API keys publicly for easy integration - Publicly sharing API keys increases the risk of unauthorized access and should be avoided.

QUESTION 33

Answer - [A] _customer_name

A) When retrieving records using a custom connector and interacting with related entities, the _customer_name attribute contains the display name of the associated customer record. You should include the _customer_name attribute in your custom connector to ensure that the customer's name is retrieved along with the order details.

Option B) _customerid - Incorrect: This attribute may contain the GUID of the associated customer record, not the customer's name.
Option C) _customer_value - Incorrect: This attribute is not typically used to retrieve the name of related records.
Option D) _customerid_name - Incorrect: This attribute combination does not exist and would not represent the customer's name.

QUESTION 34

Answer - [A] Encrypting all data in transit and at rest.

A) Encrypting all data in transit and at rest - Correct, encryption ensures that sensitive data remains protected both during transmission and when stored.

B) Storing sensitive data in plain text within API requests - Storing sensitive data in plain text exposes it to potential interception and compromise.

C) Using SSL/TLS for secure communication - SSL/TLS encryption is crucial for securing data during transmission over networks.

D) Logging sensitive data in clear text to facilitate troubleshooting - Logging sensitive data in clear text presents a significant security risk and violates data protection principles.

E) Sharing sensitive data with third-party services without encryption - Sharing sensitive data without encryption increases the risk of data breaches and non-compliance with regulations.

QUESTION 35

Answer - A

Option A - Correct: OAuth with Azure Active Directory is the standard for securing and authorizing API access.

Option B - Incorrect: Embedding API keys in URLs is not secure.

Option C - Incorrect: Basic authentication is not recommended for cloud services due to security concerns.

Option D - Incorrect: Anonymous access would compromise security.

Option E - Incorrect: Virtual networks are for connectivity, not API authentication.

QUESTION 36

Answer - B) POST

A) GET - Incorrect. Used for retrieving data, not sending it.
B) POST - Correct. Best for sending data to a server for creating logs or entries.
C) PUT - Incorrect. Used for full resource updates.
D) PATCH - Incorrect. For partial modifications.
E) DELETE - Incorrect. Used to delete data.

QUESTION 37

Answer - [B] Utilizing batch requests for simultaneous operations

A) Implementing pagination with appropriate page sizes - Pagination helps manage large data sets but may not directly improve performance or efficiency.

B) Utilizing batch requests for simultaneous operations - Correct, batch requests allow multiple operations to be grouped and processed together, reducing the number of round trips to the server and improving efficiency.

C) Increasing server-side timeouts for long-running queries - While adjusting timeouts may prevent premature termination of queries, it may not address performance issues related to large data sets.

D) Reducing data redundancy through denormalization - Denormalization may improve data storage efficiency but may not directly address performance concerns related to data retrieval.

E) Distributing data across multiple environments - Data distribution may improve scalability but may introduce complexity and management overhead.

QUESTION 38

Answer - [A] Azure Monitor

A) Azure Monitor - Correct, Azure Monitor provides comprehensive monitoring and logging capabilities for various Azure services, including Azure API calls.

B) Power Automate - While Power Automate can be used for workflow automation, it is not specifically designed for monitoring and logging API retries.

C) Power Apps Portal - Power Apps Portal is primarily used for building external-facing websites and portals, not for monitoring API calls.

D) Microsoft Dataverse - While Dataverse provides data storage and management capabilities, it does not offer monitoring features for API calls.

E) Azure DevOps - Azure DevOps is a set of tools for software development and collaboration, including version control and CI/CD pipelines, but it does not specialize in monitoring API retries.

QUESTION 39

Answer - A), B), and E)

A) Correct. Prevents the flow from attempting updates during planned outages.

B) Correct. Ensures that updates can still be processed through an alternate service.

C) Incorrect. Logging is useful for records but doesn't ensure operational continuity.

D) Incorrect. Notifies about the problem but doesn't solve it.

E) Correct. Allows the system to attempt the operation again after a failure, reducing disruption.

QUESTION 40

Answer - C)

A) Incorrect - This JavaScript snippet does not securely authenticate; it exposes the key comparison directly.

B) Incorrect - JSON configuration for binding does not include authentication details.

C) Correct - This TypeScript function includes secure header checking and proper environmental variable usage, fitting for handling HTTP-triggered functions with authentication.

D) Incorrect - The C# function should not use TraceWriter for new developments and uses outdated methods for checking headers.

E) Incorrect - HTML cannot be used for authentication in Azure Functions and is inappropriate for server-side logic.

QUESTION 41

Answer - [E] Centralizing common logic in separate child flows

A) Using nested conditionals for complex branching - Nested conditionals may increase complexity and hinder readability and maintainability of flows.

B) Employing parallel branches for concurrent execution - While parallel branches offer concurrency, they may not address the need for centralizing common logic.

C) Implementing recursive loops for iterative processing - Recursive loops may introduce complexity and potential performance issues in flow execution.

D) Utilizing custom plugins for extending flow functionality - Custom plugins are useful but may not directly relate to improving flow performance and maintainability.

E) Centralizing common logic in separate child flows - Correct, centralizing common logic in separate child flows promotes reusability, simplifies maintenance, and enhances performance by reducing redundancy.

QUESTION 42

Answer - A), B), and C)

A) Correct. Directly checks if the tag is 'Reviewed'.

B) Correct. Ensures the library in question is 'Reports'.

C) Correct. Combines both conditions ensuring both the tag and library match.

D) Incorrect. Only ensures the tags field isn't empty.

E) Incorrect. Version number checking isn't specified as a needed condition.

QUESTION 43

Answer - [C] Limiting access to Azure Key Vault based on least privilege principles

A) Sharing Azure Key Vault secrets across multiple applications - Sharing secrets across applications increases the risk of unauthorized access and violates security best practices.

B) Storing sensitive information in plain text within Azure Key Vault - Storing sensitive information in plain text exposes it to unauthorized access and violates security standards.

C) Limiting access to Azure Key Vault based on least privilege principles - Correct, restricting access to Azure Key Vault ensures that only authorized users and applications have access to sensitive information, minimizing the risk of data breaches.

D) Hard-coding Entra service principal credentials in application code - Hard-coding credentials in application code is insecure and violates security best practices.

E) Allowing unrestricted access to Entra service principals - Allowing unrestricted access increases the risk of unauthorized actions and violates the principle of least privilege.

QUESTION 44

Answer - [B] Utilizing pre-built connectors and templates for rapid development and deployment

A) Implementing error handling logic using custom JavaScript code actions - While custom JavaScript code actions can provide flexibility, utilizing pre-built connectors and templates is often more efficient for rapid development.

B) Utilizing pre-built connectors and templates for rapid development and deployment - Correct, leveraging pre-built connectors and templates allows for faster development and deployment of flow steps, reducing time-to-market and development effort.

C) Embedding complex business logic directly within flow actions for performance optimization - Embedding complex logic within flow actions may increase complexity and maintenance overhead, and it may not always optimize performance.

D) Minimizing data transformation and manipulation to reduce processing overhead - While minimizing transformation can improve performance, it may not always be feasible or advisable depending on business requirements.

E) Leveraging Power Automate Desktop for offline data processing and synchronization - Power Automate Desktop may not be the best choice for online integration scenarios and may introduce additional complexity.

QUESTION 45

Answer - B) OAuth 2.0

A) Incorrect. Client credentials are a form of OAuth 2.0 but not specific enough.
B) Correct. OAuth 2.0 with client credentials grant is suitable for application-level permissions.
C) Incorrect. API key does not provide granular permission control.
D) Incorrect. Certificate-based is more for mutual authentication.
E) Incorrect. Dynamic authentication is not a standard term.

QUESTION 46

Answer - [A, B, C, D] Triggering external workflows or processes in response to Dataverse data changes, Notifying users or stakeholders about critical system events or updates in real-time, Integrating Dataverse with external systems and services asynchronously, Orchestrating complex business logic and approvals based on Dataverse events

A) Triggering external workflows or processes in response to Dataverse data changes - Correct, this is a common use case for publishing events using IServiceEndpointNotificationService.

B) Notifying users or stakeholders about critical system events or updates in real-time - Real-time notifications are a common use case for event publication.

C) Integrating Dataverse with external systems and services asynchronously - Asynchronous integration is a common scenario for event-driven architectures.

D) Orchestrating complex business logic and approvals based on Dataverse events - Event-driven orchestration is a common use case for IServiceEndpointNotificationService.

E) Monitoring performance metrics and resource utilization in real-time - While monitoring is important, it's not a direct use case for publishing events using IServiceEndpointNotificationService.

QUESTION 47

Answer - [A, B, C, D, E] Implementing OAuth authentication for secure endpoint access, Encrypting data transmission between endpoints using SSL/TLS, Restricting endpoint access based on IP whitelisting, Enabling role-based access control (RBAC) for endpoint management, Regularly updating endpoint credentials and access tokens

A) Implementing OAuth authentication for secure endpoint access - OAuth provides secure access control mechanisms for endpoint authentication.

B) Encrypting data transmission between endpoints using SSL/TLS - SSL/TLS encryption ensures secure data transmission over the network.

C) Restricting endpoint access based on IP whitelisting - IP whitelisting helps restrict access to trusted entities, enhancing endpoint security.

D) Enabling role-based access control (RBAC) for endpoint management - RBAC enables granular access control based on user roles and permissions, enhancing endpoint security.

E) Regularly updating endpoint credentials and access tokens - Regular updates to credentials and access tokens mitigate the risk of unauthorized access to endpoints.

QUESTION 48

Answer - A) $count with $filter

A) Correct. Combining $count with $filter is appropriate for counting records that meet specific criteria, like having an email address.
B) Incorrect. $sum is not used for counting records.
C) Incorrect. $total is not a valid OData query option.
D) Incorrect. $calculate is not a valid OData query option.
E) Incorrect. $aggregate does not directly provide counting capabilities in this context.

QUESTION 49

Answer - [A, B, D] Regularly monitoring and maintaining alternate key indexes for optimal performance, Documenting the purpose and usage of each alternate key for future reference and troubleshooting, Reviewing and updating alternate key configurations as business requirements evolve over time.

A) Regularly monitoring and maintaining alternate key indexes for optimal performance. - Regular maintenance ensures that alternate key indexes remain efficient and effective for improving query performance.

B) Documenting the purpose and usage of each alternate key for future reference and troubleshooting. - Documentation helps maintain clarity and consistency in managing alternate keys, facilitating troubleshooting and knowledge transfer.

C) Avoiding excessive use of alternate keys to minimize database overhead and complexity. - While alternate keys are useful for enforcing uniqueness, excessive use can lead to increased storage overhead and complexity in database management.

D) Reviewing and updating alternate key configurations as business requirements evolve over time. - Business requirements may change, necessitating updates to alternate key configurations to ensure they remain aligned with organizational needs.

E) Implementing proper error handling mechanisms to manage exceptions related to alternate key violations. - While error handling is important, it's not specific to managing alternate keys and may involve broader aspects of application development.

QUESTION 50

Answer - [A, B, D, E] Implementing data validation rules and error handling mechanisms in the ETL process to identify and correct errors, Enforcing strict data governance policies to prevent data discrepancies at the source, Setting up alerts and notifications to notify administrators of data errors in real-time, Conducting regular data audits and reconciliations to identify and resolve discrepancies proactively.

A) Implementing data validation rules and error handling mechanisms in the ETL process to identify and correct errors. - This approach involves validating data during the ETL process and implementing error handling mechanisms to detect and address discrepancies and errors effectively.

B) Enforcing strict data governance policies to prevent data discrepancies at the source. - By enforcing data governance policies, organizations can establish standards and controls to ensure data quality and consistency, minimizing the occurrence of discrepancies at the source.

C) Increasing the frequency of data synchronization to minimize the impact of discrepancies. - While increasing synchronization frequency may help detect discrepancies sooner, it does not address the root cause or provide effective error handling mechanisms.

D) Setting up alerts and notifications to notify administrators of data errors in real-time. - Real-time alerts enable administrators to promptly respond to data errors and take corrective actions, improving data quality and integrity.

E) Conducting regular data audits and reconciliations to identify and resolve discrepancies proactively. - Regular audits and reconciliations help identify discrepancies early and facilitate proactive resolution, ensuring data accuracy and consistency.

PRACTICE TEST 4 - QUESTIONS ONLY

QUESTION 1

A healthcare organization is deploying a Power Platform solution to manage patient data and workflows. Compliance with regulatory standards such as HIPAA is critical. They need a monitoring solution that includes robust compliance auditing capabilities to ensure data security and regulatory compliance. Which aspect of monitoring and diagnostics is essential for ensuring adherence to regulatory requirements and internal policies in Power Platform solutions?

A) Application performance monitoring
B) Resource utilization tracking
C) Network traffic analysis
D) Compliance auditing
E) Data encryption techniques

QUESTION 2

A technology startup is developing a project management application using Power Platform. They need to determine when custom development should be considered to extend the functionality beyond out-of-the-box features. In which scenario is it appropriate to extend with custom development?

A) Adding custom branding and themes to the application
B) Integrating with a third-party project management tool via RESTful Web APIs
C) Creating custom reports and dashboards using Power BI
D) Configuring user roles and permissions within the application
E) Customizing email templates for automated notifications

QUESTION 3

To automate sending reminders for unpaid invoices every 2 hours during business hours (9 AM to 5 PM) on weekdays via an Azure timer function in Microsoft Dataverse, which cron expression is best?

A) 0 9-17/2 * * 1-5
B) 0 */2 9-17 * * 1-5
C) 0 9-17 */2 * * 1-5
D) 0 */2 9-17 * 1-5
E) */2 9-17 * * 1-5

QUESTION 4

An insurance company is implementing row-level security within their Power Platform solution to restrict access to sensitive customer data based on user roles. They need to evaluate the capabilities of row sharing to ensure compliance with regulatory requirements.
Which factors should they consider when assessing the row sharing capabilities of the Power Platform? Select THREE.

A) Granularity of access control based on user attributes such as department or job role.
B) Scalability of row-level security rules to accommodate large datasets.

C) Flexibility to dynamically adjust row-level security settings based on changing business needs.
D) Compatibility with external authentication providers for seamless user authentication.
E) Integration with audit logging to track user access and changes to row-level security configurations.

QUESTION 5

Develop a PowerFx formula to calculate and display the age of a contact based on their birthdate stored in Dataverse, considering today's date.

A) Age = DATEDIFF(Birthdate, Today(), Years)
B) Age = DATEDIFF(Today(), Birthdate, 'years')
C) CalculateAge = Today() - Birthdate
D) Age = YEARFRAC(Birthdate, Today())
E) Age = YEAR(Today()) - YEAR(Birthdate)

QUESTION 6

You are tasked with adding a condition to a canvas app form that only shows projects with budgets over $100,000 in a drop-down. The app is connected to Microsoft Dataverse. What is the correct PowerFx expression for the Items property?

A) Filter('Projects', Budget > 100000)
B) Collect('HighBudgetProjects', Filter(Projects, Budget > 100000))
C) Lookup('Projects', Budget > 100000)
D) 'Projects'
E) Sort('Projects', Budget, Descending)

QUESTION 7

A consulting firm is tasked with explaining the assignment and modification of roles in Dataverse to a group of business users who are new to the platform. They need to provide a clear understanding of how roles are assigned and managed to ensure effective access control within their organization.
How can roles be assigned and modified in Dataverse to control access to data and functionality?

A) Roles can be assigned manually to individual users or groups, and modifications can be made directly within the security roles configuration page.

B) Role assignment can be automated based on user attributes or membership in specific teams, and modifications can be made using role-based workflows and approval processes.

C) Roles are assigned automatically based on user roles defined in the organization's identity provider, and modifications require administrative approval and validation.

D) Role assignment and modification are handled by system administrators using specialized tools and scripts, and changes are applied globally to all users in the organization.

E) Roles are assigned dynamically based on user activity and behavior, and modifications are made through continuous monitoring and adjustment of access permissions.

QUESTION 8

A consulting firm specializing in Microsoft Power Platform solutions is advising clients on best practices for configuring business units in Microsoft Dataverse. They need to provide clear guidance on recommended configuration approaches to ensure effective data management and access control.
What are considered best practices for configuring business units in Microsoft Dataverse? Select THREE.

A) Define business unit hierarchies that mirror the organizational structure and reporting lines to facilitate data segmentation and access control.

B) Keep the number of business units to a minimum to avoid complexity and overhead in administration and maintenance.

C) Implement security roles and privileges at the business unit level to enforce fine-grained access control and data protection.

D) Regularly review and update business unit configurations to adapt to changing organizational needs and compliance requirements.

E) Integrate business unit configurations with other security features such as role-based access control (RBAC) and record-level security for comprehensive data protection.

QUESTION 9

In a Microsoft Dataverse environment, you are implementing a custom business rule that calculates the total price of an order based on the quantity and unit price entered by the user. However, users report that the total price is not calculated correctly. What could be potential reasons for this issue? Select the correct answers that apply.

A) The business rule is not activated for the target entity.
B) The order entity form is not updated to display the calculated total price field.
C) There is a JavaScript function interfering with the calculation logic of the business rule.
D) The data type of the total price field is incompatible with the calculation formula.
E) The user's browser does not support the scripting necessary for the calculation.

QUESTION 10

You need to create a RESTful API call in a Microsoft Power Platform environment to update a record in the Dataverse. Which of the following JavaScript snippets correctly makes a PATCH request to update a contact's email?

A) fetch('https://org.api.crm.dynamics.com/api/data/v9.0/contacts(0000-0000-0000-0000)', { method: 'PATCH', body: JSON.stringify({ emailaddress1: 'new@email.com' }), headers: { 'Content-Type': 'application/json' } })

B) XMLHttpRequest().open('PATCH', 'https://org.api.crm.dynamics.com/api/data/v9.0/contacts/0000-0000-0000-0000');

C) WebAPI.updateRecord('contact', '0000-0000-0000-0000', { email: 'new@email.com' })

D) API.patchContact('0000-0000-0000-0000', { email: 'new@email.com' })

E) axios.patch('https://org.api.crm.dynamics.com/api/data/v9.0/contacts/0000-0000-0000-0000', {

emailaddress1: 'new@email.com' })

QUESTION 11

A manufacturing company is implementing an inventory management system using Microsoft Dataverse. They need to configure relationships between the "Product" and "Order" entities to track product orders. Additionally, they want to ensure that when a product record is updated, associated order records reflect the changes automatically. Which type of relationship should be configured between the "Product" and "Order" entities to achieve automatic updates?

A) Many-to-Many
B) One-to-Many
C) Many-to-One
D) Self-Referential
E) Hierarchy

QUESTION 12

Your organization has identified a critical security vulnerability in one of the solutions deployed in the Microsoft Power Platform environment. As the system administrator, you need to address this vulnerability promptly to mitigate potential risks. However, you must ensure that the solution's existing functionalities remain unaffected during the remediation process. What action should you take to address the security vulnerability effectively while minimizing disruptions?

A) Create
B) Update
C) Upgrade
D) Patch

QUESTION 13

A company is experiencing issues with solution import/export processes in their Microsoft Dataverse environment. They need to troubleshoot common issues to ensure smooth operation. What are common issues that may arise during solution import/export, and how can they be addressed? Select the correct answers that apply.

A) Dependency conflicts between solution components
B) Data loss due to schema inconsistencies
C) Import/export failures due to network connectivity issues
D) Version compatibility issues between source and target environments
E) Security permissions preventing solution transfer

QUESTION 14

Security is a critical aspect of app creation in Microsoft Power Platform, especially when developing model-driven apps. What security practices should be followed during the creation of a model-driven app? Select the correct answers that apply.

A) Configure role-based permissions for entity access

B) Implement data loss prevention policies to protect sensitive information
C) Enable multi-factor authentication for app users
D) Encrypt data at rest and in transit to ensure confidentiality
E) Regularly audit user access and permissions for compliance

QUESTION 15

You are customizing a form in a model-driven app for a manufacturing company's production tracking system. The app aims to optimize production efficiency and data accuracy. What are two primary actions that you can perform by using a business rule in this context? Select the correct answers that apply.

A) Access external data.
B) Enable or disable a column based on production stage.
C) Show or hide a column based on user role.
D) Run the rule on demand.

QUESTION 16

During the development of a Power App, developers may encounter errors in their JavaScript code that require debugging. What are effective techniques for debugging JavaScript in Power Apps? Select the correct answers that apply.

A) Use browser developer tools to inspect and debug script execution
B) Utilize console logging to track variable values and execution flow
C) Implement unit tests to identify and isolate bugs systematically
D) Enable remote debugging for real-time monitoring of script behavior
E) Analyze server-side logs for insights into client-side errors

QUESTION 17

A financial institution is designing a Power App to calculate loan eligibility based on customer profiles and credit scores. They want to ensure that the Power Fx formulas are maintainable and scalable as the app evolves. What best practices should they follow to achieve this goal? Select the correct answers that apply.

A) Documenting formula logic and usage to aid future maintenance and troubleshooting
B) Organizing formulas into reusable components or functions for modularity
C) Implementing version control to track changes and collaborate effectively with team members
D) Performance testing formulas under varying load conditions to identify bottlenecks
E) Conducting regular code reviews to ensure adherence to coding standards and best practices

QUESTION 18

You are developing a model-driven app for a customer service system. The app needs to execute custom code when a user interacts with a button on the ribbon. However, only customer service representatives should have access to this functionality. Which option should you choose to implement this requirement?

A) Custom API

B) Custom process action
C) Classic workflow
D) Business rule

QUESTION 19

An organization wants to ensure the long-term health and stability of its Power Apps ecosystem. Which best practice should they prioritize to maintain app health and performance? Select the correct answers that apply.

A) Regularly review and optimize app data model and formulas
B) Implement comprehensive backup and disaster recovery strategies
C) Monitor user feedback and performance metrics for continuous improvement
D) Enforce version control and release management processes
E) Conduct regular security audits and vulnerability assessments

QUESTION 20

Optimize a Canvas app by monitoring its performance. Which tool or approach provides detailed insights into runtime behavior and load times?

A) Monitor tool in Power Apps Studio
B) App Insights integration for real-time analytics
C) Console.log() statements in the app's code
D) Using the Performance Analyzer in Power Apps
E) Set up Azure Monitor with custom logs from the app

QUESTION 21

You are developing a canvas app for a customer relationship management (CRM) system. The app requires incorporating a custom visual to display customer engagement metrics. However, you need the visual to be easily extensible to accommodate future enhancements or changes in requirements. Which approach should you select? Select the correct answers that apply.

A) Client scripting
B) Power Apps component framework code component
C) Web API
D) Liquid template

QUESTION 22

A Power Apps developer is tasked with optimizing the performance of a complex JavaScript function that runs on form load. Which of the following strategies should the developer consider to improve the function's execution time?

A) Minimize DOM manipulation operations within the function
B) Implement caching for frequently accessed data
C) Use event delegation to reduce the number of event listeners
D) Reduce the number of nested loops and conditional statements

E) Split the function into smaller, more modular components

QUESTION 23

A Power Apps developer is handling error conditions in client scripts that interact with Dataverse Web API. Which of the following represents a best practice for error handling in Web API calls?

A) Log errors to the browser console for debugging purposes
B) Display generic error messages to users without technical details
C) Retry failed requests automatically with exponential backoff
D) Ignore errors and continue script execution for seamless user experience
E) Handle errors gracefully by providing informative messages and recovery options

QUESTION 24

Your organization is implementing a compliance management solution using Microsoft Dataverse. You need to integrate an external compliance tracking system, which exposes a RESTful Web API, to capture compliance data within the solution. Considering the integration requirements, which three options should you select to ensure an efficient integration solution? Select the correct answers that apply.

A) Azure function
B) Custom connector
C) Custom API
D) HTTP request
E) Business rule

QUESTION 25

Identify the script that correctly tests a PCF component to ensure it renders correctly in different locales.

A) if (context.userSettings.languageId == 1033) { render(); } else { throw new Error('Locale not supported'); }
B) context.utils.isRTL() ? renderRTL() : renderLTR();
C) switch (context.formatting.locale) { case 'en-us': renderEnglish(); break; default: renderDefault(); }
D) locale === 'fr-fr' ? renderFrench() : render();
E) renderLocale(context.userSettings.languageId);

QUESTION 26

A Power Apps developer is testing the implementation of a PCF component interface. What aspect of the interface should be thoroughly tested to ensure data integrity and user experience?

A) Event handling logic and responsiveness.
B) Visual styling and layout consistency.
C) Data retrieval and manipulation performance.
D) Integration with external authentication providers.
E) Compatibility with legacy browser versions.

QUESTION 27

Your organization is developing a canvas app for employee training. You need to implement a feature that tracks employee progress and generates reports based on completed training modules. Which development option should you choose to implement this feature?

A) Power BI
B) Azure SQL Database
C) Power Automate flow
D) Custom connector

QUESTION 28

In a scenario where a Power Apps developer needs to access sensitive data from an external API within a PCF component, what security measure should the developer prioritize to protect the data during transmission?

A) Implement end-to-end encryption using SSL/TLS.
B) Store API credentials securely in environment variables.
C) Utilize a VPN for secure network communication.
D) Hash sensitive data before transmission.
E) Use IP whitelisting to restrict API access.

QUESTION 29

A development team is evaluating the difference between synchronous and asynchronous execution within the plug-in execution pipeline for their Power Platform solution. Which statement accurately distinguishes between the two execution modes?

A) Synchronous execution allows for parallel processing of multiple plug-ins, while asynchronous execution processes plug-ins sequentially.
B) Synchronous execution operates within the database transaction scope, while asynchronous execution operates outside the transaction scope.
C) Synchronous execution guarantees transactional consistency across multiple records, while asynchronous execution may result in eventual consistency.
D) Synchronous execution triggers immediate user notifications, while asynchronous execution delays notifications until after the transaction is committed.
E) Synchronous execution is recommended for long-running operations, while asynchronous execution is suitable for short-lived processes.

QUESTION 30

Your organization is migrating data from a legacy Microsoft Access database to Microsoft Dataverse tables using Azure Data Factory pipelines. During the migration, you encounter errors related to data type mismatches and unsupported field sizes between the Access database and Dataverse tables, resulting in failed data transfers. What are two potential strategies to address these errors and ensure the successful completion of the migration? Select the correct answers that apply.

A) Modify the schema of Dataverse tables to accommodate larger field sizes and match the data types used in the Access database, ensuring compatibility and seamless data migration.

B) Utilize Azure Data Factory's schema mapping capabilities to perform data type conversions and adjustments on-the-fly, ensuring alignment between source and destination data structures.
C) Implement data transformation logic in Azure Data Factory pipelines to preprocess data from the Access database before loading it into Dataverse tables, ensuring compliance with schema requirements.
D) Export data from the Access database to intermediate file formats, such as CSV or Excel, and then import the data into Dataverse tables using Power Query transformations to handle data type conversions and field size adjustments.

QUESTION 31

A Power Platform developer is concerned about handling exceptions and errors effectively in plug-ins using the Organization service. What is an important consideration when handling exceptions and errors?

A) Logging detailed error messages in the system event logs for easy troubleshooting.
B) Using try-catch blocks to capture and handle exceptions gracefully.
C) Ignoring errors to prevent disruption to the user experience.
D) Relying solely on platform-level error handling mechanisms.
E) Exposing detailed error information to end-users for transparency.

QUESTION 32

A Power Platform development team is discussing versioning and maintaining Custom APIs in Dataverse. What is an important consideration regarding versioning?

A) Updating existing API versions without backward compatibility.
B) Maintaining multiple versions concurrently for backward compatibility.
C) Allowing clients to specify the API version dynamically.
D) Using timestamp-based versioning for simplicity.
E) Reusing existing API endpoints for different versions.

QUESTION 33

You are designing a canvas app to display employee information retrieved from Microsoft Dataverse. The employee records contain a lookup field to the "Departments" entity. You need to ensure that the canvas app displays the name of the associated department for each employee. What attribute should you include in your canvas app to display the department's name?

A) _department_name
B) _departmentid_name
C) _department_name_value
D) _departmentid_value

QUESTION 34

A company is developing a Power Platform solution that interacts with customer data and must comply with GDPR regulations. What is a key consideration for ensuring compliance with GDPR when configuring API security?

A) Exposing customer data to unauthorized third parties.
B) Implementing access controls and permissions for sensitive data.
C) Using weak encryption algorithms for data protection.
D) Storing customer data indefinitely without consent.
E) Ignoring data subject access requests (DSARs).

QUESTION 35

How should developers handle API updates when importing definitions from Azure services to ensure continuity and consistency in Power Platform solutions?

A) Monitor Azure service updates manually and reflect changes in PowerApps.
B) Implement an automated monitoring tool in Azure that triggers updates in PowerApps when the API changes.
C) Use managed identities in Azure to automatically synchronize API updates with PowerApps.
D) Rely on built-in Power Platform alerts for any breaking changes in Azure API integrations.
E) Document API dependencies and manually review them during each sprint review.

QUESTION 36

A developer needs to implement a JavaScript API to update only a few fields of a resource without altering others in Microsoft Power Platform. Which HTTP method should they use?

A) PUT
B) GET
C) POST
D) PATCH
E) HEAD

QUESTION 37

When managing errors encountered while interacting with the Dataverse Web API, what is a best practice for effective error management?

A) Logging detailed error messages in client-side code.
B) Displaying generic error messages to users.
C) Handling errors gracefully and providing informative feedback.
D) Ignoring errors to prevent disruption to the user experience.
E) Returning HTTP status code 200 for all responses.

QUESTION 38

What is a key consideration when balancing performance and reliability in retry policies for API calls within a Power Platform solution?

A) Minimizing retry intervals to reduce latency
B) Increasing the maximum number of retry attempts for critical requests
C) Implementing fixed retry intervals for predictable behavior
D) Limiting the use of exponential backoff to prevent excessive retries

E) Prioritizing retry attempts based on request urgency

QUESTION 39

How can a Power Automate cloud flow be optimized for handling high-volume data updates from an external sales API without overwhelming the system? Select the correct answers that apply.

A) Throttle the API calls
B) Use batch processing
C) Increase API timeout settings
D) Parallel processing of API responses
E) Send alerts for high traffic volumes

QUESTION 40

A software development company needs to integrate RESTful Web APIs into their Power Platform solution to fetch real-time currency exchange rates. The Azure Function must parse JSON responses efficiently and handle possible JSON format changes without failing.

A) JavaScript: let rates = JSON.parse(res.body); console.log(rates['USD']);

B) C#: public static async Task<IActionResult> Run(HttpRequest req, ILogger log, ExecutionContext context) { HttpClient client = new HttpClient(); HttpResponseMessage response = await client.GetAsync("http://api.exchangeratesapi.io/latest"); string result = await response.Content.ReadAsStringAsync(); dynamic rates = JsonConvert.DeserializeObject(result); return new OkObjectResult(rates.USD); }

C) TypeScript: interface ExchangeRates { rates: { USD: number; }; } async function getRates(): Promise<ExchangeRates> { const response = await fetch('https://api.exchangeratesapi.io/latest'); return response.json(); }

D) JSON: { "url": "https://api.exchangeratesapi.io/latest", "method": "GET" }

E) PowerFx: Set(varResult, JSON(ParseJSON(Get('https://api.exchangeratesapi.io/latest').result), 'rates.USD'))

QUESTION 41

In the context of monitoring and analyzing flow performance, what metric is important for assessing efficiency and identifying bottlenecks?

A) Total number of flow runs executed
B) Average execution time per flow run
C) Total number of connectors used in a flow
D) Number of successful versus failed flow runs
E) Overall duration of data transfer between connectors

QUESTION 42

A Power Automate flow must trigger for documents in a SharePoint library labeled 'HR' when the 'ExpirationDate' field is less than or equal to today. What conditions should be set for the trigger? Select the correct answers that apply.

A) @lessOrEquals(triggerBody()?['ExpirationDate'], utcNow())
B) @equals(triggerBody()?['Library'], 'HR')

C) @and(lessOrEquals(triggerBody()?['ExpirationDate'], utcNow()), equals(triggerBody()?['Library'], 'HR'))

D) @not(greater(triggerBody()?['ExpirationDate'], utcNow()))
E) @contains(triggerBody()?['Title'], 'Expired')

QUESTION 43

A technology consulting firm is troubleshooting integration issues between Azure Key Vault, Microsoft Entra, and Power Platform solutions. They need to identify potential security and compliance impacts associated with misconfigured secrets and service principals. What factor should they consider when assessing security and compliance impacts?

A) Encrypting data in transit using SSL/TLS protocols
B) Implementing multi-factor authentication (MFA) for user access
C) Logging and monitoring access to Azure Key Vault and Entra
D) Sharing service principal credentials with third-party vendors
E) Exposing secrets in plain text within flow configurations

QUESTION 44

A financial services firm is deploying Power Platform solutions to automate loan approval processes. They need to monitor and optimize business process flows to ensure efficient execution and compliance with regulatory requirements. What is a key aspect of monitoring and optimizing business process flows in this scenario?

A) Implementing real-time dashboards and analytics for performance monitoring
B) Conducting periodic audits and reviews of workflow execution logs
C) Establishing service level agreements (SLAs) for workflow completion and response times
D) Enabling version control and change management for business process definitions
E) Configuring automated alerts and notifications for workflow exceptions and bottlenecks

QUESTION 45

Integrating a custom connector for a public transportation status API in Power Platform, which authentication method should you select if the API requires each request to be authenticated uniquely?

A) OAuth 2.0 with token refresh
B) API key
C) Dynamic token
D) Certificate based
E) Password based

QUESTION 46

A manufacturing company is developing a Power Platform solution to track production processes and equipment maintenance. They need to implement robust error handling and troubleshooting mechanisms for event publishing using IServiceEndpointNotificationService. What are key considerations for error handling and troubleshooting in event publishing? Select the correct answers that apply.

A) Implementing retry policies and exponential backoff strategies for failed event delivery attempts
B) Logging detailed error information and stack traces for failed event publishing attempts
C) Monitoring service health and availability of IServiceEndpointNotificationService endpoints
D) Implementing circuit breaker patterns to prevent cascading failures during event publication
E) Configuring alerting mechanisms to notify administrators about failed event publishing

QUESTION 47

An e-commerce platform is developing a Power Platform solution to manage product listings and order processing. They need to monitor and manage various service endpoints to ensure optimal performance and reliability. What are some key aspects to consider when monitoring and managing service endpoints? Select the correct answers that apply.

A) Tracking endpoint response times and latency metrics
B) Monitoring message throughput and queue lengths for asynchronous endpoints
C) Setting up alerts for endpoint availability and error rates
D) Analyzing endpoint usage patterns and traffic volumes
E) Implementing automated endpoint scaling based on workload demand

QUESTION 48

You need to create a new record in Microsoft Dataverse using the Web API that should only succeed if a similar record does not already exist. What method should you use?

A) POST with DuplicateDetection enabled
B) PUT with If-None-Match header
C) POST with $filter
D) UPSERT with If-None-Match header
E) POST with If-Match header

QUESTION 49

A healthcare organization is facing issues with alternate keys in their Power Platform solution and needs to troubleshoot common issues. What are some common issues they may encounter with alternate keys, and how can they troubleshoot them? Select the correct answers that apply.

A) Duplicate records being created despite alternate key constraints.
B) Performance degradation due to inefficient indexing of alternate keys.
C) Incorrect configuration of alternate key attributes, leading to validation errors.
D) Inconsistent enforcement of alternate key constraints across different environments.
E) Unexpected behavior during data migration processes involving entities with alternate keys.

QUESTION 50

A government agency is integrating sensitive citizen data into Microsoft Dataverse and must comply with strict security and privacy regulations. Which measure is essential for ensuring security and compliance in data integration processes? Select the correct answers that apply.

A) Implementing encryption mechanisms to protect data during transmission and storage.
B) Conducting regular vulnerability assessments and penetration testing of data integration systems.
C) Enforcing role-based access control to restrict data access based on user roles and permissions.
D) Obtaining explicit consent from citizens before integrating their data into Dataverse.
E) Implementing data anonymization techniques to protect individual privacy.

PRACTICE TEST 4 - ANSWERS ONLY

QUESTION 1

Answer - [D) Compliance auditing]

D) Compliance auditing - Compliance auditing is essential for ensuring adherence to regulatory requirements and internal policies, specifically addressing data security and regulatory compliance concerns such as HIPAA in the healthcare sector.

A) Application performance monitoring - While important, application performance monitoring does not directly address compliance auditing requirements.

B) Resource utilization tracking - Resource utilization tracking focuses on resource usage efficiency rather than compliance auditing.

C) Network traffic analysis - Network traffic analysis primarily deals with monitoring network activities and may not cover compliance auditing aspects.

E) Data encryption techniques - Data encryption techniques are important for data security but may not cover compliance auditing requirements comprehensively.

QUESTION 2

Answer - [B) Integrating with a third-party project management tool via RESTful Web APIs]

A) Adding custom branding and themes to the application - Custom branding and themes can often be achieved without custom development through configuration options.

B) Integrating with a third-party project management tool via RESTful Web APIs - Integration with external systems typically requires custom development to establish connections and exchange data.

C) Creating custom reports and dashboards using Power BI - Customizing reports and dashboards within Power BI is a configuration task rather than custom development.

D) Configuring user roles and permissions within the application - User roles and permissions can usually be configured without custom development using built-in features.

E) Customizing email templates for automated notifications - Customizing email templates is usually a configuration task rather than custom development.

QUESTION 3

Answer - A) 0 9-17/2 * * 1-5

A) Correct. Executes every 2 hours from 9 AM to 5 PM on weekdays.
B) Incorrect. Misformats the hour range and interval.
C) Incorrect. Misplaces the interval for hours.
D) Incorrect. This would not correctly restrict to business hours each day.
E) Incorrect. Lacks the necessary zero to correctly position the minute field in the cron expression.

QUESTION 4

Answer - A, B, and C) Granularity of access control based on user attributes such as department or job role. Scalability of row-level security rules to accommodate large datasets. Flexibility to dynamically adjust row-level security settings based on changing business needs.

A) - Correct. The granularity of access control based on user attributes ensures precise control over data access, enhancing compliance with regulatory requirements.

B) - Correct. Scalability of row-level security rules is essential for handling large datasets without compromising performance.

C) - Correct. Flexibility to dynamically adjust row-level security settings allows for agility in responding to evolving business requirements and compliance mandates.

D) - Incorrect. Compatibility with external authentication providers relates more to user authentication than to row-level security capabilities.

E) - Incorrect. While audit logging is important for compliance, it is not directly related to the capabilities of row sharing within the Power Platform.

QUESTION 5

Answer - B

Option A - Incorrect. DATEDIFF syntax is incorrect as the parameters are not in the correct order.

Option B - Correct. Uses the DATEDIFF function correctly to calculate the age in years based on the birthdate.

Option C - Incorrect. This calculation would result in the difference in days, not years.

Option D - Incorrect. YEARFRAC is not a function in PowerFx.

Option E - Incorrect. This method does not account for whether the birthday has occurred yet this year, potentially resulting in an inaccurate age.

QUESTION 6

Answer - A) Filter('Projects', Budget > 100000)

A) Correct. Filters the Projects to only include those with a budget over $100,000.
B) Incorrect. Collect is not needed to populate a drop-down.
C) Incorrect. Lookup is used to find a single record.
D) Incorrect. This would list all projects, without filtering by budget.
E) Incorrect. Sort orders the items but does not filter them based on budget.

QUESTION 7

Answer - A) Roles can be assigned manually to individual users or groups, and modifications can be made directly within the security roles configuration page.

A) - Correct. Roles can be assigned manually to individual users or groups, allowing administrators to specify access permissions based on user roles and responsibilities. Modifications to role assignments can be made directly within the security roles configuration page, providing flexibility and control over access control settings.

B) - Incorrect. While role assignment can be automated in some scenarios, modifications made using role-based workflows and approval processes are not standard features of Dataverse role management.

C) - Incorrect. Roles are typically not assigned automatically based on user roles defined in the identity provider, and modifications do not necessarily require administrative approval and validation.

D) - Incorrect. While system administrators may handle role assignment and modification, changes are typically made within the Dataverse environment rather than through specialized tools and scripts.

E) - Incorrect. While roles can be assigned dynamically in certain contexts, continuous monitoring and adjustment of access permissions are not standard practices for role management in Dataverse.

QUESTION 8

Answer - A, C, and D) Define business unit hierarchies that mirror the organizational structure and reporting lines to facilitate data segmentation and access control. Implement security roles and privileges at the business unit level to enforce fine-grained access control and data protection. Regularly review and update business unit configurations to adapt to changing organizational needs and compliance requirements.

A) - Correct. Defining business unit hierarchies that mirror the organizational structure helps establish clear data segmentation and access control boundaries, enhancing data management and governance.

C) - Correct. Implementing security roles and privileges at the business unit level enables fine-grained access control, ensuring that users have appropriate permissions based on their roles and responsibilities within the organization.

D) - Correct. Regularly reviewing and updating business unit configurations ensures that they remain aligned with changing organizational needs and compliance requirements, maintaining data integrity and security over time.

B) - Incorrect. While minimizing the number of business units may reduce complexity, it may not always be feasible or advisable, especially for larger organizations with diverse business units and departments.

E) - Incorrect. While integrating business unit configurations with other security features is important, it is not specifically a best practice for configuring business units but rather a broader approach to enhancing overall data protection and access control.

QUESTION 9

Answer - [A], [C], and [D].

B) Display settings wouldn't affect the calculation logic of the business rule.

E) Browser support would affect client-side scripting, not server-side business rules.

A) Inactive business rules won't execute.

C) Interference from JavaScript may disrupt calculation logic.

D) Incompatible data types can lead to calculation errors.

QUESTION 10

Answer - A

Option A - Correct: This correctly formats a PATCH request using fetch API in JavaScript for updating a contact in Dataverse.

Option B - Incorrect: This XMLHttpRequest snippet is incomplete and lacks body data.

Option C - Incorrect: WebAPI.updateRecord is not the correct method for a PATCH request.

Option D - Incorrect: API.patchContact is not a recognized function.

Option E - Incorrect: While axios could be used, the method shown is missing headers necessary for the operation.

QUESTION 11

Answer - [B] One-to-Many

Option B is correct as a One-to-Many relationship allows multiple order records to be associated with a single product, enabling automatic updates to associated order records when the product record is updated.

Option A, Many-to-Many, would imply that multiple products can be associated with multiple orders, which does not align with the requirement for automatic updates.

Option C, Many-to-One, would imply that multiple orders are associated with a single product, which does not fulfill the requirement for automatic updates.

Option D, Self-Referential, involves entities being related to themselves, which is not applicable in this scenario.

Option E, Hierarchy, represents parent-child relationships within the same entity, not between different entities like "Product" and "Order".

QUESTION 12

Answer - [D] Patch.

A) Creating a new solution would not address the existing vulnerability and could disrupt existing functionalities.
B) Updating might introduce unintended changes along with fixing the vulnerability and could pose risks to system stability.
C) Upgrading could involve significant changes and could impact existing functionalities and system stability.
D) Patching allows for addressing specific security vulnerabilities without impacting existing functionalities or system stability, minimizing disruptions and risks.

QUESTION 13

Answer - [A, B, C, D] Dependency conflicts between solution components, Data loss due to schema inconsistencies, Import/export failures due to network connectivity issues, Version compatibility issues between source and target environments

Options A, B, C, and D are correct as they represent common issues such as dependency conflicts, data loss, network connectivity issues, and version compatibility problems that may arise during solution import/export processes.

Option E, while a potential issue, is less common and may not directly affect solution import/export processes.

QUESTION 14

Answer - [A, B, C, D] Configure role-based permissions for entity access, Implement data loss prevention policies to protect sensitive information, Enable multi-factor authentication for app users, Encrypt data at rest and in transit to ensure confidentiality

Options A, B, C, and D are correct as they represent essential security practices during the creation of a model-driven app in Power Apps, including role-based access control, data protection, authentication, and encryption.

Option E, while important for compliance, is more related to ongoing security management rather than initial app creation.

QUESTION 15

Answer - [B] and [C].

A) Business rules cannot directly access external data.

B) Business rules can enable or disable a column dynamically based on production stage, facilitating efficient production tracking and ensuring data accuracy.

C) Business rules can show or hide a column based on user role, ensuring that employees have access to relevant information for their roles, thereby improving user experience and productivity.

QUESTION 16

Answer - [A, B, D] Use browser developer tools to inspect and debug script execution, Utilize console logging to track variable values and execution flow, Enable remote debugging for real-time monitoring of script behavior

Options A, B, and D are correct as they represent effective techniques for debugging JavaScript in Power Apps, including using browser developer tools, console logging, and remote debugging.

Options C and E, while useful, are not direct methods for debugging JavaScript in Power Apps.

QUESTION 17

Answer - [A, B, C, E] Documenting formula logic and usage to aid future maintenance and troubleshooting, Organizing formulas into reusable components or functions for modularity, Implementing version control to track changes and collaborate effectively with team members, Conducting regular code reviews to ensure adherence to coding standards and best practices

Options A, B, C, and E are correct as they represent best practices for maintaining and scaling Power Fx formulas, including documentation, modularization, version control, and code reviews.

Option D, while important for performance optimization, is not directly related to maintainability and scalability.

QUESTION 18

Answer - [B] Custom process action.

A) Custom APIs are typically used for integrating external systems or services with the Power Platform but do not provide user-specific execution control.

B) Custom process actions enable developers to define custom actions that can be executed by specific users, making them suitable for restricting code execution to customer service representatives. This ensures that only authorized personnel, such as customer service representatives, have access to execute the custom code, maintaining data confidentiality and integrity within the customer service system.

C) Classic workflows are automation processes but do not offer the capability to control code execution based on user roles or privileges.

D) Business rules are used for implementing simple business logic within the app's user interface but do not involve executing custom code on the ribbon.

QUESTION 19

Answer - [A, B, C, D, E] Regularly review and optimize app data model and formulas, Implement comprehensive backup and disaster recovery strategies, Monitor user feedback and performance metrics for continuous improvement, Enforce version control and release management processes, Conduct regular security audits and vulnerability assessments

Options A, B, C, D, and E represent essential best practices for maintaining app health and performance, including data model optimization, backup strategies, performance monitoring, version control, and security measures.

QUESTION 20

Answer - D

Option A - Incorrect: Monitor tool provides limited insights compared to Performance Analyzer.

Option B - Incorrect: App Insights does not directly integrate for this purpose.

Option C - Incorrect: Console.log() is useful for debugging but not for performance monitoring.

Option D - Correct: Directly provides performance metrics and optimization suggestions.

Option E - Incorrect: Azure Monitor is overkill for direct Power Apps performance monitoring.

QUESTION 21

Answer - [B] Power Apps component framework code component.

A) Client scripting may offer customization but may not provide the desired extensibility for accommodating future enhancements or changes.

B) Power Apps component framework code components allow for easy extensibility and customization, making them suitable for accommodating future enhancements or changes in requirements.

C) Web API is used for data integration and retrieval, not for creating custom visuals within the canvas app.

D) Liquid templates are primarily used for rendering dynamic content, not for creating custom visuals.

QUESTION 22

Answer - [D] Reduce the number of nested loops and conditional statements

A) Minimize DOM manipulation operations within the function - While minimizing DOM manipulation can improve performance, it may not address the primary performance bottlenecks within the JavaScript function.

B) Implement caching for frequently accessed data - Caching data can improve performance but may not directly address the execution time of the JavaScript function itself.

C) Use event delegation to reduce the number of event listeners - Event delegation can optimize event handling but may not significantly impact the execution time of a function running on form load.

D) Reduce the number of nested loops and conditional statements - This is a recommended strategy to improve performance as nested loops and conditional statements can introduce significant overhead, making it the correct answer.

E) Split the function into smaller, more modular components - While modularizing code can improve maintainability, it may not directly address performance issues related to nested loops and conditional statements.

QUESTION 23

Answer - [E] Handle errors gracefully by providing informative messages and recovery options

A) Log errors to the browser console for debugging purposes - While logging errors can aid in debugging, it doesn't provide a user-friendly experience or recovery options.

B) Display generic error messages to users without technical details - Generic error messages may frustrate users and hinder troubleshooting efforts.

C) Retry failed requests automatically with exponential backoff - While automatic retry mechanisms can improve resilience, they may not address all error scenarios and can potentially exacerbate issues.

D) Ignore errors and continue script execution for seamless user experience - Ignoring errors can lead to unpredictable behavior and data inconsistencies.

E) Handle errors gracefully by providing informative messages and recovery options - This is a best practice for error handling in client scripts, ensuring that users are informed about issues and offered potential solutions.

QUESTION 24

Answer - [A] Azure function
[B] Custom connector
[C] Custom API.

A) Azure functions can execute custom logic to facilitate real-time communication between Microsoft Dataverse and the RESTful Web API of the external compliance tracking system, enabling seamless capture of compliance data within the solution.

B) Custom connectors offer a standardized integration approach, enabling efficient connectivity between Microsoft Dataverse and the RESTful Web API of the external compliance tracking system, ensuring seamless data capture within the solution.

C) Custom APIs provide tailored integration solutions, enabling direct communication between Microsoft Dataverse and the RESTful Web API of the external compliance tracking system, ensuring data consistency and reliability in the compliance management solution.

QUESTION 25

Answer - B

Option A - Incorrect: Hard-coded language ID limits flexibility.

Option B - Correct: Uses API to determine text direction based on locale, ensuring correct rendering.

Option C - Incorrect: Locale handling is overly specific and not adaptive.

Option D - Incorrect: Only handles French, not scalable.

Option E - Incorrect: Does not handle locale specifics beyond language ID.

QUESTION 26

Answer - [A] Event handling logic and responsiveness.

A) Event handling logic and responsiveness - Testing event handling ensures that the interface behaves as expected and responds appropriately to user interactions.

B) Visual styling and layout consistency - While important for user experience, visual styling and layout consistency are not directly related to data integrity.

C) Data retrieval and manipulation performance - Performance testing is essential but focuses more on efficiency rather than data integrity and user experience.

D) Integration with external authentication providers - Authentication integration is critical but does not directly impact data integrity and user experience within the interface.

E) Compatibility with legacy browser versions - While compatibility is important, it is not the primary concern for ensuring data integrity and user experience within the interface.

QUESTION 27

Answer - [A] Power BI.

A) Power BI offers advanced analytics and reporting capabilities, making it suitable for tracking employee progress and generating reports based on completed training modules. By connecting Power BI to the canvas app, users can access insightful visualizations and reports to monitor training effectiveness.

Option B) Azure SQL Database: Azure SQL Database is a cloud-based relational database service, which can store training data, but it requires additional development effort to create reports and visualizations compared to Power BI.

Option C) Power Automate flow: While Power Automate flow can automate processes related to employee training, it does not provide the same level of analytics and reporting capabilities as Power BI.
Option D) Custom connector: Custom connectors are used for integrating external data sources with the Power Platform but are not designed for advanced analytics and reporting like Power BI.

QUESTION 28

Answer - [A] Implement end-to-end encryption using SSL/TLS.

A) Implement end-to-end encryption using SSL/TLS - SSL/TLS ensures secure communication between the PCF component and the API server, protecting sensitive data during transmission.

B) Store API credentials securely in environment variables - While important, storing credentials securely does not protect data during transmission.

C) Utilize a VPN for secure network communication - VPNs are useful for network security but do not directly protect data during transmission from the client.

D) Hash sensitive data before transmission - Hashing may provide data integrity but does not address confidentiality during transmission.

E) Use IP whitelisting to restrict API access - IP whitelisting controls access but does not secure data during transmission.

QUESTION 29

Answer - [B] Synchronous execution operates within the database transaction scope, while asynchronous execution operates outside the transaction scope.

A) Synchronous execution allows for parallel processing of multiple plug-ins, while asynchronous execution processes plug-ins sequentially - Both executions happen sequentially, but this statement incorrectly suggests parallelism for synchronous execution.

B) Synchronous execution operates within the database transaction scope, while asynchronous execution operates outside the transaction scope - Correct, synchronous execution is part of the transaction, while asynchronous occurs after the transaction is committed.

C) Synchronous execution guarantees transactional consistency across multiple records, while asynchronous execution may result in eventual consistency - Both executions ensure transactional consistency, but asynchronous may have delayed consistency due to its timing.

D) Synchronous execution triggers immediate user notifications, while asynchronous execution delays notifications until after the transaction is committed - Notification timing is not the primary distinction between the two execution modes.

E) Synchronous execution is recommended for long-running operations, while asynchronous execution is suitable for short-lived processes - The recommendation depends on various factors, not just the duration of the process.

QUESTION 30

Answer - [B] Utilize Azure Data Factory's schema mapping capabilities to perform data type conversions and adjustments on-the-fly, ensuring alignment between source and destination data structures.
Answer - [C] Implement data transformation logic in Azure Data Factory pipelines to preprocess data from the Access database before loading it into Dataverse tables, ensuring compliance with schema requirements.

B) Utilizing Azure Data Factory's schema mapping capabilities allows you to perform data type conversions and adjustments on-the-fly, ensuring alignment between the source data from the Access database and the destination data structures in Dataverse tables. By dynamically adjusting data types and field sizes, you can address compatibility issues and ensure the successful completion of the migration.

C) Implementing data transformation logic in Azure Data Factory pipelines enables you to preprocess data from the Access database before loading it into Dataverse tables. By applying transformations to handle data type mismatches and unsupported field sizes, you can ensure that the data is compliant with Dataverse schema requirements, reducing the likelihood of migration errors.

Option A) Modify Dataverse table schema: While modifying the schema may address compatibility issues, it may not be practical or desirable due to potential data loss or schema changes affecting other applications.

Option D) Export data to intermediate formats: While exporting data to intermediate formats may facilitate data type conversions, it introduces additional complexity and may not offer real-time transformation capabilities during the migration process.

QUESTION 31

Answer - [B] Using try-catch blocks to capture and handle exceptions gracefully.

A) Logging detailed error messages in the system event logs for easy troubleshooting - Logging is important, but handling errors gracefully is also necessary.

B) Using try-catch blocks to capture and handle exceptions gracefully - Correct, try-catch blocks help prevent unhandled exceptions from disrupting the execution flow and provide opportunities for error handling.

C) Ignoring errors to prevent disruption to the user experience - Ignoring errors can lead to data corruption and unexpected behavior.

D) Relying solely on platform-level error handling mechanisms - Platform-level mechanisms may not cover all scenarios, so custom error handling is often needed.

E) Exposing detailed error information to end-users for transparency - Exposing detailed error information can pose security risks and is not recommended.

QUESTION 32

Answer - [B] Maintaining multiple versions concurrently for backward compatibility.

A) Updating existing API versions without backward compatibility - This approach can break existing client integrations and cause compatibility issues.

B) Maintaining multiple versions concurrently for backward compatibility - Correct, maintaining multiple versions ensures that existing client integrations remain functional while allowing for the introduction of new features in newer versions.

C) Allowing clients to specify the API version dynamically - While flexible, dynamic versioning may lead to compatibility issues if clients are not updated accordingly.

D) Using timestamp-based versioning for simplicity - Timestamp-based versioning may not provide clear semantic versioning and can be confusing for clients.

E) Reusing existing API endpoints for different versions - Reusing endpoints for different versions may lead to confusion and conflicts between versions.

QUESTION 33

Answer - [A] _department_name

A) In this context, the _department_name attribute likely contains the display name of the associated department record. When designing a canvas app to display related information, you should include the _department_name attribute to ensure that the department's name is displayed correctly for each employee.

Option B) _departmentid_name - Incorrect: This attribute may contain the GUID of the associated department record, not the department's name.
Option C) _department_name_value - Incorrect: This attribute combination is unlikely to exist and may not provide the department's name.
Option D) _departmentid_value - Incorrect: This attribute combination is unlikely to exist and may not provide the department's name.

QUESTION 34

Answer - [B] Implementing access controls and permissions for sensitive data.

A) Exposing customer data to unauthorized third parties - Exposing customer data violates GDPR regulations and can result in significant fines.

B) Implementing access controls and permissions for sensitive data - Correct, GDPR mandates the implementation of access controls and permissions to ensure that only authorized individuals can access sensitive customer data.

C) Using weak encryption algorithms for data protection - Weak encryption algorithms do not provide adequate protection for sensitive data and may lead to non-compliance with GDPR.

D) Storing customer data indefinitely without consent - GDPR requires companies to obtain consent for data storage and to adhere to data retention policies.

E) Ignoring data subject access requests (DSARs) - Ignoring DSARs violates GDPR rights and can result in penalties.

QUESTION 35

Answer - B

Option A - Inefficient: Manual monitoring is prone to errors and delays.

Option B - Correct: Automating the monitoring and update process ensures that changes are timely and accurately reflected in PowerApps.

Option C - Incorrect: Managed identities handle access, not synchronization of updates.

Option D - Incorrect: Power Platform does not provide alerts for Azure API changes.

Option E - Inefficient: While documentation is good practice, it does not ensure timely updates.

QUESTION 36

Answer - D) PATCH

A) PUT - Incorrect. Replaces the entire entity.
B) GET - Incorrect. Only retrieves data.
C) POST - Incorrect. Used mainly for creating new resources.
D) PATCH - Correct. Allows partial update of a resource.
E) HEAD - Incorrect. Retrieves the headers only.

QUESTION 37

Answer - [C] Handling errors gracefully and providing informative feedback

A) Logging detailed error messages in client-side code - While logging errors is important for troubleshooting, it may not provide users with actionable information or a good user experience.

B) Displaying generic error messages to users - Generic error messages may confuse users and hinder troubleshooting efforts.

C) Handling errors gracefully and providing informative feedback - Correct, providing clear and actionable error messages helps users understand issues and take appropriate actions, improving overall user experience.

D) Ignoring errors to prevent disruption to the user experience - Ignoring errors may lead to unexpected behavior and frustrate users who encounter issues.

E) Returning HTTP status code 200 for all responses - Returning a success status code for error responses is misleading and violates HTTP standards.

QUESTION 38

Answer - [D] Limiting the use of exponential backoff to prevent excessive retries

A) Minimizing retry intervals to reduce latency - While reducing latency is important, it should not come at the expense of excessive retry attempts, which may overload APIs.

B) Increasing the maximum number of retry attempts for critical requests - While critical requests may warrant more retry attempts, an unlimited number of retries can lead to unnecessary load on APIs.

C) Implementing fixed retry intervals for predictable behavior - Fixed retry intervals may not adapt well to varying network conditions and API responsiveness.

D) Limiting the use of exponential backoff to prevent excessive retries - Correct, while exponential backoff is effective in reducing retries, it should be used judiciously to prevent excessive retries that may strain APIs.

E) Prioritizing retry attempts based on request urgency - While prioritization is important, it may not directly address the balance between performance and reliability in retry policies.

QUESTION 39

Answer - A), B), and D)

A) Correct. Prevents the system from hitting API rate limits.

B) Correct. Reduces the load on the system by handling large data sets in smaller chunks.

C) Incorrect. Increasing timeouts does not address the issue of system load.

D) Correct. Improves efficiency by handling multiple tasks simultaneously.

E) Incorrect. Alerts provide information but do not reduce the load.

QUESTION 40

Answer - B)

A) Incorrect - This JavaScript code is too simplistic and does not handle JSON format changes robustly.

B) Correct - The C# example uses HttpClient and JsonConvert.DeserializeObject which are appropriate for handling RESTful API calls with dynamic JSON parsing in Azure Functions.

C) Incorrect - The TypeScript function assumes a static JSON structure, making it fragile in face of format changes.

D) Incorrect - The JSON snippet is just a configuration and does not include any logic for handling or parsing the API response.

E) Incorrect - PowerFx does not have native support for making HTTP requests or parsing JSON directly in Azure Functions.

QUESTION 41

Answer - [B] Average execution time per flow run

A) Total number of flow runs executed - While the total number of runs provides insight into flow usage, it may not directly indicate efficiency or bottlenecks.

B) Average execution time per flow run - Correct, the average execution time per flow run is crucial for assessing efficiency and identifying performance bottlenecks. Longer execution times may indicate areas for optimization.

C) Total number of connectors used in a flow - The number of connectors used may impact performance but does not directly measure flow efficiency.

D) Number of successful versus failed flow runs - Success/failure counts are important but do not provide specific insights into flow performance.

E) Overall duration of data transfer between connectors - While data transfer duration is relevant, it may not capture overall flow performance comprehensively.

QUESTION 42

Answer - A), B), and C)

A) Correct. Checks if 'ExpirationDate' is today or past.

B) Correct. Ensures the document is in the 'HR' library.

C) Correct. Ensures both critical conditions for expiration and library location are met.

D) Incorrect. Not(greater) is a convoluted way to check for past or present dates.

E) Incorrect. 'Expired' in title is not required by the condition.

QUESTION 43

Answer - [C] Logging and monitoring access to Azure Key Vault and Entra

A) Encrypting data in transit using SSL/TLS protocols - While encryption is important, it does not directly address the security and compliance impacts of misconfigured secrets and service principals.

B) Implementing multi-factor authentication (MFA) for user access - MFA enhances security but may not specifically address misconfiguration issues with Azure Key Vault and Entra.

C) Logging and monitoring access to Azure Key Vault and Entra - Correct, logging and monitoring access helps identify unauthorized access attempts and potential security breaches, ensuring compliance with security policies.

D) Sharing service principal credentials with third-party vendors - Sharing credentials with third parties increases the risk of unauthorized access and violates security best practices.

E) Exposing secrets in plain text within flow configurations - Exposing secrets in plain text is a security risk but does not directly relate to assessing security and compliance impacts.

QUESTION 44

Answer - [A] Implementing real-time dashboards and analytics for performance monitoring

A) Implementing real-time dashboards and analytics for performance monitoring - Correct, real-time dashboards and analytics enable proactive monitoring and optimization of business process flows by providing insights into performance metrics and trends.

B) Conducting periodic audits and reviews of workflow execution logs - While audits are important, real-time monitoring allows for immediate action in response to performance issues.

C) Establishing service level agreements (SLAs) for workflow completion and response times - SLAs are important but may not directly address the need for real-time monitoring and optimization.

D) Enabling version control and change management for business process definitions - Version control is essential for managing changes but may not directly contribute to real-time optimization.

E) Configuring automated alerts and notifications for workflow exceptions and bottlenecks - Automated alerts are valuable but may not provide real-time insights into overall performance and trends.

QUESTION 45

Answer - A) OAuth 2.0 with token refresh

A) Correct. OAuth 2.0 with token refresh ensures each request can be uniquely authenticated through a new token.
B) Incorrect. API key is static and not unique per request.
C) Incorrect. Dynamic token, while unique, is not specified to refresh per request.
D) Incorrect. Certificate based is not typically for single request authentication.
E) Incorrect. Password based is static and not unique per request.

QUESTION 46

Answer - [A, B, C, D, E] Implementing retry policies and exponential backoff strategies for failed event delivery attempts, Logging detailed error information and stack traces for failed event publishing attempts, Monitoring service health and availability of IServiceEndpointNotificationService endpoints, Implementing circuit breaker patterns to prevent cascading failures during event publication, Configuring alerting mechanisms to notify administrators about failed event publishing

A) Implementing retry policies and exponential backoff strategies for failed event delivery attempts - Retry and backoff strategies help mitigate transient failures during event delivery.

B) Logging detailed error information and stack traces for failed event publishing attempts - Detailed logging aids in troubleshooting and identifying root causes of event publishing failures.

C) Monitoring service health and availability of IServiceEndpointNotificationService endpoints - Monitoring ensures timely detection and resolution of service disruptions.

D) Implementing circuit breaker patterns to prevent cascading failures during event publication - Circuit breakers help prevent system overload and mitigate the impact of failing IServiceEndpointNotificationService endpoints.

E) Configuring alerting mechanisms to notify administrators about failed event publishing - Alerting ensures prompt notification of failures for timely intervention and resolution.

QUESTION 47

Answer - [A, B, C, D, E] Tracking endpoint response times and latency metrics, Monitoring message throughput and queue lengths for asynchronous endpoints, Setting up alerts for endpoint availability and error rates, Analyzing endpoint usage patterns and traffic volumes, Implementing automated endpoint scaling based on workload demand

A) Tracking endpoint response times and latency metrics - Monitoring response times and latency helps assess endpoint performance and identify potential bottlenecks.

B) Monitoring message throughput and queue lengths for asynchronous endpoints - For asynchronous endpoints, monitoring message throughput and queue lengths is crucial for performance optimization.

C) Setting up alerts for endpoint availability and error rates - Proactive alerting ensures timely detection and resolution of endpoint availability issues.

D) Analyzing endpoint usage patterns and traffic volumes - Analyzing usage patterns helps forecast resource requirements and optimize endpoint configurations.

E) Implementing automated endpoint scaling based on workload demand - Automated scaling ensures that endpoints can handle varying workload demands efficiently, maintaining optimal performance and reliability.

QUESTION 48

Answer - A) POST with DuplicateDetection enabled

A) Correct. POST with DuplicateDetection enabled helps prevent creating duplicate records.
B) Incorrect. PUT with If-None-Match is not appropriate for creating records.
C) Incorrect. POST with $filter does not prevent duplicate creations.
D) Incorrect. UPSERT is a specific operation that isn't typically constrained by If-None-Match in Dataverse.
E) Incorrect. If-Match is used for updates, not for preventing duplicates in creation.

QUESTION 49

Answer - [A, C, D, E] Duplicate records being created despite alternate key constraints, Incorrect configuration of alternate key attributes, leading to validation errors, Inconsistent enforcement of alternate key constraints across different environments, Unexpected behavior during data migration processes involving entities with alternate keys.

A) Duplicate records being created despite alternate key constraints. - This issue may occur due to data integrity issues or incorrect alternate key configurations, requiring investigation and resolution.

B) Performance degradation due to inefficient indexing of alternate keys. - While alternate keys can improve performance, inefficient indexing or excessive use may lead to performance issues that need to be addressed through optimization.

C) Incorrect configuration of alternate key attributes, leading to validation errors. - Incorrect configuration of alternate key attributes can result in validation errors during data insertion or update operations, requiring review and correction of configurations.

D) Inconsistent enforcement of alternate key constraints across different environments. - Inconsistencies in alternate key enforcement across environments can lead to data integrity issues and require alignment of configurations.

E) Unexpected behavior during data migration processes involving entities with alternate keys. - Data migration processes involving entities with alternate keys may encounter unexpected behavior due to differences in data formats or configurations between source and target environments, necessitating troubleshooting and adjustment of migration strategies.

QUESTION 50

Answer - [A, C] Implementing encryption mechanisms to protect data during transmission and storage, Enforcing role-based access control to restrict data access based on user roles and permissions.

A) Implementing encryption mechanisms to protect data during transmission and storage. - Encryption helps safeguard sensitive data from unauthorized access or interception during transmission and storage, ensuring compliance with security and privacy regulations.

B) Conducting regular vulnerability assessments and penetration testing of data integration systems. - While important for overall system security, vulnerability assessments and penetration testing focus more on identifying system weaknesses rather than ensuring compliance specifically in data integration processes.

C) Enforcing role-based access control to restrict data access based on user roles and permissions. - Role-based access control ensures that only authorized users have access to sensitive data, minimizing the risk of data breaches and ensuring compliance with security regulations.

D) Obtaining explicit consent from citizens before integrating their data into Dataverse. - While consent is important for data privacy, it may not be sufficient on its own to ensure security and compliance in data integration processes.

E) Implementing data anonymization techniques to protect individual privacy. - Data anonymization helps protect privacy but may not be directly related to security and compliance measures required for data integration processes involving sensitive information.

PRACTICE TEST 5 - QUESTIONS ONLY

QUESTION 1

A telecommunications company is deploying Power Platform solutions to streamline customer support processes. They need a monitoring solution that includes clear service level agreements (SLAs) to ensure that system performance meets the needs of both internal users and external customers. Which practice directly addresses service performance and quality standards by defining expected levels of service and performance guarantees for Power Platform solutions?

A) Service Level Agreements (SLAs)
B) Incident management
C) Change tracking
D) Dependency mapping
E) Service tickets generation

QUESTION 2

A consulting firm is advising a client on the use of out-of-the-box features versus customization for their Power Platform solution. They need to assess the trade-offs associated with using out-of-the-box features. What is a potential trade-off of relying heavily on out-of-the-box features?

A) Increased development time and cost
B) Greater flexibility to meet specific business requirements
C) Higher risk of compatibility issues during updates
D) Enhanced scalability and performance
E) Improved maintainability and ease of updates

QUESTION 3

A monthly data review process needs to be triggered at midnight on the first of every month in Microsoft Dataverse using an Azure Function. What is the correct cron expression to use?

A) 0 0 1 * *
B) 0 0 * 1 *
C) 0 12 1 * *
D) 0 0 0 1 *
E) 0 0 * * 1

QUESTION 4

A financial institution is reviewing the overall security architecture of their Power Platform solutions to ensure comprehensive protection against internal and external threats. They need to assess various security features and best practices to strengthen their defenses.
Which aspects should they consider when evaluating the overall security architecture of their Power Platform solutions? Select THREE.

A) Implementation of multi-factor authentication (MFA) for user access.
B) Encryption of sensitive data stored within Microsoft Dataverse.

C) Regular monitoring and analysis of security logs for suspicious activities.
D) Integration of threat intelligence feeds to proactively identify potential security threats.
E) Adoption of role-based access controls (RBAC) for fine-grained authorization.

QUESTION 5

A company needs to ensure that its sales data entered into a Power Apps canvas app syncs in real-time with their SQL database. Which C# snippet embedded in a custom connector would best handle this requirement?

A) public async Task<IActionResult> Post([FromBody] Sale sale) { await dbContext.Sales.AddAsync(sale); await dbContext.SaveChangesAsync(); return Ok(); }

B) public void UpdateSales(Sale sale) { dbContext.Sales.Update(sale); dbContext.SaveChanges(); }

C) public Sale GetSale(int id) { return dbContext.Sales.FirstOrDefault(s => s.SaleId == id); }

D) public async Task<IActionResult> SyncSales([FromBody] IEnumerable<Sale> sales) { foreach (var sale in sales) { dbContext.Sales.Update(sale); } await dbContext.SaveChangesAsync(); return Ok(); }

E) public IActionResult DeleteSale(int id) { var sale = dbContext.Sales.Find(id); dbContext.Sales.Remove(sale); dbContext.SaveChangesAsync(); return Ok(); }

QUESTION 6

For a sales management canvas app, you need to ensure the drop-down list only shows customers from the 'North America' region in Microsoft Dataverse. What PowerFx expression should you set for the Items property of the drop-down?

A) Filter('Customers', Region = 'North America')
B) 'Customers'
C) Lookup('Customers', Region = 'North America')
D) Collect('NA Customers', Filter(Customers, Region = 'North America'))
E) Filter('Customers', Region.Value = 'North America')

QUESTION 7

A healthcare organization is evaluating the effectiveness of security roles in securing patient data within their Dataverse environment. They need to assess the impact of security roles on data confidentiality, integrity, and availability to ensure compliance with regulatory requirements and industry standards. How do security roles contribute to securing data in Dataverse environments? Select THREE.

A) Security roles enforce access controls to restrict unauthorized access to sensitive patient information, ensuring data confidentiality.

B) Security roles define permissions to prevent unauthorized modification or deletion of patient records, safeguarding data integrity.

C) Security roles regulate access to ensure that patient data is available only to authorized users when needed, preserving data availability.

D) Security roles facilitate auditing and logging of user activities to track access to patient records and maintain accountability.

E) Security roles enable encryption of patient data at rest and in transit to protect against unauthorized interception or disclosure.

QUESTION 8

A software development team is exploring the integration capabilities of business units in Microsoft Dataverse with other security features. They need to assess how business units can complement existing security mechanisms to enhance data protection and access control.
How does the integration of business units in Microsoft Dataverse with other security features enhance data protection? Select THREE.

A) Business units enable seamless integration with role-based access control (RBAC) to enforce access permissions and privileges based on user roles and responsibilities.

B) Integration with business units allows for the enforcement of record-level security to restrict access to sensitive data based on predefined criteria and access rules.

C) Implementing business units enhances data encryption and data loss prevention (DLP) capabilities to safeguard sensitive information and prevent unauthorized access or disclosure.

D) Business units support the implementation of multi-factor authentication (MFA) and single sign-on (SSO) for enhanced user authentication and identity management.

E) Integration of business units with other security features enables advanced threat detection and monitoring capabilities to identify and respond to security incidents proactively.

QUESTION 9

You are working on a project that involves integrating an external system with Microsoft Dataverse using Power Automate flows. However, users report that the flow is not triggering when expected events occur in the external system. What could be potential reasons for this issue? Select the correct answers that apply.

A) The Power Automate flow is disabled or not properly activated.
B) There is a delay in the execution of the flow due to system resource constraints.
C) The connection between the external system and Microsoft Dataverse is not properly configured.
D) The flow's trigger condition is not met based on the specified criteria.
E) The external system's API version is not compatible with the Power Automate connector.

QUESTION 10

Implementing a custom process automation requires invoking an Azure function from a Power Apps app to process sales data. Which PowerFx script should you use to correctly call the Azure function and handle its response?

A) CallAzureFunction('https://myazurefunction.azurewebsites.net/api/SalesDataProcess', { Method: 'POST', Body: Record({ SalesData: Gallery1.Selected }) })

B) AzureFunction.Post('https://myazurefunction.azurewebsites.net/api/SalesDataProcess', JSON({ 'SalesData': Gallery1.Selected }))

C) ExecuteFunction('https://myazurefunction.azurewebsites.net/api/SalesDataProcess', { 'SalesData': Gallery1.Selected })

D) PowerAutomate.Run('https://myazurefunction.azurewebsites.net/api/SalesDataProcess', Gallery1.Selected)

E) PostToFunction('https://myazurefunction.azurewebsites.net/api/SalesDataProcess', { body: JSON.stringify({ SalesData: Gallery1.Selected }) })

QUESTION 11

A financial institution is implementing a loan management system using Microsoft Dataverse. They need to configure relationships between the "Loan" and "Payment" entities to track loan repayments. Additionally, they want to ensure that when a payment record is deleted, associated loan records are updated to reflect the remaining balance accurately. Which relationship behavior should be configured for the "Loan-Payment" relationship to meet this requirement?

A) Cascade All
B) Cascade None
C) Remove Link
D) Parental
E) Referential

QUESTION 12

You are responsible for managing a complex Microsoft Power Platform environment where various solutions are deployed to support critical business operations. One of the solutions requires additional features to meet evolving business requirements, but you want to ensure that existing functionalities remain intact to avoid disruptions to ongoing operations. What should you do to add the new features effectively while preserving the stability of the existing functionalities?

A) Create
B) Update
C) Upgrade
D) Patch

QUESTION 13

A security audit is being conducted for a Power Platform environment where solutions are frequently imported and exported between environments. What security implications should be evaluated to ensure secure solution transfer in Microsoft Dataverse? Select the correct answers that apply.

A) Role-based access control (RBAC) for solution management
B) Encryption of solution files during transfer
C) Audit logging of solution import/export activities
D) IP whitelisting for solution transfer endpoints
E) Multi-factor authentication (MFA) for solution administrators

QUESTION 14

During the setup of a model-driven app in Power Apps, developers may encounter common issues that require troubleshooting to ensure smooth operation. What are some common setup issues that developers may need to troubleshoot? Select the correct answers that apply.

A) Misconfigured entity relationships causing data inconsistency
B) Performance degradation due to inefficient form design
C) Security vulnerabilities arising from weak authentication settings
D) Integration failures with external systems due to API misconfiguration
E) User interface inconsistencies across different devices and browsers

QUESTION 15

You are enhancing the user experience of a model-driven app for a real estate agency's property management system. The app aims to streamline property management processes and improve client satisfaction. What are two key functionalities that you can achieve using a business rule in this scenario? Select the correct answers that apply.

A) Access external data.
B) Enable or disable a column based on property status.
C) Show or hide a column based on user role.
D) Run the rule on demand.

QUESTION 16

When considering the use of JavaScript versus Power Fx for implementing commands and buttons in Power Apps, developers need to weigh various factors. What are some considerations when comparing JavaScript and Power Fx implementations? Select the correct answers that apply.

A) Language familiarity and developer expertise
B) Performance optimization and execution speed
C) Integration capabilities with external systems and services
D) Accessibility and support for screen readers and assistive technologies
E) Vendor lock-in and long-term platform sustainability

QUESTION 17

An e-commerce company is developing a Power App to analyze customer purchase patterns and recommend personalized products. They need to write advanced Power Fx formulas to process large volumes of transactional data efficiently. Which scenario represents a potential challenge when writing complex Power Fx formulas for this use case? Select the correct answers that apply.

A) Handling asynchronous data updates and ensuring formula consistency across datasets
B) Managing formula dependencies and avoiding circular references to prevent calculation errors
C) Integrating real-time API calls within formulas to fetch dynamic product recommendations
D) Implementing error handling mechanisms to gracefully manage unexpected data inputs or API failures
E) Balancing formula complexity with readability to maintain code maintainability and troubleshooting ease

QUESTION 18

You are designing a model-driven app for a human resources system. The app requires executing specialized code when a user clicks on a button in the app's ribbon. However, this functionality should only be accessible to HR administrators. What option should you select to fulfill this requirement?

A) Custom API
B) Custom process action
C) Classic workflow
D) Business rule

QUESTION 19

A software consultancy firm is tasked with troubleshooting a canvas app that intermittently crashes during user interactions. Which approach would be most effective for analyzing and resolving this issue? Select the correct answers that apply.

A) Analyzing crash dumps and error logs
B) Reviewing app telemetry and usage analytics
C) Engaging with Microsoft support for advanced troubleshooting assistance
D) Rebuilding the app from scratch to eliminate potential coding errors
E) Conducting a code review to identify and address programming flaws

QUESTION 20

A Power Apps developer needs to handle common performance bottlenecks in a complex Canvas app. Which method effectively reduces overhead?

A) Defer loading non-critical data using LoadData() after app start
B) Optimize data sources with incremental loading on visible galleries
C) Reduce screen complexity by limiting media elements
D) Use non-delegable queries for all data operations
E) Implement manual caching mechanisms for frequently accessed data

QUESTION 21

You are designing a canvas app for a financial reporting system. The app requires incorporating a custom visual to display financial data trends. However, you need the visual to be easily adaptable to different screen sizes and orientations for optimal user experience. Which approach should you use?

A) Client scripting
B) Power Apps component framework code component
C) Web API
D) Liquid template

QUESTION 22

A Power Apps developer is coding a JavaScript function to handle error scenarios gracefully. Which of the following represents a best practice for error handling in this context?

A) Implement custom error messages for user-friendly feedback
B) Use specific error codes to identify different types of errors
C) Log detailed error information to a central repository for analysis
D) Retry failed operations automatically after a short delay
E) Provide fallback mechanisms to maintain app functionality during errors

QUESTION 23

A Power Apps developer is seeking best practices for integrating Dataverse Web API in client scripts for a canvas app. Which of the following represents a recommended best practice for integrating Web API in client scripts?

A) Hard-code API endpoints to improve performance
B) Minimize error handling to streamline script execution
C) Implement pagination for large data sets to improve performance
D) Store sensitive data directly within client scripts for efficiency
E) Throttle API requests to avoid exceeding rate limits and prevent abuse

QUESTION 24

Your organization is deploying an asset management solution using Microsoft Dataverse. You need to integrate an external asset tracking system, which exposes a RESTful Web API, to manage asset data within the solution. Considering the integration requirements, which three options should you utilize to ensure a robust integration solution? Select the correct answers that apply.

A) Azure function
B) Custom connector
C) Custom API
D) HTTP request
E) Business rule

QUESTION 25

During the initialization of a PCF component, you encounter an issue where the data from Dataverse is not loading correctly. What TypeScript code snippet is best for debugging this issue?

A) console.log('Data load error:', context.parameters.sampleDataSet.error);
B) if (!context.parameters.sampleDataSet.loading) { console.error('Data loading failed'); }
C) context.parameters.sampleDataSet.onLoad(error => console.error('Load error:', error));
D) console.debug('Loading data:', context.parameters.sampleDataSet.records);
E) context.mode.trackContainerResize((width, height) => { console.log('Container size:', width, 'x', height); });

QUESTION 26

A Power Apps developer is troubleshooting issues with a PCF component interface. Which action is appropriate for identifying and resolving interface-related issues efficiently?

A) Debugging the component code using browser developer tools.

B) Disabling browser cache to ensure the latest component version loads.
C) Reverting recent changes to the component configuration.
D) Refactoring the interface to use a different programming language.
E) Clearing browser cookies to resolve session-related issues.

QUESTION 27

Your organization is developing a canvas app for event management. You need to implement a feature that allows users to check in attendees using a barcode scanner. Which development option should you choose to implement this feature?

A) Power Automate flow
B) Azure Blob Storage
C) Power Apps custom control
D) Custom connector

QUESTION 28

When integrating Web API features into PCF components, what is a best practice for managing API versioning to ensure long-term compatibility?

A) Hardcode API endpoints to specific versions within the PCF component.
B) Include API version information in request headers.
C) Implement dynamic API version detection based on client capabilities.
D) Utilize API versioning tools provided by the Web API service.
E) Maintain a separate PCF component for each API version.

QUESTION 29

A development team is considering the impact of transaction support within the plug-in execution pipeline for their Power Platform solution. What is a notable impact of transaction support on plug-in execution?

A) Improved performance due to reduced database locking during record processing.
B) Ensured consistency by rolling back all changes if any operation within the transaction fails.
C) Enhanced scalability through parallel execution of transactions across multiple servers.
D) Minimized risk of data corruption by enforcing strict isolation between concurrent transactions.
E) Reduced latency by prioritizing high-priority transactions over low-priority ones.

QUESTION 30

Your organization is migrating data from an existing MySQL database to Microsoft Dataverse tables using Azure Data Factory pipelines. During the migration, you encounter errors related to data format mismatches and non-ASCII characters in text fields, leading to failed data transfers. What are two potential approaches to address these errors and ensure the successful completion of the migration? Select the correct answers that apply.

A) Utilize Azure Data Factory's built-in data quality features, such as column pattern matching and regular expression validation, to identify and remediate data format inconsistencies before loading data into Dataverse tables.

B) Configure MySQL database settings to enforce strict character encoding rules and restrict text field inputs to ASCII characters only, ensuring compatibility with Dataverse table requirements.

C) Implement custom data cleansing logic in Azure Data Factory pipelines to sanitize text data from the MySQL database, removing or replacing non-ASCII characters with appropriate substitutions before transferring data to Dataverse tables.

D) Export data from the MySQL database to intermediate JSON files, apply text encoding transformations using Azure Data Factory's Data Flow activities, and then import the transformed data into Dataverse tables with enhanced compatibility and data integrity.

QUESTION 31

A Power Platform developer is evaluating the performance implications of using the Organization service in plug-ins. What is a potential performance consideration when utilizing the service?

A) The size of the plug-in assembly has no impact on performance.
B) Accessing large datasets without proper filtering can degrade performance.
C) Parallel execution of plug-ins has minimal impact on overall system performance.
D) Increasing the number of plug-in steps in a single transaction improves performance.
E) Running plug-ins synchronously instead of asynchronously enhances performance.

QUESTION 32

A Power Platform developer is integrating Custom APIs with existing data models and business logic in Dataverse. What is a recommended approach for seamless integration?

A) Hard-coding data mappings within the Custom API logic.
B) Exposing all data fields in the Custom API responses.
C) Implementing validation rules within the Custom API.
D) Leveraging existing data relationships and business rules.
E) Embedding business logic directly within the API endpoints.

QUESTION 33

You are configuring a business process flow (BPF) in Microsoft Power Automate for managing service requests. The BPF involves a custom entity named "Tickets" with a lookup field to the "Customers" entity. During the ticket resolution process, users need to view the name of the associated customer. What attribute should you reference in the BPF to display the customer's name?

A) _customer_name
B) _customerid
C) _customer_value
D) _customerid_name

QUESTION 34

A Power Platform solution requires auditing and monitoring of API access for compliance and security purposes. Which approach is suitable for achieving this requirement?

A) Logging API access in local text files without encryption.
B) Using Azure Monitor to track API calls and performance metrics.
C) Disabling audit trails to improve system performance.
D) Ignoring unauthorized API access attempts.
E) Relying solely on third-party tools for auditing.

QUESTION 35

What common issue might occur when importing API definitions from third-party services like GitHub into Power Platform, and how can it be addressed?

A) Mismatched data types leading to runtime errors, resolved by custom wrapper functions.
B) Authentication failures due to outdated OAuth tokens, fixed by refreshing connection settings.
C) API rate limits causing failed requests, addressable by implementing throttling in Power Automate.
D) Incomplete API definitions leading to function errors, correctable by manual updates to the definition files.
E) Cross-origin resource sharing (CORS) errors, mitigated by configuring proper headers in the API gateway.

QUESTION 36

To securely initiate a server-side process via a JavaScript function that performs a system cleanup on Microsoft Power Platform, which HTTP method should be employed?

A) DELETE
B) POST
C) PUT
D) GET
E) PATCH

QUESTION 37

In performance tuning and best practices for interacting with the Dataverse Web API, what is a key consideration?

A) Minimizing the number of API requests by batching operations.
B) Increasing payload size to reduce network overhead.
C) Enabling verbose error logging for detailed diagnostics.
D) Utilizing synchronous requests for real-time data retrieval.
E) Applying exponential backoff for retrying failed requests.

QUESTION 38

When defining retry policies for API calls in a Power Platform solution, what factor should developers consider to ensure effective handling of transient faults?

A) Reducing the overall number of retry attempts
B) Increasing the initial retry interval for each subsequent attempt

C) Implementing jitter to introduce randomness in retry intervals
D) Using synchronous retry mechanisms for immediate response
E) Limiting retries to specific types of HTTP status codes

QUESTION 39

To ensure compliance with data protection regulations, how should a Power Automate cloud flow that transmits sensitive data to an external API be configured? Select the correct answers that apply.

A) Encrypt data before transmission
B) Use HTTPS for all API communications
C) Log each data transfer
D) Implement API request authentication
E) Configure error alerts for transfer failures

QUESTION 40

An IT service management company wants to automate incident reporting by triggering an Azure Function whenever an incident is logged in their ERP system. The function should validate the incident data against a set of predefined rules before updating the CDS (Dataverse).

A) C#: public static async Task<IActionResult> Run([QueueTrigger("incident-queue", Connection = "StorageAccountConnection")] string incidentJson, ILogger log) { Incident incident = JsonConvert.DeserializeObject<Incident>(incidentJson); if (ValidateIncident(incident)) { // Update CDS logic here } return new OkResult(); }

B) JavaScript: module.exports = async function (context, myQueueItem) { var incident = JSON.parse(myQueueItem); if (validateIncident(incident)) { // Update CDS logic here } }

C) TypeScript: import { QueueTrigger } from '@azure/functions'; export async function processIncident(context: { bindings: { myQueueItem: string; }, log: ILogger; }): Promise<void> { let incident = JSON.parse(context.bindings.myQueueItem); if (validateIncident(incident)) { // Update CDS logic here } }

D) HTML: <form>Incident ID: <input type="text"></form>

E) SQL: SELECT * FROM Incidents WHERE IncidentID = '123';

QUESTION 41

When handling errors and exceptions in Power Automate cloud flows, what approach helps ensure resilience and fault tolerance?

A) Using inline error handling within each action
B) Implementing retries with exponential backoff for transient errors
C) Relying solely on manual intervention for error resolution
D) Disabling error notifications to avoid unnecessary alerts
E) Skipping failed actions to maintain flow continuity

QUESTION 42

To enhance operational security, a Power Automate flow should trigger only for documents in the 'Operations' SharePoint folder that are classified as 'Confidential' and were modified today. What expressions accurately define this condition? Select the correct answers that apply.

A) @equals(triggerBody()?['Classification'], 'Confidential')
B) @equals(triggerBody()?['Modified'], utcNow())
C) @and(equals(triggerBody()?['Classification'], 'Confidential'), equals(triggerBody()?['FolderName'], 'Operations'), equals(triggerBody()?['Modified'], utcNow()))
D) @contains(triggerBody()?['FolderName'], 'Operations')
E) @not(empty(triggerBody()?['Classification']))

QUESTION 43

A healthcare organization is concerned about maintaining compliance with data protection regulations while using Azure Key Vault and Microsoft Entra in their Power Platform environment. What is a recommended approach for troubleshooting integration issues related to these services?

A) Enabling verbose logging for all flows to capture detailed error messages
B) Reviewing Azure Key Vault access policies for misconfigurations
C) Disabling Azure Key Vault and Entra to prevent further issues
D) Rebooting the Power Platform environment to reset configurations
E) Ignoring integration issues to avoid disruption to operations

QUESTION 44

A retail company is facing challenges with integrated flows and processes in its customer order fulfillment system. They need to troubleshoot issues related to data synchronization and workflow dependencies to minimize order processing delays. What approach should they take for troubleshooting issues in integrated flows and processes?

A) Analyzing execution logs and error details in Azure Monitor and Log Analytics
B) Reviewing flow configurations and dependencies in the Power Platform Admin Center
C) Conducting end-to-end testing to identify and isolate integration bottlenecks
D) Implementing custom error handling logic using Power Automate Cloud Flows
E) Collaborating with cross-functional teams to identify root causes and solutions

QUESTION 45

When creating a custom connector to a healthcare system via Power Platform, the API requires encrypted communications and authenticated requests. Which authentication types should you consider?

A) Certificate based and OAuth 2.0
B) API key and Single sign-on
C) OAuth 2.0 and API key
D) Password based and API key
E) Single sign-on and OAuth 2.0

QUESTION 46

A financial services firm is developing a Power Platform solution to manage client portfolios and investment transactions. They need to address security considerations when publishing events using IServiceEndpointNotificationService. What security considerations are important in event publishing? Select the correct answers that apply.

A) Implementing OAuth 2.0 authentication for secure access to IServiceEndpointNotificationService

B) Encrypting event payloads and sensitive data transmitted through IServiceEndpointNotificationService

C) Restricting access to event publishing endpoints based on IP allowlists or firewall rules

D) Enforcing role-based access control (RBAC) to manage permissions for event publishers

E) Using secure protocols such as HTTPS for communication between Dataverse and IServiceEndpointNotificationService

QUESTION 47

A healthcare organization is developing a Power Platform solution to manage patient records and medical appointments. They need to ensure robust handling of failures and retries when interacting with service endpoints to maintain data integrity and reliability. What are some strategies for handling failures and retries effectively in this scenario? Select the correct answers that apply.

A) Implementing exponential backoff and jitter for retry logic
B) Using dead-letter queues for storing failed messages and processing them later
C) Configuring retry policies with exponential delay and maximum retry attempts
D) Monitoring error rates and automatically scaling endpoint resources
E) Implementing circuit breaker patterns to prevent cascading failures

QUESTION 48

In a scenario where you need to update a set of records in Microsoft Dataverse based on a complex filter and apply changes to a specific field, what approach should you take using the Web API?

A) PATCH with $filter
B) POST with batch operations
C) PATCH with batch operations
D) PUT with $filter
E) PATCH with a complex query in the request body

QUESTION 49

A software development company is considering when to use alternate keys in their Power Platform solutions. In what scenarios should they consider using alternate keys? Select the correct answers that apply.

A) Ensuring uniqueness for natural keys that are not primary or foreign keys.
B) Enforcing referential integrity constraints between related entities.
C) Improving query performance for frequently accessed attributes.

D) Facilitating data synchronization between Dataverse and external systems.

E) Preventing duplicate records from being created based on specific business rules.

QUESTION 50

A retail company aims to automate the integration of sales data from its online and offline stores into Microsoft Dataverse to streamline analytics and reporting processes. Which approach would best support the automation of data integration tasks in this scenario? Select the correct answers that apply.

A) Using scheduled data imports to periodically synchronize sales data from different sources.

B) Developing custom Power Automate flows to trigger data integration tasks based on predefined events.

C) Implementing event-driven architecture with Azure Functions to handle real-time data integration.

D) Utilizing Power Query to manually transform and import sales data into Dataverse.

E) Leveraging Azure Data Factory pipelines to orchestrate and automate data movement and transformation processes.

PRACTICE TEST 5 - ANSWERS ONLY

QUESTION 1

Answer - [A) Service Level Agreements (SLAs)]

A) Service Level Agreements (SLAs) - SLAs define the expected level of service and performance guarantees, directly addressing service performance and quality standards.

B) Incident management - Incident management focuses on handling incidents rather than defining service performance standards.

C) Change tracking - Change tracking monitors system changes but does not define service performance standards.

D) Dependency mapping - Dependency mapping identifies relationships between system components but does not define service performance standards.

E) Service tickets generation - Service tickets generation is part of incident management and does not specifically define service performance standards.

QUESTION 2

Answer - [C) Higher risk of compatibility issues during updates]

A) Increased development time and cost - Out-of-the-box features typically reduce development time and cost compared to customization.

B) Greater flexibility to meet specific business requirements - Customization often provides greater flexibility, while out-of-the-box features may have limitations.

C) Higher risk of compatibility issues during updates - Relying heavily on out-of-the-box features may lead to compatibility issues when updates or changes are applied, especially if the solution heavily depends on specific versions or configurations.

D) Enhanced scalability and performance - Out-of-the-box features are often designed for scalability and performance, but customization can sometimes optimize these aspects further.

E) Improved maintainability and ease of updates - Out-of-the-box features generally simplify maintenance and updates, as they are designed to be compatible with platform updates and changes.

QUESTION 3

Answer - A) 0 0 1 * *

A) Correct. Executes at midnight on the first of every month.
B) Incorrect. Misformatted for daily execution.
C) Incorrect. This schedules for noon, not midnight.
D) Incorrect. Redundant and incorrect use of hour field.
E) Incorrect. This cron expression is misformatted and would not execute as intended.

QUESTION 4

Answer - A, B, C, and D) Implementation of multi-factor authentication (MFA) for user access. Encryption of sensitive data stored within Microsoft Dataverse. Regular monitoring and analysis of security logs for suspicious activities. Integration of threat intelligence feeds to proactively identify potential security threats.

A) - Correct. Implementation of multi-factor authentication enhances user access security by requiring additional verification steps beyond passwords.

B) - Correct. Encryption of sensitive data stored within Microsoft Dataverse helps protect data confidentiality against unauthorized access.

C) - Correct. Regular monitoring and analysis of security logs enable timely detection and response to security incidents and suspicious activities.

D) - Correct. Integration of threat intelligence feeds enables proactive identification and mitigation of potential security threats before they escalate.

E) - Incorrect. While role-based access controls (RBAC) are important for authorization, they do not cover all aspects of the overall security architecture, such as encryption and threat intelligence integration.

QUESTION 5

Answer - D

Option A - Incorrect. Handles single sale insertion but not syncing a list.

Option B - Incorrect. Synchronously updates a sale which may not scale well for real-time requirements.

Option C - Incorrect. Retrieves a single sale but doesn't handle syncing.

Option D - Correct. Efficiently handles multiple sales updates asynchronously, suitable for real-time syncing requirements.

Option E - Incorrect. Handles deletion, not syncing.

QUESTION 6

Answer - A) Filter('Customers', Region = 'North America')

A) Correct. Filters the Customers data source to only include those in the 'North America' region.
B) Incorrect. This would include all customers.
C) Incorrect. Lookup is intended for finding single records.
D) Incorrect. Collect is not needed and is incorrectly used.
E) Incorrect. Incorrect syntax for accessing the Region field.

QUESTION 7

Answer - A, B, and C) Security roles enforce access controls to restrict unauthorized access to sensitive patient information, ensuring data confidentiality. Security roles define permissions to prevent unauthorized modification or deletion of patient records, safeguarding data integrity. Security roles regulate access to ensure that patient data is available only to authorized users when needed, preserving data availability.

A) - Correct. Security roles enforce access controls to restrict unauthorized access to sensitive patient information, ensuring data confidentiality and protecting patient privacy.

B) - Correct. By defining permissions, security roles prevent unauthorized modification or deletion of patient records, maintaining data integrity and accuracy.

C) - Correct. Security roles regulate access to ensure that patient data is available only to authorized users when needed, maintaining data availability and preventing unauthorized disclosure or loss.

D) - Incorrect. While auditing and logging are important for accountability, they are not direct functions of security roles in securing data within Dataverse environments.

E) - Incorrect. While encryption is a critical security measure, security roles do not directly enable encryption of patient data; encryption is typically implemented at a lower level of the technology stack, such as at the database or network layer.

QUESTION 8

Answer - A, B, and E) Business units enable seamless integration with role-based access control (RBAC) to enforce access permissions and privileges based on user roles and responsibilities. Integration with business units allows for the enforcement of record-level security to restrict access to sensitive data based on predefined criteria and access rules. Integration of business units with other security features enables advanced threat detection and monitoring capabilities to identify and respond to security incidents proactively.

A) - Correct. Business units can integrate with RBAC mechanisms to enforce access permissions based on user roles, enhancing data protection and access control within Microsoft Dataverse.

B) - Correct. Integration with business units allows for the enforcement of record-level security, enabling organizations to restrict access to sensitive data based on predefined criteria and access rules, enhancing data privacy and confidentiality.

E) - Correct. Integration of business units with other security features such as Azure Monitor and Log Analytics enables advanced threat detection and monitoring capabilities, enhancing security posture and enabling proactive incident response within the Dataverse environment.

C) - Incorrect. While implementing business units may enhance security, they are not directly related to data encryption or DLP capabilities, which are separate security features within Microsoft Dataverse.

D) - Incorrect. While business units may support authentication mechanisms, such as MFA and SSO, their integration with these features is not specifically related to enhancing data protection but rather user authentication and identity management.

QUESTION 9

Answer - [A], [C], and [D].

B) System resource constraints would affect flow execution but not trigger conditions.

E) API version compatibility is important but wouldn't prevent flow triggering.

A) Inactive flows won't execute.

C) Misconfigured connections can prevent flow activation.

D) If trigger conditions aren't met, the flow won't activate.

QUESTION 10

Answer - A

Option A - Correct: Uses the correct syntax for invoking an Azure function within PowerFx, including the proper method and body configuration.

Option B - Incorrect: AzureFunction.Post is not a recognized function in PowerFx.

Option C - Incorrect: ExecuteFunction does not exist in PowerFx for calling Azure functions.

Option D - Incorrect: PowerAutomate.Run does not directly invoke Azure functions and is incorrectly formatted.

Option E - Incorrect: PostToFunction is not a valid PowerFx function.

QUESTION 11

Answer - [A] Cascade All

Option A is correct as configuring the relationship with Cascade All behavior ensures that when a payment record is deleted, associated loan records are updated automatically to reflect the remaining balance accurately, meeting the requirement.

Option B, Cascade None, would not automatically update associated loan records upon payment deletion, which does not align with the requirement.

Option C, Remove Link, would only remove the association between loan and payment records, without affecting the remaining balance of the loan.

Option D, Parental, is not a valid relationship behavior in Microsoft Dataverse.

Option E, Referential, does not provide the necessary automatic update of associated records upon deletion.

QUESTION 12

Answer - [B] Update.

A) Creating a new solution may introduce unnecessary complexity and could disrupt existing functionalities and system stability.
B) Updating allows for adding new features to an existing solution while preserving the stability of existing functionalities, ensuring seamless integration and minimizing disruptions.
C) Upgrading might involve significant changes and could impact existing functionalities and system stability.
D) Patching is typically used for addressing specific issues or minor fixes and may not be suitable for adding new features to a solution.

QUESTION 13

Answer - [A, B, C, D, E] Role-based access control (RBAC) for solution management, Encryption of solution files during transfer, Audit logging of solution import/export activities, IP whitelisting for solution transfer endpoints, Multi-factor authentication (MFA) for solution administrators

Options A, B, C, D, and E are correct as they represent security measures such as RBAC, encryption, audit logging, IP whitelisting, and MFA that should be evaluated and implemented to ensure secure solution transfer in Microsoft Dataverse, protecting sensitive data and preventing unauthorized access or tampering.

QUESTION 14

Answer - [A, B, C, D, E] Misconfigured entity relationships causing data inconsistency, Performance degradation due to inefficient form design, Security vulnerabilities arising from weak authentication settings, Integration failures with external systems due to API misconfiguration, User interface inconsistencies across different devices and browsers

Options A, B, C, D, and E are correct as they represent common setup issues that developers may encounter during the creation of a model-driven app in Power Apps, including data consistency, performance, security, integration, and user interface issues.

QUESTION 15

Answer - [B] and [C].

A) Business rules cannot directly access external data.

B) Business rules can enable or disable a column dynamically based on property status, facilitating efficient property management and ensuring data accuracy.

C) Business rules can show or hide a column based on user role, ensuring that employees have access to relevant property information for their roles, thereby improving user experience and client satisfaction.

QUESTION 16

Answer - [A, B, C, E] Language familiarity and developer expertise, Performance optimization and execution speed, Integration capabilities with external systems and services, Vendor lock-in and long-term platform sustainability

Options A, B, C, and E are correct as they represent considerations when comparing JavaScript and Power Fx implementations in Power Apps, including language familiarity, performance, integration capabilities, and platform sustainability.

Option D, while important for accessibility, is not directly related to the comparison between JavaScript and Power Fx.

QUESTION 17

Answer - [A, B, C, D] Handling asynchronous data updates and ensuring formula consistency across datasets, Managing formula dependencies and avoiding circular references to prevent calculation errors,

Integrating real-time API calls within formulas to fetch dynamic product recommendations, Implementing error handling mechanisms to gracefully manage unexpected data inputs or API failures

Options A, B, C, and D represent potential challenges when writing complex Power Fx formulas for processing transactional data efficiently, including data consistency, dependencies, API integration, and error handling.

Option E, while important, is more about maintaining code quality and readability rather than posing a specific challenge.

QUESTION 18

Answer - [B] Custom process action.

A) Custom APIs are typically used for integrating external systems or services with the Power Platform but do not provide user-specific execution control.
B) Custom process actions enable developers to define custom actions that can be executed by specific users, making them suitable for restricting code execution to HR administrators. This ensures that only authorized personnel, such as HR administrators, have access to execute the specialized code, maintaining data confidentiality and integrity within the HR system.
C) Classic workflows are automation processes but do not offer the capability to control code execution based on user roles or privileges.
D) Business rules are used for implementing simple business logic within the app's user interface but do not involve executing custom code on the ribbon.

QUESTION 19

Answer - [A, B, C, D, E] Analyzing crash dumps and error logs, Reviewing app telemetry and usage analytics, Engaging with Microsoft support for advanced troubleshooting assistance, Rebuilding the app from scratch to eliminate potential coding errors, Conducting a code review to identify and address programming flaws

Options A, B, C, D, and E represent comprehensive approaches to troubleshooting app crashes, including crash analysis, telemetry review, support engagement, app reconstruction, and code review for identifying and addressing underlying issues.

QUESTION 20

Answer - B

Option A - Incorrect: LoadData() is not specifically for deferring loading.

Option B - Correct: Incremental loading optimizes data fetching and reduces initial load times.

Option C - Correct but less specific to data handling.

Option D - Incorrect: Non-delegable queries increase overhead.

Option E - Incorrect: Manual caching can be effective but is complex and error-prone compared to built-in solutions.

QUESTION 21

Answer - [D] Liquid template.

A) Client scripting may provide customization but may not offer optimal adaptability to different screen sizes and orientations.
B) Power Apps component framework code components offer customization but may not provide the necessary adaptability for optimal user experience across different screen sizes and orientations.
C) Web API is used for data integration and retrieval, not for creating custom visuals within the canvas app.
D) Liquid templates can dynamically adjust content based on screen sizes and orientations, making them suitable for optimal user experience in various scenarios.

QUESTION 22

Answer - [C] Log detailed error information to a central repository for analysis

A) Implement custom error messages for user-friendly feedback - While user-friendly error messages are important, logging detailed error information for analysis is a best practice for effective error handling.

B) Use specific error codes to identify different types of errors - Using specific error codes can help categorize errors, but it's not as critical as logging detailed error information.

C) Log detailed error information to a central repository for analysis - Logging detailed error information allows developers to diagnose and troubleshoot issues more effectively, making it the correct answer.

D) Retry failed operations automatically after a short delay - While automatic retries can be useful in some scenarios, they may not be appropriate for all error situations and can potentially exacerbate issues.

E) Provide fallback mechanisms to maintain app functionality during errors - Fallback mechanisms are important for maintaining app functionality, but they are not directly related to error handling or logging.

QUESTION 23

Answer - [E] Throttle API requests to avoid exceeding rate limits and prevent abuse

A) Hard-code API endpoints to improve performance - Hard-coding endpoints may reduce flexibility and maintainability, especially if endpoints change over time.

B) Minimize error handling to streamline script execution - Error handling is crucial for robustness and user experience, so minimizing it is not recommended.

C) Implement pagination for large data sets to improve performance - While pagination can enhance performance, it's not directly related to integrating Web API in client scripts.

D) Store sensitive data directly within client scripts for efficiency - Storing sensitive data in client scripts poses security risks and is generally discouraged.

E) Throttle API requests to avoid exceeding rate limits and prevent abuse - Throttling API requests helps maintain system stability and complies with service provider policies, making it a recommended best practice.

QUESTION 24

Answer - [A] Azure function
[C] Custom API
[E] Business rule.

A) Azure functions can execute custom logic to facilitate real-time communication between Microsoft Dataverse and the RESTful Web API of the external asset tracking system, enabling seamless management of asset data within the solution.

C) Custom APIs provide tailored integration solutions, enabling direct communication between Microsoft Dataverse and the RESTful Web API of the external asset tracking system, ensuring data consistency and reliability in the asset management solution.

E) Business rules can enforce specific logic and conditions to regulate data synchronization between Microsoft Dataverse and the RESTful Web API of the external asset tracking system, enhancing integration effectiveness.

QUESTION 25

Answer - A

Option A - Correct: Directly logs if there is an error during data load.

Option B - Incorrect: Incorrect condition check for loading status.

Option C - Incorrect: onLoad is not a function available in this context.

Option D - Incorrect: console.debug is not typically used for error tracking.

Option E - Incorrect: Tracks container resize, not data load issues.

QUESTION 26

Answer - [A] Debugging the component code using browser developer tools.

A) Debugging the component code using browser developer tools - Browser developer tools provide insights into component behavior and help identify and resolve interface-related issues efficiently.

B) Disabling browser cache to ensure the latest component version loads - While useful for ensuring the latest version loads, disabling browser cache is not directly related to troubleshooting interface issues.

C) Reverting recent changes to the component configuration - Reverting changes may be necessary in some cases but does not address the root cause of interface-related issues.

D) Refactoring the interface to use a different programming language - Refactoring the interface is a significant undertaking and should not be the first step in troubleshooting interface issues.

E) Clearing browser cookies to resolve session-related issues - Clearing cookies may resolve session-related issues but is unlikely to address interface-specific issues.

QUESTION 27

Answer - [C] Power Apps custom control.

C) Power Apps custom controls can integrate device features like the barcode scanner directly into canvas apps, enabling users to check in attendees by scanning their barcodes. This provides a seamless and efficient check-in process within the app interface.

Option A) Power Automate flow: While Power Automate flow can automate processes related to event management, it does not provide direct integration with device features like barcode scanners for real-time check-ins.

Option B) Azure Blob Storage: Azure Blob Storage is a cloud storage solution, which can store barcode data, but it requires additional integration and is not directly integrated into the app interface for barcode scanning.

Option D) Custom connector: Custom connectors are used for integrating external data sources with the Power Platform but are not designed for device-specific features like barcode scanning within canvas apps.

QUESTION 28

Answer - [B] Include API version information in request headers.

A) Hardcode API endpoints to specific versions within the PCF component - Hardcoding versions limits flexibility and may lead to compatibility issues with future API updates.

B) Include API version information in request headers - Including version information in headers allows for flexible version management without modifying PCF component code.

C) Implement dynamic API version detection based on client capabilities - While dynamic detection is possible, it adds complexity and may not be necessary for PCF components.

D) Utilize API versioning tools provided by the Web API service - While tools may assist, including version information in headers offers more direct control within the PCF component.

E) Maintain a separate PCF component for each API version - Managing separate components for each version increases maintenance overhead and complexity.

QUESTION 29

Answer - [B] Ensured consistency by rolling back all changes if any operation within the transaction fails.

A) Improved performance due to reduced database locking during record processing - Transaction support may increase locking to maintain consistency.

B) Ensured consistency by rolling back all changes if any operation within the transaction fails - Correct, transactions ensure data integrity by rolling back changes if any part of the operation fails.

C) Enhanced scalability through parallel execution of transactions across multiple servers - Transaction support focuses on consistency rather than scalability.

D) Minimized risk of data corruption by enforcing strict isolation between concurrent transactions - Isolation ensures data integrity but is not the primary impact of transaction support.

E) Reduced latency by prioritizing high-priority transactions over low-priority ones - Transaction priority is not a typical feature of transaction support within the plug-in pipeline.

QUESTION 30

Answer - [A] Utilize Azure Data Factory's built-in data quality features, such as column pattern matching and regular expression validation, to identify and remediate data format inconsistencies before loading data into Dataverse tables.

Answer - [C] Implement custom data cleansing logic in Azure Data Factory pipelines to sanitize text data from the MySQL database, removing or replacing non-ASCII characters with appropriate substitutions before transferring data to Dataverse tables.

A) Utilizing Azure Data Factory's built-in data quality features allows you to identify and remediate data format inconsistencies, such as non-ASCII characters, before loading data into Dataverse tables. By applying column pattern matching and regular expression validation, you can ensure that the data meets the required format specifications, reducing the likelihood of migration errors.

C) Implementing custom data cleansing logic in Azure Data Factory pipelines enables you to sanitize text data from the MySQL database, removing or replacing non-ASCII characters with appropriate substitutions. By preprocessing the data to address format mismatches and character encoding issues, you can ensure the integrity and compatibility of the migrated data with Dataverse tables.

Option B) Configure MySQL database settings: While configuring database settings may enforce character encoding rules, it may not address existing non-ASCII characters or format mismatches in the data, requiring additional preprocessing or cleansing steps.

Option D) Export data to intermediate JSON files: While using JSON files may facilitate transformations, it introduces complexity and may not offer real-time data cleansing capabilities during the migration process.

QUESTION 31

Answer - [B] Accessing large datasets without proper filtering can degrade performance.

A) The size of the plug-in assembly has no impact on performance - Larger assemblies can impact load times and memory consumption, affecting performance.

B) Accessing large datasets without proper filtering can degrade performance - Correct, querying large datasets can result in increased processing time and resource consumption.

C) Parallel execution of plug-ins has minimal impact on overall system performance - Parallel execution can increase system load and affect performance, especially under heavy usage.

D) Increasing the number of plug-in steps in a single transaction improves performance - More plug-in steps can increase transaction overhead and degrade performance.

E) Running plug-ins synchronously instead of asynchronously enhances performance - Synchronous execution can block user interaction and may not always be the best choice for performance.

QUESTION 32

Answer - [D] Leveraging existing data relationships and business rules.

A) Hard-coding data mappings within the Custom API logic - Hard-coding mappings may lead to inflexible integrations and maintenance challenges.

B) Exposing all data fields in the Custom API responses - Exposing unnecessary data fields can increase payload size and compromise security.

C) Implementing validation rules within the Custom API - Validation rules should be enforced at the data source or in the consuming applications, not within the Custom API itself.

D) Leveraging existing data relationships and business rules - Correct, leveraging existing relationships and business rules ensures consistency and integrity across the integrated systems.

E) Embedding business logic directly within the API endpoints - Business logic should be separated from API endpoints to maintain modularity and scalability.

QUESTION 33

Answer - [A] _customer_name

A) In the context of business process flows (BPFs) and related entities, the _customer_name attribute contains the display name of the associated customer record. When configuring a BPF to display related information, you should reference the _customer_name attribute to ensure that the customer's name is displayed correctly.

Option B) _customerid - Incorrect: This attribute may contain the GUID of the associated customer record, not the customer's name.
Option C) _customer_value - Incorrect: This attribute is not typically used to display the name of related records.
Option D) _customerid_name - Incorrect: This attribute combination is unlikely to exist and would not represent the customer's name.

QUESTION 34

Answer - [B] Using Azure Monitor to track API calls and performance metrics.

A) Logging API access in local text files without encryption - Storing logs in plaintext without encryption poses a security risk and is not compliant with data protection regulations.

B) Using Azure Monitor to track API calls and performance metrics - Correct, Azure Monitor provides comprehensive monitoring and auditing capabilities for tracking API calls, performance metrics, and system health.

C) Disabling audit trails to improve system performance - Disabling audit trails compromises security and compliance with regulatory requirements.

D) Ignoring unauthorized API access attempts - Ignoring unauthorized access attempts can lead to security breaches and data leaks.

E) Relying solely on third-party tools for auditing - While third-party tools may complement monitoring efforts, relying solely on them may overlook crucial insights provided by native monitoring solutions like Azure Monitor.

QUESTION 35

Answer - C

Option A - Incorrect: Data types should be handled at the definition phase.

Option B - Incorrect: OAuth issues should be managed via Azure AD, not typically an import issue.

Option C - Correct: API rate limits are a common issue and handling them via throttling in Power Automate is an effective solution.

Option D - Incorrect: Manual updates are not a scalable solution for incomplete definitions.

Option E - Incorrect: CORS is generally a browser-side issue, not relevant for server-side API integrations in Power Platform.

QUESTION 36

Answer - B) POST

A) DELETE - Incorrect. Used for deleting resources, not for initiating processes.
B) POST - Correct. Best for initiating server-side processes that may change the state.
C) PUT - Incorrect. Used for complete updates to an existing record.
D) GET - Incorrect. Retrieves data only.
E) PATCH - Incorrect. Used for partial updates only.

QUESTION 37

Answer - [A] Minimizing the number of API requests by batching operations

A) Minimizing the number of API requests by batching operations - Correct, reducing the number of requests by batching operations can improve performance by reducing network overhead and server load.

B) Increasing payload size to reduce network overhead - Increasing payload size may actually increase network overhead and latency, especially for slow or unreliable connections.

C) Enabling verbose error logging for detailed diagnostics - While error logging is important, verbose logging may introduce performance overhead and should be used judiciously.

D) Utilizing synchronous requests for real-time data retrieval - Synchronous requests may introduce latency, especially for large data sets, and may not be suitable for real-time scenarios.

E) Applying exponential backoff for retrying failed requests - Exponential backoff helps mitigate server overload during high-traffic periods but may not directly address performance tuning for individual requests.

QUESTION 38

Answer - [C] Implementing jitter to introduce randomness in retry intervals

A) Reducing the overall number of retry attempts - While reducing retries may prevent overload, it may also decrease the likelihood of successful retries for transient faults.

B) Increasing the initial retry interval for each subsequent attempt - Increasing intervals may help with exponential backoff but may not address the timing of retries effectively.

C) Implementing jitter to introduce randomness in retry intervals - Correct, introducing randomness in retry intervals helps prevent synchronized retries and distributed denial-of-service attacks while still providing exponential backoff benefits.

D) Using synchronous retry mechanisms for immediate response - Synchronous retries may increase load on APIs and may not effectively handle transient faults.

E) Limiting retries to specific types of HTTP status codes - Transient faults can occur for various reasons beyond specific HTTP status codes, so limiting retries based on status codes may not cover all cases.

QUESTION 39

Answer - A), B), and D)

A) Correct. Ensures data confidentiality and integrity during transmission.

B) Correct. Secures data in transit against interception.

C) Incorrect. Logging does not protect data during transfer, though it's good for auditing.

D) Correct. Prevents unauthorized data access.

E) Incorrect. Alerts on failures are important but do not contribute to the protection of data during transmission.

QUESTION 40

Answer - A)

A) Correct - This C# function uses a QueueTrigger for asynchronous processing, includes JSON deserialization, and contains logic to validate and update records in CDS effectively.

B) Incorrect - The JavaScript example lacks the detailed setup and error handling required for robust integration with Dataverse.

C) Incorrect - This TypeScript function lacks the complete setup needed for integration with CDS and handling of queue messages.

D) Incorrect - HTML is unsuitable for backend logic and cannot trigger Azure Functions.

E) Incorrect - Direct SQL does not address the scenario's requirement for an Azure Function and does not involve incident validation or CDS updates.

QUESTION 41

Answer - [B] Implementing retries with exponential backoff for transient errors

A) Using inline error handling within each action - Inline error handling may clutter the flow design and does not ensure consistent error management across actions.

B) Implementing retries with exponential backoff for transient errors - Correct, implementing retries with exponential backoff helps handle transient errors gracefully, improving flow resilience and fault tolerance.

C) Relying solely on manual intervention for error resolution - Manual intervention may introduce delays and reduce automation effectiveness, especially for transient errors.

D) Disabling error notifications to avoid unnecessary alerts - Error notifications are important for proactive issue resolution and should not be disabled indiscriminately.

E) Skipping failed actions to maintain flow continuity - Skipping failed actions may lead to data loss or incomplete processes and is not a reliable error handling strategy.

QUESTION 42

Answer - A), D), and C)

A) Correct. Ensures the document is classified as 'Confidential'.

B) Incorrect. 'Modified' equal to 'utcNow()' is too precise and unlikely to be true except at the exact moment of modification.

C) Correct. Combines all required conditions for the specific scenario.

D) Correct. Ensures the document is in the 'Operations' folder.

E) Incorrect. Ensures classification is not empty, but doesn't specify 'Confidential'.

QUESTION 43

Answer - [B] Reviewing Azure Key Vault access policies for misconfigurations

A) Enabling verbose logging for all flows to capture detailed error messages - While logging is important for troubleshooting, enabling verbose logging may generate excessive noise and complicate issue identification.

B) Reviewing Azure Key Vault access policies for misconfigurations - Correct, misconfigured access policies can lead to integration issues and compliance violations, making it essential to review and adjust them as needed.

C) Disabling Azure Key Vault and Entra to prevent further issues - Disabling services is a drastic measure and may not resolve underlying integration issues.

D) Rebooting the Power Platform environment to reset configurations - Rebooting may temporarily resolve issues but does not address the root cause of integration problems.

E) Ignoring integration issues to avoid disruption to operations - Ignoring issues can lead to data breaches and compliance violations, posing significant risks to the organization.

QUESTION 44

Answer - [A] Analyzing execution logs and error details in Azure Monitor and Log Analytics

A) Analyzing execution logs and error details in Azure Monitor and Log Analytics - Correct, Azure Monitor and Log Analytics provide insights into flow execution, errors, and performance metrics, facilitating effective troubleshooting.

B) Reviewing flow configurations and dependencies in the Power Platform Admin Center - While reviewing configurations is important, Azure Monitor offers more detailed insights into execution and performance.

C) Conducting end-to-end testing to identify and isolate integration bottlenecks - End-to-end testing is valuable but may not provide real-time insights into production issues.

D) Implementing custom error handling logic using Power Automate Cloud Flows - Custom error handling logic is useful but may not address the need for real-time monitoring and troubleshooting.

E) Collaborating with cross-functional teams to identify root causes and solutions - Collaboration is essential, but Azure Monitor provides specific insights into flow execution and errors.

QUESTION 45

Answer - A) Certificate based and OAuth 2.0

A) Correct. Certificate-based ensures encrypted communications, and OAuth 2.0 provides authenticated access control.
B) Incorrect. API key and SSO don't address encryption requirements.
C) Incorrect. API key doesn't ensure encryption.
D) Incorrect. Password-based is less secure for healthcare.
E) Incorrect. SSO does not guarantee encrypted communications.

QUESTION 46

Answer - [A, B, C, D, E] Implementing OAuth 2.0 authentication for secure access to IServiceEndpointNotificationService, Encrypting event payloads and sensitive data transmitted through IServiceEndpointNotificationService, Restricting access to event publishing endpoints based on IP allowlists or firewall rules, Enforcing role-based access control (RBAC) to manage permissions for event publishers, Using secure protocols such as HTTPS for communication between Dataverse and IServiceEndpointNotificationService

A) Implementing OAuth 2.0 authentication for secure access to IServiceEndpointNotificationService - OAuth 2.0 ensures secure access to IServiceEndpointNotificationService endpoints.

B) Encrypting event payloads and sensitive data transmitted through IServiceEndpointNotificationService - Encryption safeguards data privacy during transmission.

C) Restricting access to event publishing endpoints based on IP allowlists or firewall rules - Access restrictions enhance the security posture of IServiceEndpointNotificationService endpoints.

D) Enforcing role-based access control (RBAC) to manage permissions for event publishers - RBAC helps control access to IServiceEndpointNotificationService based on predefined roles and permissions.

E) Using secure protocols such as HTTPS for communication between Dataverse and IServiceEndpointNotificationService - Secure protocols ensure data integrity and confidentiality during transit between systems.

QUESTION 47

Answer - [A, B, C, D, E] Implementing exponential backoff and jitter for retry logic, Using dead-letter queues for storing failed messages and processing them later, Configuring retry policies with exponential delay and maximum retry attempts, Monitoring error rates and automatically scaling endpoint resources, Implementing circuit breaker patterns to prevent cascading failures

A) Implementing exponential backoff and jitter for retry logic - Exponential backoff and jitter help mitigate the risk of overload when retrying failed requests.

B) Using dead-letter queues for storing failed messages and processing them later - Dead-letter queues provide a mechanism for handling failed messages and facilitating manual or automated retries.

C) Configuring retry policies with exponential delay and maximum retry attempts - Configuring retry policies ensures that failed requests are retried with appropriate delays and limits to prevent excessive load on endpoints.

D) Monitoring error rates and automatically scaling endpoint resources - Monitoring error rates helps detect issues, while automatic scaling ensures that endpoint resources can handle increased demand during retries.

E) Implementing circuit breaker patterns to prevent cascading failures - Circuit breaker patterns help prevent cascading failures by temporarily suspending requests to failing endpoints, allowing them time to recover.

QUESTION 48

Answer - C) PATCH with batch operations

A) Incorrect. PATCH cannot be directly combined with $filter in a single request.
B) Incorrect. POST is used for creating new records, not updating multiple records.
C) Correct. Using PATCH with batch operations allows for updating multiple records based on specific criteria.
D) Incorrect. PUT is not used for updating multiple records with a filter.
E) Incorrect. PATCH does not typically accept complex queries in the request body.

QUESTION 49

Answer - [A, E] Ensuring uniqueness for natural keys that are not primary or foreign keys, Preventing duplicate records from being created based on specific business rules.

A) Ensuring uniqueness for natural keys that are not primary or foreign keys. - Alternate keys are commonly used to enforce uniqueness for attributes that are not primary or foreign keys, ensuring data integrity and consistency.

B) Enforcing referential integrity constraints between related entities. - Referential integrity constraints are typically enforced through primary and foreign keys, rather than alternate keys.

C) Improving query performance for frequently accessed attributes. - While alternate keys can improve query performance, their primary purpose is to enforce uniqueness rather than optimize attribute access.

D) Facilitating data synchronization between Dataverse and external systems. - Data synchronization may involve other mechanisms such as integration connectors or APIs, rather than alternate keys.

E) Preventing duplicate records from being created based on specific business rules. - Alternate keys are effective in preventing duplicate records based on business rules, ensuring data integrity and adherence to organizational standards.

QUESTION 50

Answer - [B, C, E] Developing custom Power Automate flows to trigger data integration tasks based on predefined events, Implementing event-driven architecture with Azure Functions to handle real-time data integration, Leveraging Azure Data Factory pipelines to orchestrate and automate data movement and transformation processes.

A) Using scheduled data imports to periodically synchronize sales data from different sources. - Scheduled imports are suitable for periodic synchronization but may not provide the real-time automation required for immediate data integration.

B) Developing custom Power Automate flows to trigger data integration tasks based on predefined events. - Power Automate flows allow for flexible automation based on events, enabling real-time or near-real-time integration of sales data from multiple sources.

C) Implementing event-driven architecture with Azure Functions to handle real-time data integration. - Event-driven architecture with Azure Functions enables real-time processing of events, making it ideal for handling immediate data integration tasks triggered by events such as sales transactions.

D) Utilizing Power Query to manually transform and import sales data into Dataverse. - Manual transformation and import processes are not suitable for automation and may require significant manual effort for each data integration task.

E) Leveraging Azure Data Factory pipelines to orchestrate and automate data movement and transformation processes. - Azure Data Factory provides robust capabilities for orchestrating and automating data movement and transformation, making it well-suited for streamlining the automation of data integration tasks in the scenario described.

PRACTICE TEST 6 - QUESTIONS ONLY

QUESTION 1

A company is developing a Power Platform solution for its HR department. They need to implement authentication methods that align with their security policies and provide a seamless user experience. Which authentication method in the Power Platform allows users to sign in with their organizational credentials without requiring them to enter a username and password?

A) OAuth
B) SAML
C) Forms authentication
D) Active Directory Federation Services (ADFS)
E) Multi-factor authentication (MFA)

QUESTION 2

A logistics company is considering implementing automation for their shipment tracking process using either Logic Apps or Power Automate. They need to understand the use cases for each tool to make an informed decision. Which scenario is best suited for Logic Apps over Power Automate?

A) Integrating with external services using complex RESTful Web API calls
B) Automating routine tasks with simple trigger-based workflows
C) Orchestrating complex workflows involving multiple conditional steps
D) Building chatbots for customer service interactions
E) Creating approval workflows for document review processes

QUESTION 3

You are tasked with configuring a timer-triggered Azure Function to generate a report every Monday at 2:00 PM for Microsoft Dataverse. Which cron expression should you use?

A) 0 14 * * 1
B) 0 0 14 * * 1
C) 0 14 * * MON
D) 0 2 * * 1
E) 0 14 1 * *

QUESTION 4

A multinational corporation is planning to design a comprehensive Dataverse data model to support their enterprise-wide operations. They need to ensure scalability, flexibility, and maintainability of the data model to accommodate future growth and changes in business requirements.
 Which considerations should they include when planning the structure of their Dataverse data model? Select THREE.

A) Normalize data to minimize redundancy and improve data integrity.
B) Denormalize data to optimize query performance and simplify data retrieval.
C) Define appropriate relationships between entities to represent business processes accurately.

D) Implement complex calculated fields to derive data dynamically at runtime.
E) Partition data across multiple environments based on geographic locations to comply with data residency regulations.

QUESTION 5

Given the requirement to synchronize SQL database changes with Dataverse, identify the correct C# method to handle this integration using an Azure function.

A) public static async Task Run([HttpTrigger(AuthorizationLevel.Function, "get", "post", Route = null)] HttpRequest req, ILogger log) {...}

B) public static void Run([TimerTrigger("0 */5 * * * *")] TimerInfo myTimer, ILogger log) {...}

C) public static async Task<IActionResult> SyncToDataverse([SqlTrigger("SELECT * FROM Changes")] IEnumerable<SqlData> data, ILogger log) {...}

D) public static void Run([ServiceBusTrigger("myqueue", Connection = "ServiceBusConnection")] string myQueueItem, ILogger log) {...}

E) public static async Task SyncDataverse([SqlTrigger("SELECT * FROM Changes")] HttpRequest req, ILogger log) {...}

QUESTION 6

In a canvas app for asset tracking, you need to display assets assigned to the currently logged-in user. The app uses Microsoft Dataverse. What PowerFx expression should you use for the Items property of the gallery displaying the assets?

A) Filter('Assets', AssignedTo = User().Email)
B) 'Assets'
C) Filter('Assets', AssignedTo.Email = User().Email)
D) Lookup('Assets', AssignedTo = User().Email)
E) Collect('UserAssets', Filter(Assets, AssignedTo.Email = User().Email))

QUESTION 7

A large enterprise is implementing column-level security in Dataverse to control access to sensitive data fields across multiple departments. They need to understand the setup process for column-level security and its implications for their data management strategy.
What details are involved in setting up column-level security in Dataverse? Select THREE.

A) Define column-level security profiles specifying which columns users can read, write, or update.

B) Configure security roles to assign users access to specific columns based on their job roles or responsibilities.

C) Establish field-level security privileges for individual users or groups to control access to sensitive data fields.

D) Implement column-level security rules to enforce data access policies and restrictions based on user attributes or conditions.

E) Create field-level security profiles to define access controls for specific data fields within tables or entities.

QUESTION 8

A large organization is restructuring its teams within Microsoft Dataverse to improve collaboration and data management across departments. They need to understand the setup and management of teams to ensure a smooth transition and efficient teamwork.
How should teams be set up and managed in Microsoft Dataverse? Select FOUR.

A) Define teams to represent functional units or project groups within the organization, assigning users and permissions based on their roles and responsibilities.

B) Configure team membership dynamically using rules and criteria based on user attributes or organizational metadata, ensuring flexibility and scalability in team management.

C) Implement team-based security roles and privileges to control access to data and resources, ensuring that team members have appropriate permissions for their tasks.

D) Utilize team templates to streamline the creation and provisioning of new teams, ensuring consistency and standardization across the organization.

E) Monitor team performance and collaboration using built-in analytics and reporting tools, identifying areas for improvement and optimization.

QUESTION 9

You are developing a Power Apps canvas app that retrieves data from Microsoft Dataverse. However, users report that they are unable to see the expected data in the app. What could be potential reasons for this issue? Select the correct answers that apply.

A) The app's connection to Dataverse is not properly configured.
B) The users' security roles do not have read access to the Dataverse entity.
C) The data source for the app does not include the required entity.
D) The app's filter or sort functions are incorrectly applied.
E) The app's version is not compatible with the Dataverse schema changes.

QUESTION 10

Given the need to enhance application security within a Power Apps environment, you are tasked with configuring a Dataverse table to store user roles and their permissions. Write a script to create this table with columns for role name and permissions using TypeScript.

A) const table = new Entity('UserRoles', [new Column('RoleName', 'string'), new Column('Permissions', 'string')]);

B) const table = { entityName: 'UserRoles', columns: [{ name: 'RoleName', type: 'string' }, { name: 'Permissions', type: 'string' }] };

C) let table = Entity.create('UserRoles', ['RoleName: string', 'Permissions: string']);

D) var table = new DataverseTable('UserRoles', ['RoleName', 'Permissions']);

E) const table = new Table('UserRoles', [new Field('RoleName', FieldType.String), new Field('Permissions', FieldType.String)]);

QUESTION 11

A retail company is developing a sales management application using Power Apps and Microsoft Dataverse. They need to ensure that certain business rules are applied automatically to improve data quality and enforce consistency. Which statement accurately describes the setup and application of business rules in Microsoft Dataverse?

A) Business rules are configured using JavaScript code embedded within Power Apps
B) Business rules can only be applied to text fields within Dataverse entities
C) Business rules execute automatically on the client-side when data is entered or modified
D) Business rules can be deactivated once applied to a specific entity
E) Business rules can trigger server-side actions such as workflows or plugins

QUESTION 12

You are developing a model-driven Power Apps app for a healthcare organization's patient management system. The app requires various functionalities to optimize patient data entry and management. Which two tasks can you accomplish using business rules to enhance the app's usability and efficiency? Select the correct answers that apply.

A) Clear column values for discharged patients.
B) Enable and disable columns based on user roles.
C) Show and hide tabs for different departments.
D) Show and hide sections based on patient status.

QUESTION 13

A large enterprise is developing a comprehensive Microsoft Power Platform solution consisting of multiple components. They need to define solution dependencies within the platform to ensure smooth development and deployment processes. How can solution dependencies be defined within Microsoft Power Platform?

A) Specify component dependencies in solution metadata
B) Establish parent-child relationships between solution components
C) Utilize solution import/export settings to manage dependencies
D) Define dependency rules in solution configuration files
E) Implement custom dependency resolution algorithms

QUESTION 14

A multinational corporation is implementing a model-driven app in Power Apps to streamline its sales processes. They require extensive customization of forms to capture specific data points. Which options are valid for customizing forms in model-driven apps? Select the correct answers that apply.

A) Add custom JavaScript for client-side validation
B) Configure business rules to control field visibility

C) Apply form themes to enhance visual appearance
D) Implement server-side logic using TypeScript
E) Use embedded Canvas Apps for complex UI elements

QUESTION 15

You are customizing a form in a model-driven app for an educational institution's student management system. The app aims to streamline student information management and improve administrative efficiency. What are two actions that you can perform by using a business rule in this scenario? Select the correct answers that apply.

A) Access external data.
B) Enable or disable a column based on enrollment status.
C) Show or hide a column based on user role.
D) Run the rule on demand.

QUESTION 16

A manufacturing company wants to create a canvas app to streamline their inventory management process. They need guidance on the steps involved in creating a canvas app. Which steps should they follow to create a canvas app in Power Apps? Select the correct answers that apply.

A) Design the user interface using drag-and-drop controls
B) Define data sources and connect to external databases or services
C) Configure app settings such as permissions and access control
D) Implement business logic using Power Fx formulas or JavaScript
E) Publish the app to make it available to users

QUESTION 17

A software development firm is tasked with creating a library of reusable components for their internal Power Apps projects. Which considerations should they prioritize when designing components for reuse? Select the correct answers that apply.

A) Ensuring modular design to promote component independence and reusability
B) Implementing clear documentation and usage guidelines for each component
C) Enforcing version control to track changes and updates across component libraries
D) Optimizing components for performance and scalability to accommodate varying app requirements
E) Integrating automated testing frameworks to validate component functionality and behavior

QUESTION 18

You are developing a model-driven app for a procurement management system. The app requires executing custom code when a user selects a button on the ribbon. However, only procurement managers should be able to run this code. What should you use to achieve this requirement?

A) Custom API
B) Custom process action
C) Classic workflow

D) Business rule

QUESTION 19

A software development team is encountering frequent errors when integrating external APIs into their Power Apps solution. Which tool or feature is most suitable for identifying and resolving these API integration issues?

A) Azure Monitor
B) Log Analytics
C) Power Apps Monitor
D) API Management
E) Error Reporting Dashboard

QUESTION 20

You need to optimize the loading time for a model-driven app by preloading data when the app starts. Which JavaScript code snippet should you use?

A) Xrm.WebApi.retrieveMultipleRecords("account", "?$select=name&$top=50")

B) fetch('/api/data/v9.1/accounts?$select=name&$top=50')

C) Xrm.Page.data.entity.load("accounts", "$select=name&$top=50")

D) document.onload = function() {Xrm.WebApi.retrieveMultipleRecords("account", {select: ["name"], top: 50})}

E) window.onload = () => {Xrm.WebApi.retrieveMultipleRecords("account", "?$select=name&$top=50")}

QUESTION 21

You are tasked with integrating a legacy HR system, which exposes a SOAP API, with Microsoft Dataverse to synchronize employee data. Considering the complexity and requirements of the integration, which three options should you choose to create a comprehensive solution? Select the correct answers that apply.

A) Azure function
B) Custom connector
C) Custom API
D) HTTP request
E) Business rule

QUESTION 22

A Power Apps developer is tasked with registering event handlers for various user interactions in a custom canvas app. Which of the following methods represents a common approach to registering event handlers in client scripting?

A) Inline event handlers in HTML elements
B) Using the addEventListener method in JavaScript

C) Defining event handlers within the app's manifest file
D) Attaching event handlers via jQuery
E) Embedding event handling logic directly in Power Apps controls

QUESTION 23

A Power Apps developer is tasked with understanding the Client API object model for a canvas app project. Which of the following statements provides an accurate overview of the Client API object model components?

A) The Client API object model consists of entities, attributes, forms, views, and actions for interacting with data in Dataverse.

B) The Client API object model primarily comprises HTML elements, CSS styles, and JavaScript functions for building user interfaces.

C) Components of the Client API object model include user authentication, role-based access control, and data encryption mechanisms.

D) The Client API object model is focused on managing cloud resources, deploying infrastructure, and monitoring system performance.

E) Client API object model components encompass server-side logic, database schemas, and RESTful API endpoints for data manipulation.

QUESTION 24

Your organization is developing a model-driven app for managing customer accounts. You need to create a custom control that allows users to view customer account details in a visually appealing and interactive manner. The control should be reusable across multiple forms and support modern client frameworks like React and Fluent UI. Considering the requirements, which development option should you choose?

A) Power Apps custom control
B) Custom API
C) Azure Functions
D) Power Automate flow

QUESTION 25

What XML element is crucial when defining a new property for a PCF component in the manifest file to link it to a Dataverse field?

A) <property name="dataField" type="SingleLine.Text" usage="input" />
B) <property name="dataField" type="SingleLine.Text" usage="bound" />
C) <control name="dataField" type="SingleLine.Text" bind="true" />
D)
E) <field name="dataField" type="String" />

QUESTION 26

A Power Apps developer is preparing to package a PCF component for deployment. Which step is typically involved in the packaging process?

A) Generating a solution file from Power Apps Maker Portal.
B) Manually copying component files to the destination environment.
C) Exporting component metadata as a JSON file.
D) Creating a custom connector for component integration.
E) Executing a PowerShell script to compile component code.

QUESTION 27

Your organization is migrating legacy data into Dataverse tables using a custom-built data migration tool written in TypeScript. Due to the complexity of the legacy data, the migration tool occasionally encounters errors related to data format mismatches, resulting in failed data inserts. You need to implement a solution to handle these errors and ensure the successful completion of the migration. What are two possible approaches to achieve this goal? Select the correct answers that apply.

A) Implement error handling logic to skip invalid data records and continue with the migration.
B) Split the migration process into smaller batches to reduce the likelihood of encountering data format mismatches.
C) Upgrade the TypeScript compiler to the latest version to leverage improved error handling capabilities.
D) Increase the timeout duration for each data insertion operation to allow more time for processing complex data records.

QUESTION 28

A company plans to integrate a new PCF component with an existing CRM system to streamline customer data management. What security measure should the development team prioritize to ensure the integrity and confidentiality of sensitive customer information during integration?

A) Implement OAuth 2.0 for secure authentication and authorization.
B) Utilize SSL/TLS encryption for secure data transmission.
C) Apply role-based access controls (RBAC) to restrict data access within the CRM system.
D) Encrypt sensitive data stored within the PCF component.
E) Implement multi-factor authentication (MFA) for user access to the PCF component.

QUESTION 29

A company is developing a Power Apps solution that requires extensive customization using plug-ins. They need to understand what is included in the plug-in execution context to optimize their development process. Which of the following accurately defines what is included in the execution context?

A) Input parameters, secure configuration data, pre/post image data
B) Target entity attributes, organization service, execution mode
C) Caller ID, shared variables, database transaction
D) Execution mode, target entity, pre/post image data

E) Execution mode, shared variables, secure configuration data

QUESTION 30

You are developing a Power Automate flow to automate the process of sending approval requests for expense reports. The flow should retrieve the manager's email address from a custom entity named "Employees." What attribute should you reference in your flow to retrieve the manager's email address?

A) _manager_email
B) _manager_emailaddress
C) _manager_emailaddress_value
D) _manager_email_value

QUESTION 31

A development team is facing performance issues with plug-ins in their Power Platform solution. Which technique can help enhance plug-in performance effectively?

A) Increasing the frequency of plug-in execution intervals.
B) Implementing asynchronous processing for long-running operations.
C) Adding additional try-catch blocks for error handling.
D) Utilizing synchronous execution for all plug-ins.
E) Increasing the complexity of plug-in logic to optimize performance.

QUESTION 32

A team of Power Platform developers needs to register custom assemblies using the Plug-in Registration Tool. What is a critical step in this process?

A) Exporting the assembly from Visual Studio.
B) Creating a new solution in the Power Platform admin center.
C) Generating a new client ID for authentication.
D) Importing the assembly into the Dataverse environment.
E) Specifying the assembly's deployment type.

QUESTION 33

A system needs to update a specific record in Microsoft Power Platform using a custom JavaScript action. Which HTTP method should be used in the Web API call?

A) GET
B) POST
C) PUT
D) PATCH
E) DELETE

QUESTION 34

A company is developing a Power Platform solution that requires modifying the behavior of connectors dynamically based on specific conditions. Which approach allows for modifying connector behavior at runtime?

A) Using custom code snippets within Power Automate flows.
B) Leveraging policy templates to define connector behavior.
C) Manually updating connector configurations in the Power Platform Admin Center.
D) Creating separate connector instances for each scenario.
E) Building custom connectors from scratch.

QUESTION 35

How do you create a custom connector in Power Apps to integrate with an Azure service using OpenAPI definitions?

A) Go to Power Apps > Data > Custom Connectors > Create from blank > Import an OpenAPI file.
B) Navigate to Azure Portal > Create API Management service > Export to Power Apps/Power Automate.
C) Use Power Automate to set up a new custom connector via importing an OpenAPI specification directly.
D) In Power Apps, select Connectors > New custom connector > Import an OpenAPI from GitHub.
E) Create a new custom connector directly within the Azure portal and link it to Power Apps.

QUESTION 36

You are designing a Power Automate cloud flow for a financial services company to integrate with a credit scoring API. How can you ensure robust error handling when the API occasionally fails? Select the correct answers that apply.

A) Add a parallel branch with an email notification action
B) Use the "Configure run after" setting to only run on action success
C) Use a scope to group actions
D) Set the email notification action to run after an action has failed
E) Add an instant flow trigger

QUESTION 37

A company is developing a Power Platform solution that requires advanced data manipulation capabilities with the Organization service API. Which of the following operations are supported by the Organization service API?

A) Querying, creating, updating, and deleting records
B) Generating reports and dashboards
C) Managing user roles and permissions
D) Triggering Power Automate flows
E) Handling email notifications

QUESTION 38

A company is developing a Power Platform solution that heavily relies on API calls to integrate with external systems. They are concerned about optimizing these API calls for better performance. Which technique is most suitable for optimizing API calls in this scenario?

A) Implementing synchronous API calls for real-time data retrieval
B) Minimizing payload sizes to reduce network latency
C) Using caching mechanisms to store frequently accessed data
D) Employing asynchronous processing for non-blocking operations
E) Increasing the number of API requests to parallelize data fetching

QUESTION 39

A Power Automate flow must start whenever a new document is uploaded to a SharePoint library and the document status is marked as 'Under Review'. Which two expressions would correctly trigger this flow? Select the correct answers that apply.

A) @equals(triggerBody()?['DocumentStatus'], 'Under Review')
B) @contains(triggerBody()?['DocumentStatus'], 'Review')
C) @not(empty(triggerBody()?['DocumentStatus']))
D) @equals(triggerBody()?['DocumentStatus'], null)
E) @contains(triggerBody()?['FileRef'], 'Documents')

QUESTION 40

A financial institution is migrating its existing on-premises applications to Azure. They aim to leverage managed identities for Azure services to enhance security and simplify authentication processes. The team needs to understand the configuration process for managed identities and evaluate the associated benefits and limitations.

A) PowerShell: New-AzureADServicePrincipal -ApplicationId $appId -DisplayName "ManagedIdentityApp"

B) C#: ManagedIdentityAppServicePrincipal = new ServicePrincipal(appId, displayName: "ManagedIdentityApp");

C) JSON: { "type": "Microsoft.ManagedIdentity/userAssignedIdentities", "apiVersion": "2018-11-30", "name": "ManagedIdentityApp" }

D) TypeScript: az ad sp create-for-rbac -n "ManagedIdentityApp"

E) HTML: <button onclick="createManagedIdentity()">Create Managed Identity</button>

QUESTION 41

A company is implementing a Power Platform solution for managing customer interactions. They need to configure a cloud flow to create new records in Dataverse whenever a customer submits a form on their website. What is a crucial step in configuring the flow to use the Dataverse connector actions?

A) Enabling row-level security for data access
B) Defining appropriate triggers based on form submissions
C) Configuring connection references for authentication
D) Implementing custom error handling for fault tolerance
E) Optimizing query filters for efficient data retrieval

QUESTION 42

You are tasked to create a custom connector in Power Platform that connects to a financial data service. The service exposes a RESTful API requiring an API key for access. What type of authentication should you configure?

A) Password based
B) API key
C) OAuth 2.0
D) Certificate based
E) No authentication

QUESTION 43

A multinational retail corporation is developing a Power Platform solution to automate inventory management across its global supply chain. They need to ensure that their workflows can handle errors gracefully and recover from failures without manual intervention. What strategy should they employ to implement retries and compensatory actions effectively?

A) Utilizing the "Retry Policy" action in Power Automate to retry failed steps with exponential backoff
B) Implementing custom error handling logic using JavaScript code actions
C) Triggering email notifications to administrators for manual intervention on errors
D) Redirecting failed flows to alternative pathways using conditional branching
E) Pausing failed flows until manual approval is obtained

QUESTION 44

A large financial institution is developing a complex Power Platform solution for risk assessment and compliance management. They need to implement advanced techniques in plug-in development to enhance the functionality of their Dataverse environment. What is a key aspect of advanced plug-in development techniques in this scenario?

A) Utilizing multithreading for parallel execution of plug-in operations
B) Implementing complex business logic using JavaScript within plug-in assemblies
C) Leveraging dependency injection for managing plug-in dependencies and services
D) Integrating external APIs directly within plug-in code for seamless data exchange
E) Implementing custom error handling mechanisms using try-catch blocks in plug-in code

QUESTION 45

You need to retrieve multiple contacts from Microsoft Dataverse Web API where the last name is 'Smith'. What is the best practice to filter these records in the GET request?

A) Use $filter=lastname eq 'Smith'
B) Use $search=lastname:'Smith'
C) Set the MSCRM.SearchOnlyLastName header to 'Smith'
D) Use lastname=Smith in the URL query
E) Include a custom query option using $custom='lastname:Smith'

QUESTION 46

A healthcare organization is developing a Power Platform solution to manage patient appointments and medical records. They need to utilize the Plug-in Registration Tool for event publishing to integrate with their existing patient management system. What are the essential steps involved in using the Plug-in Registration Tool for event publishing?

A) Registering a new webhook endpoint and configuring event subscriptions
B) Creating a new plugin assembly and registering it with Dataverse
C) Defining custom events and event handlers for publishing events
D) Configuring event properties and mappings for accurate event publication
E) Generating a new application registration and granting necessary permissions for event publishing

QUESTION 47

A manufacturing company is developing a Power Platform solution to monitor production line efficiency and track equipment maintenance schedules. They need to listen to Dataverse events to trigger notifications and alerts based on specific conditions. Which overview best describes methods for event consumption in this scenario? Select the correct answers that apply.

A) Subscribing to Dataverse change events using Power Automate
B) Using Azure Functions with Event Grid triggers to process Dataverse events
C) Implementing polling mechanisms to periodically check for Dataverse record updates
D) Directly querying the Dataverse database for real-time event data
E) Leveraging Dataverse webhooks to push event notifications to external services

QUESTION 48

You need to ensure a Power Apps solution sends out daily reminders for a project deadline using Azure Durable Functions. What method should you use to create a daily reminder timer in an orchestrator function?

A) createTimer() method
B) setInterval() function
C) setTimeout() function
D) Task.Delay() method
E) setDaily() function

QUESTION 49

A multinational corporation is integrating multiple legacy systems with Microsoft Dataverse to streamline data synchronization processes. They need to ensure that updates from these systems are accurately reflected in Dataverse without creating duplicate records. When should they consider using UpsertRequest in this scenario? Select the correct answers that apply.

A) When inserting new records from legacy systems to Dataverse.
B) When updating existing records in Dataverse based on data changes from legacy systems.
C) When deleting records in Dataverse that have corresponding records in legacy systems.
D) When querying Dataverse to retrieve data for reporting purposes.
E) When performing batch operations to synchronize large volumes of data between legacy systems and

Dataverse.

QUESTION 50

A multinational corporation is implementing a data integration solution to synchronize customer data between its CRM system and Microsoft Dataverse. The solution must handle large volumes of data efficiently while ensuring minimal latency. Which strategy would best optimize data transfer and processing in this scenario? Select the correct answers that apply.

A) Implementing parallel processing to distribute data transfer across multiple threads or instances.
B) Utilizing batch processing to group and process data in predefined intervals.
C) Employing in-memory caching to accelerate data retrieval and processing.
D) Enabling compression techniques to reduce data size during transfer.
E) Implementing data partitioning to divide large datasets into smaller chunks for parallel processing.

PRACTICE TEST 6 - ANSWERS ONLY

QUESTION 1

Answer - [D) Active Directory Federation Services (ADFS)]

A) OAuth - OAuth is used for authorization and delegation, not specifically for seamless sign-in without entering credentials.

B) SAML - SAML is used for single sign-on (SSO) but may still require users to enter their credentials.

C) Forms authentication - Forms authentication typically requires users to enter their credentials.

D) Active Directory Federation Services (ADFS) - ADFS allows users to sign in using their organizational credentials without entering a username and password, providing a seamless experience.

E) Multi-factor authentication (MFA) - MFA adds an extra layer of security but does not eliminate the need for entering credentials.

QUESTION 2

Answer - [A) Integrating with external services using complex RESTful Web API calls]

A) Integrating with external services using complex RESTful Web API calls - Logic Apps are well-suited for integrating with external services and handling complex API calls, making them the preferable choice for this scenario.

B) Automating routine tasks with simple trigger-based workflows - Power Automate is designed for automating routine tasks and simple workflows triggered by events.

C) Orchestrating complex workflows involving multiple conditional steps - Logic Apps excel at orchestrating complex workflows with conditional logic and multiple steps.

D) Building chatbots for customer service interactions - While both Logic Apps and Power Automate can be used for chatbot development, Power Automate offers more tailored features for this purpose.

E) Creating approval workflows for document review processes - Power Automate is commonly used for creating approval workflows and document review processes due to its user-friendly interface and integration with Microsoft Office applications.

QUESTION 3

Answer - A) 0 14 * * 1

A) Correct. This expression correctly schedules the function for every Monday at 2 PM.
B) Incorrect. The minutes and hours are reversed in this pattern.
C) Incorrect. Azure Functions do not use day names like 'MON' in cron expressions.
D) Incorrect. This sets the time to 2 AM instead of 2 PM.
E) Incorrect. This would run monthly on the first day of the month at 2 PM, not every Monday.

QUESTION 4

Answer - A, C, and E) Normalize data to minimize redundancy and improve data integrity. Define appropriate relationships between entities to represent business processes accurately. Partition data across multiple environments based on geographic locations to comply with data residency regulations.

A) - Correct. Normalizing data helps minimize redundancy and improve data integrity by reducing the risk of inconsistencies across entities.

B) - Incorrect. Denormalizing data may improve query performance but can introduce redundancy and complicate data management.

C) - Correct. Defining appropriate relationships between entities ensures the accurate representation of business processes and facilitates data consistency.

D) - Incorrect. Implementing complex calculated fields may impact performance and maintainability without providing significant benefits in terms of data structure.

E) - Correct. Partitioning data across multiple environments based on geographic locations helps organizations comply with data residency regulations and ensures data sovereignty.

QUESTION 5

Answer - B

Option A - Incorrect. Uses HttpTrigger which is not suitable for database synchronization.

Option B - Incorrect. TimerTrigger does not directly capture changes from SQL.

Option C - Correct. The SqlTrigger attribute correctly captures changes from a SQL query, making it ideal for the scenario.

Option D - Incorrect. ServiceBusTrigger is unrelated to direct SQL changes.

Option E - Incorrect. Mismatch of SqlTrigger usage and HttpRequest which is not applicable.

QUESTION 6

Answer - C) Filter('Assets', AssignedTo.Email = User().Email)

A) Incorrect. This assumes that 'AssignedTo' directly stores an email, which is usually not the case.
B) Incorrect. This expression does not filter the assets based on the user.
C) Correct. This filters assets where the 'AssignedTo' field's email matches the logged-in user's email.
D) Incorrect. Lookup is used for finding a single record, not suitable here.
E) Incorrect. Collect is unnecessary and incorrectly used for displaying items.

QUESTION 7

Answer - A, B, and C) Define column-level security profiles specifying which columns users can read, write, or update. Configure security roles to assign users access to specific columns based on their job roles or responsibilities. Establish field-level security privileges for individual users or groups to control access to sensitive data fields.

A) - Correct. Setting up column-level security involves defining security profiles that specify which columns users can read, write, or update, ensuring data protection and access control.

B) - Correct. Configuring security roles allows for the assignment of access to specific columns based on users' job roles or responsibilities, aligning access permissions with organizational needs.

C) - Correct. Establishing field-level security privileges enables the granular control of access to sensitive data fields, ensuring that only authorized users or groups can view or modify certain data elements.

D) - Incorrect. While column-level security rules may be part of the implementation, they are not the primary method for setting up column-level security in Dataverse.

E) - Incorrect. Field-level security profiles are used to control access to individual data fields, rather than entire columns, making them less suitable for managing column-level security across multiple departments.

QUESTION 8

Answer - A, B, C, and D) Define teams to represent functional units or project groups within the organization, assigning users and permissions based on their roles and responsibilities. Configure team membership dynamically using rules and criteria based on user attributes or organizational metadata. Implement team-based security roles and privileges to control access to data and resources. Utilize team templates to streamline the creation and provisioning of new teams.

A) - Correct. Defining teams to represent functional units or project groups helps organize users and resources within Microsoft Dataverse, facilitating collaboration and access control based on roles and responsibilities.

B) - Correct. Configuring team membership dynamically using rules and criteria ensures that team composition adapts to organizational changes, promoting flexibility and scalability in team management.

C) - Correct. Implementing team-based security roles and privileges enables granular access control, ensuring that team members have appropriate permissions for their tasks while maintaining data security and compliance.

D) - Correct. Utilizing team templates streamlines the creation and provisioning of new teams, promoting consistency and standardization in team setup across the organization, reducing administrative overhead.

E) - Incorrect. While monitoring team performance is important, it is not specifically related to the setup and management of teams within Microsoft Dataverse, which focuses more on organizational structure and access control.

QUESTION 9

Answer - [A], [B], and [C].

D) Incorrect application of filter or sort functions would not prevent data retrieval.

E) App version compatibility is less likely to cause data visibility issues.

A) Misconfigured connection can prevent data retrieval.

B) Lack of read access would block users from viewing data.

C) Absence of required entities in the data source would result in missing data.

QUESTION 10

Answer - A

Option A - Correct: Proper TypeScript syntax for defining a new Dataverse entity with columns.

Option B - Incorrect: Incorrect object structure for creating a table.

Option C - Incorrect: Incorrect method and parameters for creating an entity.

Option D - Incorrect: There is no such constructor as DataverseTable in the context.

Option E - Incorrect: Incorrect class and method names; 'Table' and 'Field' are not valid for this context.

QUESTION 11

Answer - [C] Business rules execute automatically on the client-side when data is entered or modified

Option C is correct as business rules in Microsoft Dataverse execute automatically on the client-side when data is entered or modified, ensuring immediate validation and enforcement of defined rules.

Option A is incorrect as business rules are configured using a point-and-click interface within the Dataverse environment, without the need for JavaScript code.

Option B is incorrect as business rules can be applied to various data types, not limited to text fields only.

Option D is incorrect as once applied, business rules cannot be deactivated but can be modified or deleted.

Option E is incorrect as business rules are limited to client-side execution and cannot directly trigger server-side actions such as workflows or plugins.

QUESTION 12

Answer - [A] and [B].

C) Business rules cannot directly control tab visibility, which might require more advanced customization or use of other features.

D) Business rules cannot directly control section visibility based on dynamic patient statuses, which might require more complex logic or integration with other components.

A) Business rules can clear column values for discharged patients, ensuring data accuracy and compliance.

B) Business rules can enable or disable columns based on user roles, providing a personalized and secure data entry experience.

QUESTION 13

Answer - [A] Specify component dependencies in solution metadata

Option A is correct as specifying component dependencies in solution metadata allows developers to define the relationships between solution components, ensuring proper dependency management within Microsoft Power Platform.

Options B, C, D, and E are incorrect as they do not directly relate to the standard method of defining solution dependencies within the platform.

QUESTION 14

Answer - [A, B, C, E] Add custom JavaScript for client-side validation, Configure business rules to control field visibility, Apply form themes to enhance visual appearance, Use embedded Canvas Apps for complex UI elements

Options A, B, C, and E are correct as they represent valid methods for customizing forms in model-driven apps, including client-side validation, field visibility control, visual enhancement, and integration with Canvas Apps.

Option D is incorrect because TypeScript is primarily used for client-side scripting and is not directly applicable to server-side logic in model-driven apps.

QUESTION 15

Answer - [B] and [C].

A) Business rules cannot directly access external data.

B) Business rules can enable or disable a column dynamically based on enrollment status, facilitating efficient student information management and ensuring data accuracy.

C) Business rules can show or hide a column based on user role, ensuring that administrative staff have access to relevant information for their roles, thereby improving user experience and administrative efficiency.

QUESTION 16

Answer - [A, B, C, D, E] Design the user interface using drag-and-drop controls, Define data sources and connect to external databases or services, Configure app settings such as permissions and access control, Implement business logic using Power Fx formulas or JavaScript, Publish the app to make it available to users

Options A, B, C, D, and E are correct as they outline the steps involved in creating a canvas app in Power Apps, including designing the UI, defining data sources, configuring app settings, implementing business logic, and publishing the app.

QUESTION 17

Answer - [A, B, C, D, E] Ensuring modular design to promote component independence and reusability, Implementing clear documentation and usage guidelines for each component, Enforcing version control to track changes and updates across component libraries, Optimizing components for performance and scalability to accommodate varying app requirements, Integrating automated testing frameworks to validate component functionality and behavior

Options A, B, C, D, and E represent essential considerations when designing reusable components for Power Apps projects, including modular design, documentation, version control, performance optimization, and automated testing.

QUESTION 18

Answer - [B] Custom process action.

A) Custom APIs are typically used for integrating external systems or services with the Power Platform but do not provide user-specific execution control.

B) Custom process actions allow developers to define custom actions that can be executed by specific users, making them suitable for restricting code execution to procurement managers. This ensures that only authorized personnel can access and execute the custom code, maintaining data integrity and security within the procurement management system.

C) Classic workflows are automation processes but do not offer the capability to control code execution based on user roles or privileges.

D) Business rules are used for implementing simple business logic within the app's user interface but do not involve executing custom code on the ribbon.

QUESTION 19

Answer - [D] API Management

A) Azure Monitor - Azure Monitor is primarily used for monitoring Azure resources and applications, not specifically for API integration issues.

B) Log Analytics - Log Analytics provides centralized log management and analytics but may not be tailored for API integration issues.

C) Power Apps Monitor - Power Apps Monitor focuses on app usage and performance, not API integration issues.

D) API Management - API Management is designed for managing, monitoring, and troubleshooting API integrations, making it the ideal choice for identifying and resolving API integration issues.

E) Error Reporting Dashboard - Error Reporting Dashboard may provide insights into app errors but may not offer detailed API integration troubleshooting capabilities.

QUESTION 20

Answer - E

Option A - Incorrect: Correct method but lacks handling for onload event.

Option B - Incorrect: Incorrect URL format and not using Xrm.WebApi.

Option C - Incorrect: Incorrect method load for retrieving records.

Option D - Incorrect: Use of document.onload not suitable in this context.

Option E - Correct: Properly handles preloading on window load with correct API usage.

QUESTION 21

Answer - [A] Azure function
[B] Custom connector
[D] HTTP request.

A) Azure functions can be used to create serverless applications, enabling seamless integration with external systems like the legacy HR system via its SOAP API.

B) Custom connectors provide a streamlined way to connect Microsoft Dataverse with external systems, facilitating data exchange and synchronization with the legacy HR system's SOAP API.

D) HTTP requests can facilitate real-time communication and data exchange between the legacy HR system's SOAP API and Microsoft Dataverse, supporting the required synchronization of employee data.

QUESTION 22

Answer - [B] Using the addEventListener method in JavaScript

A) Inline event handlers in HTML elements - While this method is valid, it's not considered a best practice for larger, maintainable applications.

B) Using the addEventListener method in JavaScript - This is a common and recommended approach for registering event handlers in client scripting, making it the correct answer.

C) Defining event handlers within the app's manifest file - Event handlers are typically defined in JavaScript code rather than in the app's manifest file.

D) Attaching event handlers via jQuery - While jQuery can be used for event handling, it's not a native approach and may introduce unnecessary dependencies.

E) Embedding event handling logic directly in Power Apps controls - While Power Apps allows for some level of event handling within controls, it's not as flexible or scalable as using JavaScript with the addEventListener method.

QUESTION 23

Answer - [A] The Client API object model consists of entities, attributes, forms, views, and actions for interacting with data in Dataverse.

A) The Client API object model consists of entities, attributes, forms, views, and actions for interacting with data in Dataverse - This statement accurately describes the key components of the Client API object model in the context of Power Apps development.

B) The Client API object model primarily comprises HTML elements, CSS styles, and JavaScript functions for building user interfaces - This description aligns more with web development concepts rather than the Power Apps Client API object model.

C) Components of the Client API object model include user authentication, role-based access control, and data encryption mechanisms - While these are important aspects of application development, they are not direct components of the Client API object model.

D) The Client API object model is focused on managing cloud resources, deploying infrastructure, and monitoring system performance - This description pertains more to Azure services management rather than the Power Apps Client API object model.

E) Client API object model components encompass server-side logic, database schemas, and RESTful API endpoints for data manipulation - This description conflates different layers of application development and does not accurately represent the Client API object model.

QUESTION 24

Answer - [A] Power Apps custom control.

A) Power Apps custom controls are specifically designed to create reusable and interactive controls within model-driven apps. They support modern client frameworks like React and Fluent UI, making them ideal for visually appealing and interactive solutions for managing customer accounts.

Option B) Custom API: Custom APIs are used for integrating external systems with the Power Platform but are not suitable for creating custom controls within model-driven apps.

Option C) Azure Functions: Azure Functions are serverless compute services used for executing code in response to events but are not meant for creating custom controls in Power Apps.

Option D) Power Automate flow: Power Automate flows are used for automating workflows and processes but are not suitable for creating custom controls in model-driven apps.

QUESTION 25

Answer - B

Option A - Incorrect: 'input' usage does not bind the field to Dataverse.

Option B - Correct: 'bound' usage correctly specifies that the property is bound to a Dataverse field.

Option C - Incorrect: 'control' is not a valid element for defining properties in a PCF manifest.

Option D - Incorrect: 'parameter' is used for function arguments, not component properties.

Option E - Incorrect: 'field' is not a recognized XML element in PCF manifest files.

QUESTION 26

Answer - [A] Generating a solution file from Power Apps Maker Portal.

A) Generating a solution file from Power Apps Maker Portal - Packaging a PCF component often involves creating a solution file that encapsulates all necessary components for deployment.

B) Manually copying component files to the destination environment - Manual copying is not a standard packaging practice and may lead to inconsistencies and errors during deployment.

C) Exporting component metadata as a JSON file - While metadata export may be part of the process, it is not the primary step for packaging a PCF component.

D) Creating a custom connector for component integration - Custom connectors are used for integrating external services and are not directly related to packaging PCF components.

E) Executing a PowerShell script to compile component code - PowerShell scripts may be used for automation but are not typically involved in packaging PCF components.

QUESTION 27

Answer - [A] Implement error handling logic to skip invalid data records and continue with the migration.
Answer - [B] Split the migration process into smaller batches to reduce the likelihood of encountering data format mismatches.

A) Implementing error handling logic within the migration tool allows you to identify and skip invalid data records, ensuring that the migration can continue uninterrupted despite encountering errors. This approach helps maintain progress and enables the successful completion of the migration.

B) Splitting the migration process into smaller batches reduces the risk of encountering data format mismatches by processing smaller volumes of data at a time. This approach improves data quality and increases the likelihood of successful migration.

Option C) Upgrade the TypeScript compiler: While upgrading the compiler may offer benefits, such as improved error handling, it does not directly address the issue of handling data format mismatches during migration.

Option D) Increase the timeout duration: While increasing the timeout duration may provide more time for processing complex data records, it does not address the underlying issue of data format mismatches and may not be effective in resolving migration errors.

QUESTION 28

Answer - [B] Utilize SSL/TLS encryption for secure data transmission.

A) Implement OAuth 2.0 for secure authentication and authorization - OAuth addresses authentication but may not directly protect data during transmission.

B) Utilize SSL/TLS encryption for secure data transmission - SSL/TLS ensures data integrity and confidentiality during transmission, crucial for protecting sensitive customer information.

C) Apply role-based access controls (RBAC) to restrict data access within the CRM system - While RBAC is important, it focuses on access control within the CRM system rather than data transmission security.

D) Encrypt sensitive data stored within the PCF component - Encryption at rest addresses data security within the component but does not directly address data transmission.

E) Implement multi-factor authentication (MFA) for user access to the PCF component - MFA enhances authentication but is not directly related to data transmission security.

QUESTION 29

Answer - [A] Input parameters, secure configuration data, pre/post image data

A) Input parameters, secure configuration data, pre/post image data - Correct, these are all included in the plug-in execution context.

B) Target entity attributes, organization service, execution mode - Some elements are included, but not comprehensive enough.

C) Caller ID, shared variables, database transaction - These are not all included in the plug-in execution context.

D) Execution mode, target entity, pre/post image data - Missing secure configuration data.

E) Execution mode, shared variables, secure configuration data - Missing pre/post image data.

QUESTION 30

Answer - [B] _manager_emailaddress

B) In this scenario, the _manager_emailaddress attribute likely contains the email address of the manager associated with the employee record. When developing a Power Automate flow to retrieve the manager's email address, you should reference the _manager_emailaddress attribute to ensure that the correct email address is retrieved and used for approval requests.

Option A) _manager_email - Incorrect: This attribute does not follow the standard naming convention and may not exist in the context of the "Employees" entity.

Option C) _manager_emailaddress_value - Incorrect: This attribute combination is unlikely to exist and may not provide the manager's email address.

Option D) _manager_email_value - Incorrect: This attribute combination is unlikely to exist and may not provide the manager's email address.

QUESTION 31

Answer - [B] Implementing asynchronous processing for long-running operations.

A) Increasing the frequency of plug-in execution intervals - This may overload the system and worsen performance issues.

B) Implementing asynchronous processing for long-running operations - Correct, asynchronous processing prevents blocking and improves overall system responsiveness.

C) Adding additional try-catch blocks for error handling - While error handling is important, it does not directly address performance issues.

D) Utilizing synchronous execution for all plug-ins - Synchronous execution can lead to delays and impact user experience.

E) Increasing the complexity of plug-in logic to optimize performance - Increasing complexity can exacerbate performance problems rather than solve them.

QUESTION 32

Answer - [D] Importing the assembly into the Dataverse environment.

A) Exporting the assembly from Visual Studio - While necessary, exporting occurs before importing into the environment.

B) Creating a new solution in the Power Platform admin center - This step is unrelated to registering custom assemblies using the Plug-in Registration Tool.

C) Generating a new client ID for authentication - Authentication steps typically come before assembly registration and involve separate processes.

D) Importing the assembly into the Dataverse environment - Correct, this step involves bringing the custom assembly into the environment for registration.

E) Specifying the assembly's deployment type - Deployment type specification occurs within the Plug-in Registration Tool interface after importing the assembly.

QUESTION 33

Answer - C) PUT

A) GET - Incorrect. Used for retrieving data, not updating it.
B) POST - Incorrect. Used for creating new resources.
C) PUT - Correct. Used for updating existing records.
D) PATCH - Incorrect. Used for partial updates.
E) DELETE - Incorrect. Used for deleting resources.

QUESTION 34

Answer - [B] Leveraging policy templates to define connector behavior.

A) Using custom code snippets within Power Automate flows - While possible, this approach may not provide the flexibility and scalability needed for runtime modification of connector behavior.

B) Leveraging policy templates to define connector behavior - Correct, policy templates allow for defining and applying policies that modify connector behavior dynamically based on specific conditions, ensuring flexibility and scalability.

C) Manually updating connector configurations in the Power Platform Admin Center - Manual updates are not ideal for dynamic modification and may introduce human error and maintenance overhead.

D) Creating separate connector instances for each scenario - Creating separate instances increases complexity and management overhead, especially for scenarios requiring frequent changes.

E) Building custom connectors from scratch - While custom connectors offer flexibility, they are time-consuming to develop and may not be suitable for runtime modification.

QUESTION 35

Answer - A

Option A - Correct: Direct and correct path to create a custom connector in Power Apps using an OpenAPI file.

Option B - Incorrect: API Management exports to Power Apps are not direct.

Option C - Incorrect: Power Automate does not import OpenAPI specifications directly for creating connectors.

Option D - Incorrect: GitHub is not directly integrated in this path for importing OpenAPI.

Option E - Incorrect: Azure portal does not create connectors that directly link to Power Apps.

QUESTION 36

Answer - A) and D)

A) Correct. Allows handling errors while the main flow continues, ensuring stakeholders are immediately informed.

B) Incorrect. This setting would not address failures.

C) Incorrect. Useful for grouping but doesn't handle notifications on failure.

D) Correct. Ensures notifications are sent when preceding actions fail, crucial for timely responses in financial services.

E) Incorrect. Instant triggers do not relate to handling failures within a flow.

QUESTION 37

Answer - [A] Querying, creating, updating, and deleting records

A) Querying, creating, updating, and deleting records - Correct, the Organization service API supports CRUD operations for interacting with Dataverse records.

B) Generating reports and dashboards - Reporting and dashboard generation are typically performed using other components of the Power Platform, such as Power BI.

C) Managing user roles and permissions - User role management is usually handled through the Power Platform admin interface, not directly through the Organization service API.

D) Triggering Power Automate flows - While Power Automate can be integrated with the Power Platform, triggering flows is not a direct function of the Organization service API.

E) Handling email notifications - Email notifications are often managed through Power Automate or other messaging services, not directly through the Organization service API.

QUESTION 38

Answer - [D] Employing asynchronous processing for non-blocking operations

A) Implementing synchronous API calls for real-time data retrieval - Synchronous calls may introduce latency and block other operations, impacting performance.

B) Minimizing payload sizes to reduce network latency - While reducing payload sizes can improve performance, it may not directly optimize API calls.

C) Using caching mechanisms to store frequently accessed data - Caching can improve performance but may not optimize API calls themselves.

D) Employing asynchronous processing for non-blocking operations - Correct, asynchronous processing allows concurrent execution of API calls, improving overall system responsiveness and performance.

E) Increasing the number of API requests to parallelize data fetching - Increasing the number of requests may overload the system and worsen performance due to contention.

QUESTION 39

Answer - A) and C)

A) Correct. Triggers the flow when the status exactly matches 'Under Review'.

B) Incorrect. 'Review' is not the exact status needed.

C) Correct. Ensures the trigger only fires when the status field is not empty.

D) Incorrect. This expression triggers the flow when the status is null.

E) Incorrect. Checks if file reference contains 'Documents', irrelevant to the status.

QUESTION 40

Answer - C)

A) Incorrect - PowerShell cmdlet is for creating service principals, not managed identities.

B) Incorrect - This C# code snippet is not related to managing Azure managed identities.

C) Correct - This JSON represents the configuration for a user-assigned managed identity, suitable for Azure services authentication.

D) Incorrect - This is a command-line interface (CLI) command for Azure Active Directory, not related to managed identities configuration.

E) Incorrect - HTML button click cannot be used to create managed identities in Azure.

QUESTION 41

Answer - [C] Configuring connection references for authentication

A) Enabling row-level security for data access - Row-level security may be important but is not directly related to configuring connection references for authentication.

B) Defining appropriate triggers based on form submissions - While triggers are crucial, they are not specific to configuring connection references for authentication.

C) Configuring connection references for authentication - Correct, configuring connection references ensures proper authentication to Dataverse, allowing the flow to interact with data securely.

D) Implementing custom error handling for fault tolerance - Error handling is important but does not directly relate to configuring connection references.

E) Optimizing query filters for efficient data retrieval - Query optimization is important but not the primary focus during connector authentication configuration.

QUESTION 42

Answer - B) API key

A) Incorrect. Uses a password for user authentication, not suitable for services.
B) Correct. API keys are commonly used for service APIs without user context.
C) Incorrect. OAuth 2.0 is used for delegating access, not typical for direct service access.

D) Incorrect. Uses certificates, not keys.

E) Incorrect. Access without authentication is not secure.

QUESTION 43

Answer - [A] Utilizing the "Retry Policy" action in Power Automate to retry failed steps with exponential backoff

A) Utilizing the "Retry Policy" action in Power Automate to retry failed steps with exponential backoff - Correct, the "Retry Policy" action in Power Automate allows for automatic retries of failed steps with exponential backoff, ensuring robust error handling and workflow resilience.

B) Implementing custom error handling logic using JavaScript code actions - While custom error handling is possible with JavaScript code actions, using built-in retry policies is often more efficient and less error-prone.

C) Triggering email notifications to administrators for manual intervention on errors - Email notifications for manual intervention may introduce delays and increase the risk of errors not being addressed promptly.

D) Redirecting failed flows to alternative pathways using conditional branching - While conditional branching can be useful, it may not address the need for automatic retries and compensatory actions.

E) Pausing failed flows until manual approval is obtained - Manual approval introduces delays and may not be suitable for automated error recovery in real-time workflows.

QUESTION 44

Answer - [C] Leveraging dependency injection for managing plug-in dependencies and services

A) Utilizing multithreading for parallel execution of plug-in operations - While multithreading can improve performance, it's not directly related to plug-in development techniques.

B) Implementing complex business logic using JavaScript within plug-in assemblies - JavaScript is not typically used within plug-in assemblies; C# is the standard language for plug-in development.

C) Leveraging dependency injection for managing plug-in dependencies and services - Correct, dependency injection helps manage dependencies and improve testability and maintainability of plug-ins.

D) Integrating external APIs directly within plug-in code for seamless data exchange - While integrating external APIs is common, it may not be considered an advanced plug-in development technique.

E) Implementing custom error handling mechanisms using try-catch blocks in plug-in code - While error handling is important, it's not specific to advanced plug-in development techniques.

QUESTION 45

Answer - A) Use $filter=lastname eq 'Smith'

A) Correct. The $filter query option correctly restricts the results to entries where the last name equals 'Smith'.

B) Incorrect. The $search query option does not exist in OData used by Dataverse.

C) Incorrect. MSCRM.SearchOnlyLastName header does not exist.
D) Incorrect. Direct URL query without OData query options is not valid.
E) Incorrect. $custom is not a recognized OData query option.

QUESTION 46

Answer - [B] Creating a new plugin assembly and registering it with Dataverse

A) Registering a new webhook endpoint and configuring event subscriptions - This choice is not directly related to using the Plug-in Registration Tool for event publishing.

B) Creating a new plugin assembly and registering it with Dataverse - Correct, using the Plug-in Registration Tool involves creating a new plugin assembly and registering it with Dataverse.

C) Defining custom events and event handlers for publishing events - While important, this step typically occurs within the plugin code and is not directly related to the Plug-in Registration Tool.

D) Configuring event properties and mappings for accurate event publication - Event properties and mappings are configured within the plugin code, not through the Plug-in Registration Tool.

E) Generating a new application registration and granting necessary permissions for event publishing - This step is related to authentication and permissions, not the Plug-in Registration Tool itself.

QUESTION 47

Answer - [A, B, C, E] Subscribing to Dataverse change events using Power Automate, Using Azure Functions with Event Grid triggers to process Dataverse events, Implementing polling mechanisms to periodically check for Dataverse record updates, Leveraging Dataverse webhooks to push event notifications to external services

A) Subscribing to Dataverse change events using Power Automate - Power Automate allows for easy integration with Dataverse change events, enabling automation based on data changes.

B) Using Azure Functions with Event Grid triggers to process Dataverse events - Azure Functions with Event Grid triggers provide a scalable and event-driven approach to processing Dataverse events.

C) Implementing polling mechanisms to periodically check for Dataverse record updates - Polling mechanisms are less efficient and may introduce delays compared to event-driven approaches.

D) Directly querying the Dataverse database for real-time event data - Directly querying the database bypasses event-driven architecture and may not capture all relevant events in real-time.

E) Leveraging Dataverse webhooks to push event notifications to external services - Webhooks offer a real-time push notification mechanism for reacting to Dataverse events externally.

QUESTION 48

Answer - A) createTimer() method

A) Correct. The createTimer() method is used in Azure Durable Functions orchestrator to set up a timer.
B) Incorrect. setInterval() is used in JavaScript for repeating intervals, not suitable here.
C) Incorrect. setTimeout() is a JavaScript function for delays, not used here.
D) Incorrect. Task.Delay() is used in C# for delays but not for durable timers.

E) Incorrect. setDaily() function does not exist.

QUESTION 49

Answer - [A, B, E] When inserting new records from legacy systems to Dataverse, When updating existing records in Dataverse based on data changes from legacy systems, When performing batch operations to synchronize large volumes of data between legacy systems and Dataverse.

A) When inserting new records from legacy systems to Dataverse. - UpsertRequest is useful when inserting new records, allowing for both insertion and update operations based on specified criteria.

B) When updating existing records in Dataverse based on data changes from legacy systems. - UpsertRequest enables updating existing records if they exist or inserting new records if they don't, facilitating synchronization between systems.

C) When deleting records in Dataverse that have corresponding records in legacy systems. - UpsertRequest is not designed for deleting records; it focuses on inserting or updating data based on specified conditions.

D) When querying Dataverse to retrieve data for reporting purposes. - UpsertRequest is not used for querying data; it's specifically for inserting or updating records.

E) When performing batch operations to synchronize large volumes of data between legacy systems and Dataverse. - UpsertRequest can be efficient for batch operations, ensuring that data synchronization occurs accurately and efficiently.

QUESTION 50

Answer - [A, E] Implementing parallel processing to distribute data transfer across multiple threads or instances, Implementing data partitioning to divide large datasets into smaller chunks for parallel processing.

A) Implementing parallel processing to distribute data transfer across multiple threads or instances. - Parallel processing can effectively distribute the workload across multiple threads or instances, improving data transfer performance and reducing latency, especially for large volumes of data.

B) Utilizing batch processing to group and process data in predefined intervals. - While batch processing is suitable for managing data in intervals, it may not provide the real-time processing capabilities required for minimal latency in this scenario.

C) Employing in-memory caching to accelerate data retrieval and processing. - While caching can improve performance, it may not be sufficient for handling large volumes of data and minimizing latency in real-time data integration scenarios.

D) Enabling compression techniques to reduce data size during transfer. - Compression can help reduce bandwidth usage but may not address the efficiency and latency requirements of processing large volumes of data.

E) Implementing data partitioning to divide large datasets into smaller chunks for parallel processing. - Data partitioning enables parallel processing by dividing large datasets into smaller segments, allowing for efficient data transfer and processing with minimal latency.

PRACTICE TEST 7 - QUESTIONS ONLY

QUESTION 1

A multinational corporation is deploying a Power Platform solution to manage its supply chain operations. They need to ensure secure access to Power Apps while minimizing the risk of unauthorized access. Which strategy is recommended for secure access to Power Apps in this scenario?

A) Implement role-based access control (RBAC)
B) Enable anonymous access
C) Use a shared access signature (SAS)
D) Restrict access by IP address
E) Disable authentication

QUESTION 2

A software development company is evaluating integration capabilities between Logic Apps and Power Automate for their DevOps processes. They need to understand the integration capabilities of each tool to make an informed decision. Which statement best describes the integration capabilities of Logic Apps and Power Automate?

A) Logic Apps support integration with Azure services, while Power Automate supports integration with third-party services.

B) Logic Apps allow for complex data transformations, while Power Automate is limited to simple data mappings.

C) Logic Apps offer direct integration with Azure DevOps, while Power Automate requires custom connectors for integration.

D) Logic Apps are suitable for real-time event-driven integrations, while Power Automate is better suited for batch processing.

E) Logic Apps provide built-in connectors for popular SaaS applications, while Power Automate requires custom development for such integrations.

QUESTION 3

An Azure Function needs to be triggered on the last day of each month at midnight to update records in Microsoft Dataverse. What is the correct cron expression to use?

A) 0 0 L * *
B) 0 0 28-31 * *
C) 0 0 31 * *
D) 0 0 * * L
E) 59 23 L * *

QUESTION 4

A manufacturing company is designing reusable components in Power Apps to streamline their

production processes and improve efficiency. They need to ensure that the reusable components are flexible, customizable, and easy to maintain across different applications and scenarios.
Which strategies should they employ when designing reusable components in Power Apps? Select THREE.

A) Use component libraries to encapsulate common UI elements and functionalities.

B) Implement design patterns such as Model-View-ViewModel (MVVM) to separate concerns and promote reusability.

C) Parameterize components to allow dynamic configuration and adaptation to varying requirements.

D) Hard-code business logic within components to ensure consistent behavior across applications.

E) Embed external dependencies directly into components to reduce external dependencies.

QUESTION 5

Implement a JavaScript function to fetch and display records from a Dataverse entity using the Web API. Which snippet correctly handles the API call and result parsing?

A) fetch('https://org.api.crm.dynamics.com/api/data/v9.0/accounts').then(res => res.json()).then(data => console.log(data));

B) fetch('https://org.api.crm.dynamics.com/api/data/v9.0/accounts', {headers: {'Authorization': 'Bearer ' + token}}).then(res => res.text()).then(data => console.log(data));

C) XMLHttpRequest('GET', 'https://org.api.crm.dynamics.com/api/data/v9.0/accounts', true).send();

D) fetch('https://org.api.crm.dynamics.com/api/data/v9.0/accounts').then(res => res.blob()).then(data => console.log(data));

E) fetch('https://org.api.crm.dynamics.com/api/data/v9.0/accounts').then(res => res.json()).then(data => displayData(data));

QUESTION 6

You are creating a canvas app to manage conference registrations in Microsoft Dataverse. Only active conferences should be shown in a dropdown. What PowerFx expression should you apply to the Items property of the drop-down list?

A) Filter('Conferences', Status = 'Active')
B) 'Conferences'
C) Collect('Active Conferences', Filter(Conferences, Status = 'Active'))
D) Lookup('Conferences', Status = 'Active')
E) Filter('Conferences', IsActive = true)

QUESTION 7

A manufacturing company is considering implementing column-level security in Dataverse to restrict access to proprietary product information within their organization. They need to evaluate potential use cases for column-level security to determine its applicability to their data management requirements.
In which scenarios would column-level security be beneficial in Dataverse implementations? Select

THREE.

A) Protecting personally identifiable information (PII) fields in customer records to comply with data privacy regulations.

B) Restricting access to financial data fields to employees in the finance department only.

C) Controlling access to sensitive research and development (R&D) project details to authorized team members.

D) Securing access to employee salary information based on hierarchical roles within the organization.

E) Enforcing data access restrictions for specific product categories based on geographic regions.

QUESTION 8

A company is evaluating the data access capabilities of teams and business units within Microsoft Dataverse to determine the most suitable organizational structure for their requirements. They need to compare teams to business units in terms of data access to make an informed decision.
How do teams and business units differ in terms of data access within Microsoft Dataverse?

A) Teams provide granular control over data access and permissions within a specific functional group or project team, while business units establish broader access boundaries based on organizational hierarchies.

B) Business units restrict data access to records owned by users within the same organizational unit, whereas teams enable collaboration and data sharing across different departments or functional areas.

C) Teams facilitate role-based access control (RBAC) within a defined team structure, while business units enforce strict data segregation and isolation to prevent unauthorized access across organizational units.

D) Business units define geographical regions for data localization and compliance, while teams focus on optimizing data visibility and collaboration within a specific team or department.

E) Teams and business units both provide similar levels of data access and permissions, with differences primarily in their organizational scope and structure.

QUESTION 9

You are implementing a custom plugin in Microsoft Dataverse to perform additional validation on record creation. However, users report that records are being created without triggering the plugin validation. What could be potential reasons for this issue? Select the correct answers that apply.

A) The plugin is registered on the wrong event pipeline.
B) The plugin assembly is not deployed to the correct Dataverse environment.
C) The plugin registration is inactive.
D) The plugin logic contains an error, causing it to fail silently.
E) The plugin registration lacks necessary execution permissions.

QUESTION 10

You are implementing a feature in a Power Apps application that requires dynamic data loading from an

SQL database based on user input. Write a SQL statement in PowerFx that retrieves all records from the 'Customers' table where the 'Country' column matches the user's input.

A) Collect(CustomerData, LookUp('dbo.Customers', "Country = '" & TextInput1.Text & "'"))

B) ClearCollect(CustomerData, Filter(dbo.Customers, Country = TextInput1.Text))

C) ClearCollect(CustomerData, SQL("SELECT * FROM Customers WHERE Country = '" + TextInput1.Text + "'"))

D) Collect(CustomerData, Query("SELECT * FROM Customers WHERE Country = '" & TextInput1.Text & "'"))

E) ClearCollect(CustomerData, 'SELECT * FROM Customers WHERE Country = "' + TextInput1.Text + '"')

QUESTION 11

A manufacturing company is building a quality control system using Power Apps and Dataverse. They need to ensure that when a product's quantity falls below a certain threshold, an alert is displayed to the user. Which scenario is suitable for implementing a business rule in this context?

A) Calculating the total cost of an order based on quantity and unit price
B) Enforcing data consistency by validating email addresses entered in a customer record
C) Automatically assigning a unique identifier to new product records
D) Displaying a warning message when the quantity of a product reaches a predefined minimum level
E) Updating the status of an order to "Shipped" when all associated products have been delivered

QUESTION 12

Your organization is developing a model-driven Power Apps app to streamline inventory management processes in a retail environment. The app needs to dynamically adjust user interface elements based on inventory levels and employee roles. What are two key functionalities that you can implement using business rules to enhance the app's usability and efficiency? Select the correct answers that apply.

A) Automatically clear column values for out-of-stock items.
B) Enable and disable columns for different user roles.
C) Show and hide tabs based on product categories.
D) Show and hide sections based on inventory status.

QUESTION 13

A development team is tasked with managing solution dependencies effectively to ensure a streamlined development process. What strategies can be employed to manage dependencies within Microsoft Power Platform? Select the correct answers that apply.

A) Utilize solution versioning to track changes and dependencies
B) Maintain clear documentation of dependency relationships
C) Implement automated dependency validation during solution deployment
D) Leverage dependency visualization tools for better understanding
E) Establish regular dependency review meetings with stakeholders

QUESTION 14

When implementing business logic in forms of model-driven apps, developers need to ensure efficient execution and proper handling of data. Which strategies can be employed to implement business logic effectively? Select the correct answers that apply.

A) Use Power Automate flows for asynchronous operations
B) Utilize JavaScript for client-side calculations and validations
C) Implement plugins for complex server-side processing
D) Leverage Canvas Apps for business process automation
E) Configure form rules to enforce data integrity

QUESTION 15

Your task is to customize a form in a model-driven app for a hospitality company's reservation management system. The app aims to streamline the reservation process and enhance guest satisfaction. What are two key actions that you can perform using a business rule in this context? Select the correct answers that apply.

A) Access external data.
B) Enable or disable a column based on reservation status.
C) Show or hide a column based on user role.
D) Run the rule on demand.

QUESTION 16

A software development firm is designing a custom page for a client's Power App to provide a tailored user experience. What design principles should they consider to ensure an effective user interface? Select the correct answers that apply.

A) Consistency in layout and navigation across different screens
B) Prioritization of essential features and information for user accessibility
C) Use of responsive design techniques to optimize display on various devices
D) Incorporation of visual cues and feedback to guide user interactions
E) Integration of complex animations and transitions for visual appeal

QUESTION 17

A multinational corporation is managing a centralized repository of component libraries for their subsidiaries' Power Apps development teams. What challenges might arise when managing these component libraries across different geographical locations and teams? Select the correct answers that apply.

A) Ensuring consistent naming conventions and coding standards across diverse development teams
B) Coordinating version updates and compatibility checks between different instances of the component library
C) Addressing language and cultural barriers that may impact communication and collaboration among teams
D) Managing licensing and compliance issues associated with the distribution of proprietary components

E) Resolving conflicts arising from simultaneous modifications or customizations of shared components by multiple teams

QUESTION 18

You are building a model-driven app for a compliance tracking system. The app requires executing specialized code when a user clicks on a button in the app's ribbon. However, this functionality should be restricted to compliance officers only. Which option should you choose to meet this requirement?

A) Custom API
B) Custom process action
C) Classic workflow
D) Business rule

QUESTION 19

A Power Apps developer is implementing error handling mechanisms for connector operations in a canvas app. Which best practice should they follow to ensure effective error handling?

A) Suppress all error messages to avoid confusing end users
B) Implement retry logic with exponential backoff for transient errors
C) Log detailed error information to an external database
D) Redirect users to a generic error page for all connector errors
E) Retry failed operations indefinitely until successful execution

QUESTION 20

Implement a query that delegates processing to the server to improve performance in a large dataset within a Canvas app. What is the correct PowerFx command?

A) Filter(LargeDataset, StartsWith(CompanyName, TextSearchBox1.Text))

B) LookUp(LargeDataset, CompanyName = TextSearchBox1.Text)

C) Search(LargeDataset, TextSearchBox1.Text, "CompanyName")

D) SortByColumns(Filter(LargeDataset, StartsWith(CompanyName, TextSearchBox1.Text)), "CompanyName", Ascending)

E) Filter(LargeDataset, CompanyName.Contains(TextSearchBox1.Text))

QUESTION 21

You are developing a solution to integrate an inventory management system, which exposes a SOAP API, with Microsoft Dataverse. The integration needs to support real-time data synchronization and transaction processing. Considering the technical requirements, which three integration options should you select to achieve the desired solution? Select the correct answers that apply.

A) Azure function
B) Custom connector
C) Custom API

D) HTTP request
E) Business rule

QUESTION 22

A Power Apps developer is implementing event handlers for a canvas app that requires high performance. Which of the following best practices should the developer follow for event handler registration to minimize performance impacts?

A) Register event handlers for all elements on the canvas to ensure comprehensive coverage
B) Consolidate multiple event handlers into a single function to reduce overhead
C) Use synchronous event handling to prioritize responsiveness over performance
D) Avoid using event delegation to minimize the propagation of events
E) Implement inline event handlers directly in HTML elements for simplicity

QUESTION 23

A Power Apps developer is studying the relationships between components in the Client API object model. Which of the following relationships accurately depicts the interaction between entities and forms in the context of the Client API object model?

A) Entities encapsulate forms, which define the data structure and behavior of records within Dataverse.
B) Forms contain entities, which manage the display and interaction of data records in canvas apps.
C) Entities and forms are independent components within the Client API object model and do not have direct relationships.
D) Entities and forms are connected through JavaScript functions, allowing for dynamic manipulation of record data and UI elements.
E) Forms inherit properties and methods from entities, enabling seamless integration of UI elements with underlying data structures.

QUESTION 24

Your organization is developing a model-driven app for managing inventory. You need to create a custom control that displays real-time inventory levels and allows users to update inventory quantities from within the app. The control should be reusable across multiple forms and support modern client frameworks like React and Fluent UI. Considering the requirements, which development option should you choose?

A) Power Apps custom control
B) Custom connector
C) Azure Logic Apps
D) Power Automate Desktop

QUESTION 25

How should you configure the dependencies for a PCF component to ensure it correctly loads the Power Apps component framework?

A) <dependencies><sdkversion>9.0</sdkversion></dependencies>

B) <dependencies><libraries><library name="PowerApps-ComponentFramework" version="1.0" /></libraries></dependencies>

C) <dependencies><component name="PowerApps-ComponentFramework" /></dependencies>

D) <dependencies><packages><package name="Microsoft.PowerApps.ComponentFramework" /></packages></dependencies>

E) <dependencies><files><file path="ComponentFramework.js" /></files></dependencies>

QUESTION 26

When deploying a PCF component, what deployment strategy helps ensure seamless updates and minimal disruption to existing applications?

A) Full deployment of all components at once.
B) Incremental deployment with version rollback capability.
C) Manual deployment using command-line tools.
D) Parallel deployment across multiple environments simultaneously.
E) Random deployment to different regions for load balancing.

QUESTION 27

Your organization is migrating data from an on-premises SQL Server database to Dataverse tables using a C# console application. During the migration, you encounter intermittent network connectivity issues that disrupt the data transfer process, resulting in incomplete data migration. What are two possible strategies to mitigate the impact of network connectivity issues and ensure the successful completion of the data migration? Select the correct answers that apply.

A) Implement retry logic with exponential backoff to automatically retry failed data transfer operations.
B) Increase the buffer size for data transfer operations to reduce the frequency of network calls.
C) Configure a secondary network connection as a failover option to maintain continuous data transfer.
D) Modify the data migration tool to compress data packets for more efficient network utilization.

QUESTION 28

A Power Apps developer is tasked with integrating a PCF component with an ERP system to facilitate real-time data synchronization. Which approach should the developer prioritize to minimize performance impacts during integration?

A) Implement asynchronous data processing to reduce latency.
B) Optimize API calls by batching requests for multiple data operations.
C) Utilize server-side caching to store frequently accessed data.
D) Minimize data payload size by selecting only essential fields for synchronization.
E) Implement request throttling to manage API call rates and prevent overload.

QUESTION 29

A development team is analyzing how the plug-in execution context affects plug-in behavior in their Power Platform solution. Which statement best describes the impact of the context?

A) The context determines the order of plug-in execution during record processing.
B) It controls the data access permissions for plug-ins within the system.
C) The context defines the runtime environment and available resources for plug-in execution.
D) It ensures transactional consistency across multiple plug-in executions within a single transaction.
E) The context governs the scheduling and execution frequency of plug-ins based on system load.

QUESTION 30

You are designing a model-driven app that includes a custom entity named "Orders" with a lookup field to the "Customers" entity. Users should be able to view the related customer's details when viewing an order. What attribute should you specify in your model-driven app to display the customer's name?

A) _customerid_value
B) _customer_name
C) _customer_value
D) _customerid_name

QUESTION 31

A Power Platform developer is troubleshooting performance bottlenecks in plug-ins. Which action can help identify performance bottlenecks effectively?

A) Reviewing system event logs for plug-in execution details.
B) Analyzing network traffic between plug-ins and external systems.
C) Profiling plug-in execution using Azure Monitor.
D) Increasing the timeout settings for plug-in execution.
E) Disabling plug-ins temporarily to observe system performance.

QUESTION 32

When registering custom assemblies using the Plug-in Registration Tool, what is an essential consideration for managing assembly updates?

A) Overwriting existing assemblies without validation.
B) Ensuring backward compatibility with existing plug-ins.
C) Keeping multiple versions of the same assembly for redundancy.
D) Modifying the assembly's namespace for each update.
E) Ignoring versioning to simplify maintenance.

QUESTION 33

You are tasked to create a JavaScript function that triggers when a new contact is added via a form, invoking a custom action. What HTTP method should be applied to execute this action through the Web API?

A) GET
B) POST
C) DELETE
D) HEAD

E) OPTIONS

QUESTION 34

In a Power Platform solution, the development team needs to implement a policy template to modify the behavior of a connector that interacts with a third-party API. Which scenario is suitable for modifying connector behavior using policy templates?

A) Dynamically adjusting rate limits based on API usage.
B) Encrypting data transmitted through the connector.
C) Changing the authentication method from OAuth to Basic.
D) Redirecting API requests to different endpoints based on user roles.
E) Logging connector activity for auditing purposes.

QUESTION 35

What authentication method should be configured in a custom connector to secure communications between Power Apps and an Azure service?

A) OAuth 2.0 with Azure Active Directory
B) API Key based authentication directly in the header
C) Basic authentication using username and password
D) Client certificate authentication for enhanced security
E) No authentication to allow unrestricted access

QUESTION 36

In managing a healthcare system's patient data synchronization flow, how can you configure Power Automate to alert administrators immediately if synchronization with the external API fails? Select the correct answers that apply.

A) Add a notification action in the main flow
B) Configure a condition that checks for failure status codes
C) Add a delay before checking API responses
D) Set the "Configure run after" for a notification to handle failures
E) Add a termination action if an error occurs

QUESTION 37

When comparing the Organization service API with other service APIs in the Power Platform ecosystem, what distinguishes the Organization service API?

A) Real-time data synchronization capabilities
B) Integration with external systems via RESTful APIs
C) Direct access to underlying database tables
D) Tight integration with Power BI for analytics
E) Support for custom code execution on the server side

QUESTION 38

In a Power Platform solution with multiple concurrent users, maintaining transactional integrity is crucial. Which strategy is recommended for managing concurrency and transactional integrity effectively?

A) Using optimistic concurrency control with timestamp-based validation
B) Employing pessimistic concurrency control with exclusive locks
C) Implementing distributed transactions with two-phase commit
D) Applying row-level locking to prevent conflicts
E) Utilizing long-running transactions for comprehensive data processing

QUESTION 39

You need a Power Automate flow to trigger when a document is updated in a SharePoint library, and its approval status changes to 'Approved'. What expressions should be used? Select the correct answers that apply.

A) @equals(triggerBody()?['ApprovalStatus'], 'Approved')
B) @not(equals(triggerBody()?['ApprovalStatus'], null))
C) @contains(triggerBody()?['Editor'], 'user')
D) @isEmpty(triggerBody()?['ApprovalStatus'])
E) @greater(triggerOutputs()?['VersionNumber'], 1)

QUESTION 40

A multinational corporation is deploying a Power Platform solution across its subsidiaries worldwide. They want to ensure a robust authentication mechanism using managed identities for Azure services. The team must identify security best practices to safeguard sensitive data and prevent unauthorized access.

A) C#: ManagedIdentityCredential credential = new ManagedIdentityCredential(clientId);
B) TypeScript: const tokenCredential = new ManagedIdentityCredential(clientId);
C) PowerShell: az ad sp create-for-rbac --name "MyServicePrincipal" --skip-assignment
D) JSON: { "identity": { "type": "SystemAssigned" } }
E) JavaScript: const credential = new DefaultAzureCredential();

QUESTION 41

In a Power Platform solution, developers are designing a cloud flow triggered by updates in Dataverse records to perform specific actions. What is a best practice for using Dataverse triggers in this scenario?

A) Triggering the flow on any record update without filtering
B) Applying conditional logic directly within the trigger settings
C) Configuring polling intervals for real-time trigger updates
D) Using custom connectors instead of Dataverse triggers for flexibility
E) Filtering trigger conditions based on specific record attributes

QUESTION 42

An organization needs a Power Platform custom connector to interface with an internal HR system using OpenAPI. The system requires authentication via company credentials. Which method should you use?

A) Single sign-on
B) API key
C) OAuth 2.0
D) Password based
E) Client certificate

QUESTION 43

A software development company is building a Power Platform solution to manage customer support tickets. They need to ensure that their workflows can detect and handle errors effectively to maintain service-level agreements (SLAs) with clients. What approach should they take to configure flow control actions for robust workflows?

A) Using the "Terminate" action to stop execution immediately upon encountering an error
B) Implementing conditional branching to handle different error scenarios
C) Enabling verbose logging for detailed error tracking and analysis
D) Automatically restarting failed flows using the "Restart on Error" feature
E) Designing workflows with single-step actions to minimize complexity

QUESTION 44

A healthcare organization is implementing a Power Platform solution to automate patient records management. They require plug-ins to perform asynchronous operations for improved performance and scalability. What is a key consideration when implementing asynchronous plug-in operations in this scenario?

A) Ensuring synchronous communication between plug-ins and external systems
B) Managing transaction boundaries and data consistency across asynchronous operations
C) Minimizing latency by optimizing network communication between plug-ins and databases
D) Implementing batch processing for grouping and optimizing asynchronous plug-in executions
E) Utilizing shared memory for inter-process communication between asynchronous plug-in instances

QUESTION 45

To update a specific contact's email in Microsoft Dataverse without affecting other properties, what should you include in your PATCH request?

A) Set If-Match: * header to ensure data integrity
B) Use the UPSERT operation
C) Include only the email property in the request body
D) Set CalculateMatchCodeSynchronously parameter
E) Use the $select query option to specify email

QUESTION 46

A manufacturing company is developing a Power Platform solution to monitor equipment performance and maintenance schedules. They want to ensure best practices are followed when setting up events for event publishing using the Plug-in Registration Tool. What are some best practices for setting up events with the Plug-in Registration Tool? Select the correct answers that apply.

A) Using descriptive names and clear descriptions for events and event handlers
B) Implementing efficient event filtering to minimize unnecessary event processing
C) Avoiding circular event dependencies to prevent infinite event loops
D) Verifying event handler logic and error handling mechanisms before deployment
E) Versioning event definitions and maintaining backward compatibility for event consumers

QUESTION 47

A marketing agency is developing a Power Platform solution to track customer interactions and analyze campaign performance. They want to ensure efficient event listening practices to minimize latency and maximize responsiveness. What best practices should they consider for efficient event listening in this scenario? Select the correct answers that apply.

A) Minimizing the use of polling mechanisms to reduce unnecessary requests
B) Utilizing Azure Event Hubs for high-throughput event ingestion and processing
C) Implementing caching mechanisms to store frequently accessed event data
D) Scaling event listeners dynamically based on workload demand
E) Optimizing network latency by colocating event listeners with data sources

QUESTION 48

In a Power Apps application managing loan approvals, you need to implement a follow-up process using Azure Durable Functions that triggers every 48 hours. Which method should you use in the orchestrator function?

A) setInterval() function
B) createTimer() method
C) Task.Delay() method
D) setTimeout() function
E) createInterval() method

QUESTION 49

A retail company is implementing a real-time inventory management system using Microsoft Power Platform and needs to synchronize inventory data across multiple stores. What are the benefits of using UpsertRequest in this data synchronization scenario? Select the correct answers that apply.

A) Minimizes data redundancy and inconsistency by updating existing records and inserting new records as needed.
B) Improves data accuracy and integrity by enforcing business rules during upsert operations.
C) Enhances performance and efficiency by minimizing API calls required for synchronization.
D) Facilitates conflict resolution by automatically resolving data conflicts during upsert operations.
E) Streamlines data synchronization processes by supporting batch operations for large data sets.

QUESTION 50

A critical business application relies on real-time data updates from various sources integrated into Microsoft Dataverse. To ensure high availability and fault tolerance, which approach should be prioritized? Select the correct answers that apply.

A) Implementing redundant data pipelines with failover mechanisms to switch to backup pipelines in case of failure.
B) Deploying multiple instances of integration components across geographically distributed regions.
C) Utilizing load balancing to evenly distribute data processing tasks across multiple servers or instances.
D) Implementing automated monitoring and alerting systems to detect and respond to integration failures promptly.
E) Configuring backup and disaster recovery mechanisms to restore data in case of system failures.

PRACTICE TEST 7 - ANSWERS ONLY

QUESTION 1

Answer - [A) Implement role-based access control (RBAC)]

A) Implement role-based access control (RBAC) - RBAC allows organizations to control access based on roles and permissions, ensuring secure access to Power Apps.

B) Enable anonymous access - Enabling anonymous access poses security risks by allowing anyone to access Power Apps without authentication.

C) Use a shared access signature (SAS) - SAS is typically used for providing limited access to storage resources, not for securing Power Apps access.

D) Restrict access by IP address - Restricting access by IP address may be too restrictive and could hinder legitimate users' access.

E) Disable authentication - Disabling authentication would expose Power Apps to unauthorized access and security threats.

QUESTION 2

Answer - [D) Logic Apps are suitable for real-time event-driven integrations, while Power Automate is better suited for batch processing]

A) Logic Apps support integration with Azure services, while Power Automate supports integration with third-party services - Both Logic Apps and Power Automate support integration with Azure services as well as third-party services.

B) Logic Apps allow for complex data transformations, while Power Automate is limited to simple data mappings - Both Logic Apps and Power Automate support complex data transformations, but Logic Apps are typically used for more extensive transformations.

C) Logic Apps offer direct integration with Azure DevOps, while Power Automate requires custom connectors for integration - Both Logic Apps and Power Automate offer integration with Azure DevOps, with Logic Apps providing direct integration and Power Automate allowing integration through custom connectors.

D) Logic Apps are suitable for real-time event-driven integrations, while Power Automate is better suited for batch processing - Logic Apps are designed for real-time event-driven integrations, while Power Automate is often used for batch processing or scheduled workflows.

E) Logic Apps provide built-in connectors for popular SaaS applications, while Power Automate requires custom development for such integrations - Both Logic Apps and Power Automate offer built-in connectors for popular SaaS applications, but Power Automate also allows for custom connectors if needed.

QUESTION 3

Answer - B) 0 0 28-31 * *

A) Incorrect. 'L' is not a valid designation in Azure cron expressions.
B) Correct. This setting ensures the function checks each day from 28 to 31, effectively catching the last day of any month.
C) Incorrect. This would only trigger on the 31st, missing shorter months.
D) Incorrect. 'L' is not recognized in Azure cron syntax.
E) Incorrect. The expression uses 'L' incorrectly and the wrong time (one minute before midnight).

QUESTION 4

Answer - A, B, and C) Use component libraries to encapsulate common UI elements and functionalities. Implement design patterns such as Model-View-ViewModel (MVVM) to separate concerns and promote reusability. Parameterize components to allow dynamic configuration and adaptation to varying requirements.

A) - Correct. Using component libraries facilitates the encapsulation of common UI elements and functionalities for reuse across different applications.

B) - Correct. Implementing design patterns such as Model-View-ViewModel (MVVM) helps separate concerns and promotes reusability by isolating UI logic from business logic.

C) - Correct. Parameterizing components enables dynamic configuration and adaptation to varying requirements, enhancing their flexibility and versatility.

D) - Incorrect. Hard-coding business logic within components limits their reusability and flexibility, making them less adaptable to different scenarios.

E) - Incorrect. Embedding external dependencies directly into components increases their coupling and reduces their portability and maintainability, contrary to the goal of reusability.

QUESTION 5

Answer - E

Option A - Incorrect. Does not handle authorization which may be required.

Option B - Incorrect. Converts response to text which isn't helpful for JSON data.

Option C - Incorrect. Incorrect usage of XMLHttpRequest syntax.

Option D - Incorrect. Converts response to a blob, not useful for JSON.

Option E - Correct. Properly fetches JSON data and assumes a function displayData to handle the display, reflecting best practices.

QUESTION 6

Answer - A) Filter('Conferences', Status = 'Active')

A) Correct. This filters the 'Conferences' data source to include only those with a status of 'Active'.
B) Incorrect. This includes all conferences, regardless of status.
C) Incorrect. Collect is not the correct function for filtering items in a drop-down list.
D) Incorrect. Lookup is used for finding a single record.
E) Incorrect. Assumes an 'IsActive' field which is not specified.

QUESTION 7

Answer - A, B, and C) Protecting personally identifiable information (PII) fields in customer records to comply with data privacy regulations. Restricting access to financial data fields to employees in the finance department only. Controlling access to sensitive research and development (R&D) project details to authorized team members.

A) - Correct. Column-level security can be used to protect personally identifiable information (PII) fields in customer records, ensuring compliance with data privacy regulations such as GDPR or CCPA.

B) - Correct. Restricting access to financial data fields to employees in the finance department only helps prevent unauthorized access and ensures data confidentiality and integrity.

C) - Correct. Column-level security enables the control of access to sensitive research and development (R&D) project details, ensuring that only authorized team members can view or modify critical data, protecting intellectual property and confidentiality.

D) - Incorrect. While securing employee salary information is important, hierarchical role-based access control may be better suited for this scenario than column-level security.

E) - Incorrect. Enforcing data access restrictions based on geographic regions may require a different access control mechanism, such as record-level security, rather than column-level security.

QUESTION 8

Answer - A) Teams provide granular control over data access and permissions within a specific functional group or project team, while business units establish broader access boundaries based on organizational hierarchies.

A) - Correct. Teams typically offer granular control over data access and permissions within a specific functional group or project team, allowing for more fine-tuned access control compared to the broader access boundaries established by business units based on organizational hierarchies.

B) - Incorrect. While teams enable collaboration and data sharing, business units may also facilitate similar functionalities, but their primary purpose is to establish organizational boundaries rather than enable cross-departmental collaboration.

C) - Incorrect. While both teams and business units may enforce access control mechanisms, their approaches and scopes differ, with teams focusing on internal collaboration and business units on organizational structure and hierarchy.

D) - Incorrect. Business units may impact data localization and compliance, but their primary purpose is not localization; teams focus more on optimizing collaboration and data sharing within specific teams or departments.

E) - Incorrect. Teams and business units serve different purposes and have distinct scopes in terms of data access and permissions, with teams typically offering more granular control within specific functional groups or project teams compared to the broader organizational boundaries established by business units.

QUESTION 9

Answer - [A] and [C].

B) Deployment issues would prevent the plugin from executing, not just validation.

D) Errors in plugin logic would likely result in visible failures, not silent ones.

E) Execution permissions would cause the plugin to fail altogether, not silently.

A) Registering the plugin on the wrong event would prevent it from triggering.

C) An inactive plugin registration would cause the validation to be skipped.

QUESTION 10

Answer - C

Option A - Incorrect: Incorrect use of LookUp function syntax.

Option B - Incorrect: Filter function does not execute SQL queries.

Option C - Correct: Proper use of PowerFx to execute a SQL query with dynamic input.

Option D - Incorrect: Query is not a recognized function in PowerFx.

Option E - Incorrect: Syntax and method combination is incorrect for executing SQL queries in PowerFx.

QUESTION 11

Answer - [D] Displaying a warning message when the quantity of a product reaches a predefined minimum level

Option D is correct as this scenario involves triggering an action (displaying a warning message) based on a specific condition (product quantity falling below a threshold), which aligns with the purpose of implementing a business rule.

Option A, B, C, and E are incorrect as they involve different scenarios unrelated to the requirement of triggering an alert based on a data threshold.

QUESTION 12

Answer - [A] and [B].

C) Business rules cannot directly control tab visibility based on product categories, which might require additional customization or integration with other components.

D) Business rules cannot directly control section visibility based on dynamic inventory statuses, which might require more advanced logic or use of other features.

A) Business rules can automatically clear column values for out-of-stock items, ensuring accurate inventory tracking and management.

B) Business rules can enable or disable columns based on user roles, providing a personalized and efficient data entry experience.

QUESTION 13

Answer - [A, B, C, D] Utilize solution versioning to track changes and dependencies, Maintain clear documentation of dependency relationships, Implement automated dependency validation during solution deployment, Leverage dependency visualization tools for better understanding

Options A, B, C, and D are correct as they represent effective strategies for managing solution dependencies within Microsoft Power Platform, including versioning, documentation, validation, and visualization.

Option E, while a potential practice, is not as directly related to the technical management of dependencies.

QUESTION 14

Answer - [A, B, C, E] Use Power Automate flows for asynchronous operations, Utilize JavaScript for client-side calculations and validations, Implement plugins for complex server-side processing, Configure form rules to enforce data integrity

Options A, B, C, and E are correct as they represent effective strategies for implementing business logic in forms of model-driven apps, including asynchronous operations, client-side scripting, server-side processing, and data integrity enforcement.

Option D is incorrect because Canvas Apps are not directly related to business logic implementation within model-driven app forms.

QUESTION 15

Answer - [B] and [C].

A) Business rules cannot directly access external data.

B) Business rules can enable or disable a column dynamically based on reservation status, facilitating efficient reservation management and ensuring accurate guest information.

C) Business rules can show or hide a column based on user role, ensuring that staff members have access to relevant reservation details for their roles, thereby improving user experience and guest satisfaction.

QUESTION 16

Answer - [A, B, C, D] Consistency in layout and navigation across different screens, Prioritization of essential features and information for user accessibility, Use of responsive design techniques to optimize display on various devices, Incorporation of visual cues and feedback to guide user interactions

Options A, B, C, and D are correct as they represent key design principles for creating an effective user interface in a Power App, including consistency, prioritization, responsiveness, and providing guidance through visual cues.

Option E is incorrect as complex animations and transitions may hinder usability rather than enhance it.

QUESTION 17

Answer - [A, B, C, D, E] Ensuring consistent naming conventions and coding standards across diverse development teams, Coordinating version updates and compatibility checks between different instances of the component library, Addressing language and cultural barriers that may impact communication and collaboration among teams, Managing licensing and compliance issues associated with the distribution of proprietary components, Resolving conflicts arising from simultaneous modifications or customizations of shared components by multiple teams

Options A, B, C, D, and E highlight the challenges associated with managing component libraries across diverse geographical locations and teams, including consistency, coordination, communication, compliance, and conflict resolution.

QUESTION 18

Answer - [B] Custom process action.

A) Custom APIs are typically used for integrating external systems or services with the Power Platform but do not provide user-specific execution control.

B) Custom process actions enable developers to define custom actions that can be executed by specific users, making them suitable for restricting code execution to compliance officers. This ensures that only authorized personnel, such as compliance officers, have access to execute the specialized code, maintaining data confidentiality and integrity within the compliance tracking system.

C) Classic workflows are automation processes but do not offer the capability to control code execution based on user roles or privileges.

D) Business rules are used for implementing simple business logic within the app's user interface but do not involve executing custom code on the ribbon.

QUESTION 19

Answer - [B] Implement retry logic with exponential backoff for transient errors

A) Suppress all error messages to avoid confusing end users - Suppressing error messages may hinder troubleshooting efforts and leave users unaware of potential issues.

B) Implement retry logic with exponential backoff for transient errors - Implementing retry logic with exponential backoff improves resilience by automatically retrying failed operations with increasing delays.

C) Log detailed error information to an external database - While logging errors is essential, storing detailed error information in an external database may introduce additional complexity and overhead.

D) Redirect users to a generic error page for all connector errors - Redirecting users to a generic error page may not provide specific guidance on how to resolve connector errors.

E) Retry failed operations indefinitely until successful execution - Retrying failed operations indefinitely may lead to performance issues and potentially infinite loops in case of persistent errors.

QUESTION 20

Answer - A

Option A - Correct: Uses StartsWith, which supports delegation.

Option B - Incorrect: LookUp does not support delegation.

Option C - Incorrect: Search does not delegate when used with large datasets.

Option D - Correct but more complex than necessary.

Option E - Incorrect: Contains does not support delegation.

QUESTION 21

Answer - [A] Azure function
[C] Custom API
[E] Business rule.

A) Azure functions provide the flexibility to execute code in response to events, making them suitable for real-time data synchronization and transaction processing between the inventory management system's SOAP API and Microsoft Dataverse.

C) Custom APIs offer tailored integration solutions, allowing direct communication between Microsoft Dataverse and the SOAP API of the inventory management system, ensuring data consistency and reliability.

E) Business rules can enforce data validation and business logic within Microsoft Dataverse, enhancing the integrity of synchronized data from the inventory management system.

QUESTION 22

Answer - [B] Consolidate multiple event handlers into a single function to reduce overhead

A) Register event handlers for all elements on the canvas to ensure comprehensive coverage - While comprehensive event handling may be necessary, registering event handlers for all elements can introduce unnecessary overhead.

B) Consolidate multiple event handlers into a single function to reduce overhead - This is a recommended best practice to minimize the number of event listeners and improve performance, making it the correct answer.

C) Use synchronous event handling to prioritize responsiveness over performance - Synchronous event handling can block the UI thread and degrade performance, so it's not recommended for high-performance scenarios.

D) Avoid using event delegation to minimize the propagation of events - Event delegation can actually improve performance by reducing the number of event listeners, so it's not necessary to avoid it for performance reasons.

E) Implement inline event handlers directly in HTML elements for simplicity - While inline event handlers may be simpler to implement, they can lead to maintenance challenges and are not as performant as consolidated event handlers.

QUESTION 23

Answer - [B] Forms contain entities, which manage the display and interaction of data records in canvas apps.

A) Entities encapsulate forms, which define the data structure and behavior of records within Dataverse - This description reverses the relationship between entities and forms and is inaccurate.

B) Forms contain entities, which manage the display and interaction of data records in canvas apps - This statement accurately reflects the relationship where forms define the presentation layer for entities' data records.

C) Entities and forms are independent components within the Client API object model and do not have direct relationships - This statement is incorrect as forms and entities are closely related in the Power Apps development context.

D) Entities and forms are connected through JavaScript functions, allowing for dynamic manipulation of record data and UI elements - While JavaScript functions can interact with both entities and forms, this statement does not accurately describe their fundamental relationship.

E) Forms inherit properties and methods from entities, enabling seamless integration of UI elements with underlying data structures - This description suggests inheritance, which is not the typical relationship between forms and entities in Power Apps development.

QUESTION 24

Answer - [B] Custom connector.

B) Custom connectors are used to integrate external data sources with the Power Platform, allowing real-time access to inventory levels and enabling users to update quantities directly within the app. They can be reused across multiple forms and support modern client frameworks like React and Fluent UI.

Option A) Power Apps custom control: While custom controls can provide interactive displays, they are not designed for direct data integration like custom connectors.

Option C) Azure Logic Apps: Azure Logic Apps are used for workflow automation and integration, but they do not provide direct data access and user interaction within model-driven apps.

Option D) Power Automate Desktop: Power Automate Desktop is used for desktop automation, which is not suitable for real-time inventory management within a model-driven app.

QUESTION 25

Answer - B

Option A - Incorrect: 'sdkversion' does not specify dependency on PCF library.

Option B - Correct: Specifies the required library for PCF component development.

Option C - Incorrect: 'component' is not a valid tag for defining dependencies.

Option D - Incorrect: 'packages' is not the correct tag for specifying framework dependencies.

Option E - Incorrect: Direct file paths are not used to declare framework dependencies in PCF.

QUESTION 26

Answer - [B] Incremental deployment with version rollback capability.

A) Full deployment of all components at once - Full deployment may cause disruption and is not conducive to seamless updates.

B) Incremental deployment with version rollback capability - Incremental deployment allows for gradual updates with the ability to roll back to previous versions in case of issues, ensuring minimal disruption.

C) Manual deployment using command-line tools - Manual deployment is error-prone and does not provide rollback capabilities inherent in incremental deployments.

D) Parallel deployment across multiple environments simultaneously - While parallel deployment may speed up the process, it does not inherently provide version rollback capability.

E) Random deployment to different regions for load balancing - Random deployment does not ensure version control or rollback capability and may lead to inconsistencies across environments.

QUESTION 27

Answer - [A] Implement retry logic with exponential backoff to automatically retry failed data transfer operations.
Answer - [C] Configure a secondary network connection as a failover option to maintain continuous data transfer.

A) Implementing retry logic with exponential backoff allows the application to automatically retry failed data transfer operations, mitigating the impact of intermittent network connectivity issues. This approach helps ensure the successful completion of the data migration by handling transient network errors effectively.

C) Configuring a secondary network connection as a failover option provides redundancy and continuity in data transfer, minimizing the impact of network connectivity issues on the migration process. By leveraging a backup connection, the application can maintain continuous data transfer even in the event of network disruptions.

Option B) Increase the buffer size: While increasing the buffer size may improve data transfer efficiency, it does not address the root cause of intermittent network connectivity issues and may not be effective in mitigating their impact.

Option D) Modify the data migration tool to compress data packets: While compression may reduce the size of data packets, it may not necessarily improve network reliability or mitigate the impact of network connectivity issues on data migration.

QUESTION 28

Answer - [B] Optimize API calls by batching requests for multiple data operations.

A) Implement asynchronous data processing to reduce latency - While asynchronous processing can be beneficial, batching API requests directly addresses performance optimization for integration.

B) Optimize API calls by batching requests for multiple data operations - Batching requests reduces overhead and improves efficiency, minimizing performance impacts during integration.

C) Utilize server-side caching to store frequently accessed data - Server-side caching can improve performance but may not directly address integration latency.

D) Minimize data payload size by selecting only essential fields for synchronization - While payload size impacts performance, batching requests is a more direct optimization for integration.

E) Implement request throttling to manage API call rates and prevent overload - Request throttling addresses scalability but may not directly optimize integration performance.

QUESTION 29

Answer - [C] The context defines the runtime environment and available resources for plug-in execution.

A) The context determines the order of plug-in execution during record processing - This is controlled by the plug-in registration, not the context.

B) It controls the data access permissions for plug-ins within the system - Security roles control data access, not the context.

C) The context defines the runtime environment and available resources for plug-in execution - Correct, the context provides information about the runtime environment and resources available for plug-in execution.

D) It ensures transactional consistency across multiple plug-in executions within a single transaction - This is the role of transaction support, not the context.

E) The context governs the scheduling and execution frequency of plug-ins based on system load - This is more related to platform behavior rather than the plug-in context.

QUESTION 30

Answer - [B] _customer_name

B) In this scenario, the _customer_name attribute contains the display name of the related customer record. When designing a model-driven app to display related information, you should specify the _customer_name attribute to ensure that the customer's name is shown correctly.

Option A) _customerid_value - Incorrect: This attribute may contain the GUID of the related customer record, not the customer's name.

Option C) _customer_value - Incorrect: This attribute is not typically used to display the name of related records.

Option D) _customerid_name - Incorrect: This attribute combination does not exist and would not represent the customer's name.

QUESTION 31

Answer - [C] Profiling plug-in execution using Azure Monitor.

A) Reviewing system event logs for plug-in execution details - System event logs may not provide granular performance insights needed for troubleshooting.

B) Analyzing network traffic between plug-ins and external systems - Network analysis may be useful but does not directly address plug-in performance within the Power Platform environment.

C) Profiling plug-in execution using Azure Monitor - Correct, Azure Monitor provides performance profiling capabilities for monitoring and diagnosing plug-in execution.

D) Increasing the timeout settings for plug-in execution - Increasing timeouts may alleviate timeout errors but does not address underlying performance bottlenecks.

E) Disabling plug-ins temporarily to observe system performance - Disabling plug-ins disrupts functionality and does not provide real-time performance insights.

QUESTION 32

Answer - [B] Ensuring backward compatibility with existing plug-ins.

A) Overwriting existing assemblies without validation - Overwriting without validation can lead to functionality loss or conflicts with existing plug-ins.

B) Ensuring backward compatibility with existing plug-ins - Correct, maintaining backward compatibility ensures that existing plug-ins continue to function correctly with updated assemblies.

C) Keeping multiple versions of the same assembly for redundancy - While feasible, it may lead to confusion and increased management overhead.

D) Modifying the assembly's namespace for each update - Namespace modification can introduce inconsistencies and affect plug-in functionality.

E) Ignoring versioning to simplify maintenance - Ignoring versioning may lead to compatibility issues and hinder troubleshooting efforts.

QUESTION 33

Answer - B) POST

A) GET - Incorrect. Used for data retrieval only.
B) POST - Correct. Used for executing actions that could change the state.
C) DELETE - Incorrect. Used for removing data.
D) HEAD - Incorrect. Retrieves headers only.
E) OPTIONS - Incorrect. Used to describe communication options.

QUESTION 34

Answer - [D] Redirecting API requests to different endpoints based on user roles.

A) Dynamically adjusting rate limits based on API usage - While possible with policy templates, this scenario typically involves implementing rate limiting policies rather than modifying connector behavior directly.

B) Encrypting data transmitted through the connector - Encryption is a security measure applied at the data level and is not typically managed through connector behavior modification.

C) Changing the authentication method from OAuth to Basic - Authentication methods are typically configured separately from connector behavior modification and may not be managed through policy templates.

D) Redirecting API requests to different endpoints based on user roles - Correct, this scenario involves modifying connector behavior dynamically based on specific conditions, making it suitable for policy template implementation.

E) Logging connector activity for auditing purposes - Logging and auditing are separate concerns and may not directly involve modifying connector behavior using policy templates.

QUESTION 35

Answer - A

Option A - Correct: OAuth 2.0 with Azure AD is the recommended secure method for authentications in Azure services.

Option B - Incorrect: Less secure and not recommended for sensitive data.

Option C - Incorrect: Not advisable for cloud services due to security risks.

Option D - Incorrect: Not commonly used in Power Apps custom connectors.

Option E - Incorrect: No authentication is highly insecure and not recommended.

QUESTION 36

Answer - B) and D)

A) Incorrect. Does not specifically address failures.

B) Correct. Allows checking for specific failure codes, ensuring targeted response to API errors.

C) Incorrect. Delays do not facilitate immediate error notification.

D) Correct. Configures the flow to send alerts specifically when failures occur, essential for timely admin responses in healthcare environments.

E) Incorrect. Termination does not facilitate communication.

QUESTION 37

Answer - [C] Direct access to underlying database tables

A) Real-time data synchronization capabilities - Real-time synchronization is a feature of the Common Data Service (Dataverse), not specific to the Organization service API.

B) Integration with external systems via RESTful APIs - While the Organization service API allows integration with external systems, this capability is not unique to it and can be achieved through various Power Platform components.

C) Direct access to underlying database tables - Correct, the Organization service API provides direct access to Dataverse tables, enabling CRUD operations on data records.

D) Tight integration with Power BI for analytics - Power BI integration is a broader feature of the Power Platform and is not specific to the Organization service API.

E) Support for custom code execution on the server side - Custom code execution can be achieved through plugins or custom workflow activities but is not inherent to the Organization service API itself.

QUESTION 38

Answer - [A] Using optimistic concurrency control with timestamp-based validation

A) Using optimistic concurrency control with timestamp-based validation - Correct, optimistic concurrency control allows multiple users to access data concurrently and resolves conflicts based on timestamp validation.

B) Employing pessimistic concurrency control with exclusive locks - Pessimistic concurrency control may lead to contention and reduced performance due to locking resources.

C) Implementing distributed transactions with two-phase commit - Distributed transactions can be complex to implement and may introduce latency and coordination overhead.

D) Applying row-level locking to prevent conflicts - Row-level locking may lead to contention and reduced concurrency, impacting system performance.

E) Utilizing long-running transactions for comprehensive data processing - Long-running transactions may increase the risk of deadlock and hinder concurrency.

QUESTION 39

Answer - A) and B)

A) Correct. Directly checks for 'Approved' status as required.

B) Correct. Ensures that the field is not null, typically used in conjunction with another condition.

C) Incorrect. This checks for a specific editor, not related to approval status.

D) Incorrect. Checks if the status is empty, opposite of what's needed.

E) Incorrect. Version checking isn't relevant here.

QUESTION 40

Answer - A)

A) Correct - This C# code correctly initializes a managed identity credential for Azure services authentication.

B) Incorrect - TypeScript snippet is correct, but it lacks context on how to use it within Power Platform solutions.

C) Incorrect - PowerShell command is for creating service principals, not configuring managed identities.

D) Incorrect - JSON represents system-assigned identity, but it's not specific to Power Platform scenarios or best practices.

E) Incorrect - JavaScript snippet is for default Azure credentials, not specific to managed identities, and lacks context on usage within Power Platform solutions.

QUESTION 41

Answer - [E] Filtering trigger conditions based on specific record attributes

A) Triggering the flow on any record update without filtering - Triggering on any update may result in unnecessary flow executions and processing overhead.

B) Applying conditional logic directly within the trigger settings - While conditional logic is important, it may be better implemented within flow actions rather than trigger settings.

C) Configuring polling intervals for real-time trigger updates - Polling intervals may introduce delays and are not ideal for real-time trigger updates.

D) Using custom connectors instead of Dataverse triggers for flexibility - Custom connectors may offer flexibility but may not directly replace the functionality provided by Dataverse triggers.

E) Filtering trigger conditions based on specific record attributes - Correct, filtering trigger conditions ensures that the flow is triggered only for relevant record updates, improving efficiency and reducing unnecessary executions.

QUESTION 42

Answer - A) Single sign-on

A) Correct. Enables use of existing company credentials.
B) Incorrect. API key is not used for personal credentials.
C) Incorrect. OAuth 2.0 is typically for external services.
D) Incorrect. Not typically used for internal systems requiring company credentials.
E) Incorrect. Used for machine to machine communication.

QUESTION 43

Answer - [B] Implementing conditional branching to handle different error scenarios

A) Using the "Terminate" action to stop execution immediately upon encountering an error - Terminating the flow immediately may not allow for error handling or recovery actions.

B) Implementing conditional branching to handle different error scenarios - Correct, conditional branching allows workflows to handle errors based on specific conditions, enabling customized error handling and recovery strategies.

C) Enabling verbose logging for detailed error tracking and analysis - While logging is important, it may not directly address the need for error handling within workflows.

D) Automatically restarting failed flows using the "Restart on Error" feature - Automatically restarting flows may not address the underlying cause of errors and could lead to endless loops if not carefully configured.

E) Designing workflows with single-step actions to minimize complexity - While minimizing complexity can be beneficial, it may not provide sufficient flexibility for error handling in complex workflows.

QUESTION 44

Answer - [B] Managing transaction boundaries and data consistency across asynchronous operations

A) Ensuring synchronous communication between plug-ins and external systems - Asynchronous operations do not require synchronous communication; they are designed for improved performance and scalability.

B) Managing transaction boundaries and data consistency across asynchronous operations - Correct, managing transaction boundaries and ensuring data consistency are crucial considerations when implementing asynchronous plug-in operations to maintain data integrity.

C) Minimizing latency by optimizing network communication between plug-ins and databases - While latency optimization is important, it's not specifically related to managing asynchronous operations.

D) Implementing batch processing for grouping and optimizing asynchronous plug-in executions - Batch processing can improve performance but may not address transaction management concerns.

E) Utilizing shared memory for inter-process communication between asynchronous plug-in instances - Shared memory is not typically used for communication between asynchronous plug-in instances.

QUESTION 45

Answer - C) Include only the email property in the request body

A) Incorrect. If-Match: * is used for concurrency control, not for partial updates.
B) Incorrect. UPSERT is used for insert or update operations, but not specifically for partial updates.
C) Correct. Including only the email property in the request body ensures that only this field will be updated.
D) Incorrect. This parameter is irrelevant to updating properties.
E) Incorrect. $select is used in GET requests, not PATCH.

QUESTION 46

Answer - [A, B, C, D, E] Using descriptive names and clear descriptions for events and event handlers, Implementing efficient event filtering to minimize unnecessary event processing, Avoiding circular event dependencies to prevent infinite event loops, Verifying event handler logic and error handling mechanisms before deployment, Versioning event definitions and maintaining backward compatibility for event consumers

A) Using descriptive names and clear descriptions for events and event handlers - Clear naming and descriptions enhance readability and maintainability of event-related components.

B) Implementing efficient event filtering to minimize unnecessary event processing - Efficient filtering improves performance and reduces unnecessary resource consumption during event processing.

C) Avoiding circular event dependencies to prevent infinite event loops - Circular dependencies can lead to system instability and should be avoided.

D) Verifying event handler logic and error handling mechanisms before deployment - Ensuring correctness and robustness of event handler logic is crucial for reliable event processing.

E) Versioning event definitions and maintaining backward compatibility for event consumers -

Versioning enables seamless updates and ensures compatibility with existing event consumers.

QUESTION 47

Answer - [A, B, C, D, E] Minimizing the use of polling mechanisms to reduce unnecessary requests, Utilizing Azure Event Hubs for high-throughput event ingestion and processing, Implementing caching mechanisms to store frequently accessed event data, Scaling event listeners dynamically based on workload demand, Optimizing network latency by colocating event listeners with data sources

A) Minimizing the use of polling mechanisms to reduce unnecessary requests - Polling mechanisms introduce unnecessary overhead and latency compared to event-driven approaches.

B) Utilizing Azure Event Hubs for high-throughput event ingestion and processing - Event Hubs provide a scalable and efficient platform for processing high volumes of events.

C) Implementing caching mechanisms to store frequently accessed event data - Caching frequently accessed event data can reduce latency and improve responsiveness.

D) Scaling event listeners dynamically based on workload demand - Dynamic scaling ensures that event listeners can handle varying workload demands effectively.

E) Optimizing network latency by colocating event listeners with data sources - Colocating event listeners with data sources reduces network latency and improves overall performance.

QUESTION 48

Answer - B) createTimer() method

A) Incorrect. setInterval() is a JavaScript function for setting repeated intervals, not applicable in this scenario.
B) Correct. createTimer() method is appropriate for setting up scheduled follow-ups in Azure Durable Functions.
C) Incorrect. Task.Delay() is used for simple delays.
D) Incorrect. setTimeout() sets a one-time delay.
E) Incorrect. createInterval() method does not exist.

QUESTION 49

Answer - [A, B, C] Minimizes data redundancy and inconsistency by updating existing records and inserting new records as needed, Improves data accuracy and integrity by enforcing business rules during upsert operations, Enhances performance and efficiency by minimizing API calls required for synchronization.

A) Minimizes data redundancy and inconsistency by updating existing records and inserting new records as needed. - UpsertRequest helps maintain data integrity by ensuring that existing records are updated and new records are inserted as necessary, reducing redundancy and inconsistency.

B) Improves data accuracy and integrity by enforcing business rules during upsert operations. - Business rules can be enforced during upsert operations to ensure that data meets quality standards and adheres to organizational policies.

C) Enhances performance and efficiency by minimizing API calls required for synchronization. - By combining insert and update operations into a single call, UpsertRequest reduces the number of API calls needed for synchronization, improving performance and efficiency.

D) Facilitates conflict resolution by automatically resolving data conflicts during upsert operations. - UpsertRequest does not automatically resolve conflicts; it relies on predefined rules or manual intervention for conflict resolution.

E) Streamlines data synchronization processes by supporting batch operations for large data sets. - While UpsertRequest can handle batch operations, its primary benefits lie in maintaining data integrity and efficiency rather than solely supporting batch processing.

QUESTION 50

Answer - [A, B, D, E] Implementing redundant data pipelines with failover mechanisms to switch to backup pipelines in case of failure, Deploying multiple instances of integration components across geographically distributed regions, Implementing automated monitoring and alerting systems to detect and respond to integration failures promptly, Configuring backup and disaster recovery mechanisms to restore data in case of system failures.

A) Implementing redundant data pipelines with failover mechanisms to switch to backup pipelines in case of failure. - Redundant pipelines with failover mechanisms ensure continuous data flow even in the event of pipeline failures, improving high availability and fault tolerance.

B) Deploying multiple instances of integration components across geographically distributed regions. - Deploying components across multiple regions reduces the risk of single-point failures and improves fault tolerance by ensuring redundancy and resilience.

C) Utilizing load balancing to evenly distribute data processing tasks across multiple servers or instances. - While load balancing improves performance, it may not directly address high availability and fault tolerance concerns related to integration failures.

D) Implementing automated monitoring and alerting systems to detect and respond to integration failures promptly. - Automated monitoring and alerting systems help identify and address integration failures quickly, minimizing downtime and improving fault tolerance.

E) Configuring backup and disaster recovery mechanisms to restore data in case of system failures. - Backup and disaster recovery mechanisms ensure data resilience and facilitate rapid recovery in the event of system failures, enhancing high availability and fault tolerance.

PRACTICE TEST 8 - QUESTIONS ONLY

QUESTION 1

An organization is extending its Power Platform solution to external partners for collaborative project management. They need to manage access for external users securely while maintaining control over data and resources. Which approach should be followed to manage access for external users effectively?

A) Guest access in Azure Active Directory (AAD)
B) Sharing links with expiration dates
C) Assigning user licenses
D) Creating separate environments for external users
E) Using service principals

QUESTION 2

An e-commerce company is concerned about the performance implications of choosing between Logic Apps and Power Automate for their order processing system. They need to evaluate the performance implications of each tool to make an informed decision. Which statement accurately reflects the performance implications of Logic Apps and Power Automate?

A) Logic Apps offer higher performance due to their serverless architecture, while Power Automate may experience latency issues for complex workflows.

B) Power Automate provides better performance for real-time event processing, while Logic Apps are more efficient for batch processing.

C) Logic Apps and Power Automate have similar performance characteristics, with slight variations depending on the complexity of the workflow.

D) Power Automate is more scalable than Logic Apps, making it a better choice for handling large volumes of data.

E) Logic Apps have lower operational costs compared to Power Automate, but Power Automate offers better performance optimization features.

QUESTION 3

A financial department requires a quarterly financial summary on the first day of each quarter at 6:00 AM using Azure Functions connected to Microsoft Dataverse. Which cron expression fits this requirement?

A) 0 6 1 1,4,7,10 *
B) 0 0 6 1 1,4,7,10
C) 0 6 * * 1,4,7,10
D) 0 6 1 JAN,APR,JUL,OCT *
E) 0 0 6 * 1,4,7,10

QUESTION 4

A technology startup is developing custom connectors for specific integration needs as part of their Power Platform solution. They need to ensure that the custom connectors are secure, reliable, and compliant with industry standards for data exchange.
Which considerations should they prioritize when designing custom connectors for their Power Platform solution? Select THREE.

A) Implement OAuth authentication to securely authenticate users and authorize access to external resources.
B) Ensure compliance with OpenAPI specifications to standardize the interface and improve interoperability with other systems.
C) Use proprietary protocols for data exchange to maximize performance and minimize overhead.
D) Embed API keys directly into the connector code to simplify authentication and access control.
E) Design connectors to handle transient faults gracefully and implement retry policies for robustness.

QUESTION 5

You need to write a TypeScript function to update a specific record in Dataverse using the Web API. Identify the correct code to perform an upsert operation.

A) const updateRecord = async (id: string, data: any) => { await fetch('https://org.api.crm.dynamics.com/api/data/v9.0/accounts/' + id, { method: 'PATCH', body: JSON.stringify(data), headers: { 'Content-Type': 'application/json' } }); }

B) function updateRecord(id: string, data: any) { fetch('https://org.api.crm.dynamics.com/api/data/v9.0/accounts/' + id, { method: 'PUT', body: JSON.stringify(data), headers: { 'Accept': 'application/json', 'Content-Type': 'application/json' } }); }

C) async function updateRecord(id: string, data: any) { const response = await fetch('https://org.api.crm.dynamics.com/api/data/v9.0/accounts/' + id, { method: 'PUT', body: JSON.stringify(data), headers: { 'Content-Type': 'application/json', 'Prefer': 'return=representation' } }); return await response.json(); }

D) async function updateRecord(id: string, data: any) { const response = await fetch('https://org.api.crm.dynamics.com/api/data/v9.0/accounts/' + id, { method: 'POST', body: JSON.stringify(data), headers: { 'Content-Type': 'application/json', 'Prefer': 'return=representation' } }); return await response.json(); }

E) async function updateRecord(id: string, data: any) { const response = await fetch('https://org.api.crm.dynamics.com/api/data/v9.0/accounts/' + id, { method: 'PATCH', body: JSON.stringify(data), headers: { 'Content-Type': 'application/json', 'Prefer': 'return=representation' } }); return await response.json(); }

QUESTION 6

A canvas app needs to list only those products in Microsoft Dataverse that have stock levels below a certain threshold. Which PowerFx expression should be used for the Items property of a list control?

A) Filter('Products', StockLevel < 5)
B) 'Products'

C) Collect('LowStockProducts', Filter(Products, StockLevel < 5))
D) Lookup('Products', StockLevel < 5)
E) Filter('Products', 'StockLevel' < 5)

QUESTION 7

A software development company is implementing column-level security in Dataverse to restrict access to proprietary algorithms and code snippets stored in their database. They need to understand the performance implications of column-level security to optimize their system's efficiency.
What are the potential performance implications of implementing column-level security in Dataverse? Select THREE.

A) Increased latency and response times due to additional security checks and access validation for each data query.

B) Higher resource utilization and storage overhead resulting from the maintenance of access control lists (ACLs) for individual columns.

C) Reduced throughput and data processing speed due to the enforcement of fine-grained access controls for each data access operation.

D) Enhanced scalability and performance optimization through caching mechanisms and query optimizations in the underlying database engine.

E) Improved data integrity and reliability through redundant backups and failover mechanisms in the event of security breaches or data corruption.

QUESTION 8

A security team is responsible for managing team security within Microsoft Dataverse to ensure data protection and compliance with regulatory requirements. They need to establish best practices for managing team security effectively.
What are considered best practices for managing team security in Microsoft Dataverse? Select THREE.

A) Implement role-based access control (RBAC) to assign granular permissions and privileges to team members based on their roles and responsibilities within the organization.

B) Regularly review and update team memberships and permissions to reflect changes in organizational structure, personnel, or access requirements.

C) Utilize team-based security roles and privileges to control access to sensitive data and resources, ensuring that team members have appropriate permissions for their tasks.

D) Enable multi-factor authentication (MFA) and single sign-on (SSO) for team members to enhance user authentication and identity management, reducing the risk of unauthorized access.

E) Monitor team activities and access patterns using audit logs and reporting tools to detect and mitigate security threats or policy violations proactively.

QUESTION 9

You are configuring security roles in Microsoft Dataverse to restrict access to sensitive data. However, users with the assigned security role report that they can still access the restricted data. What could be potential reasons for this issue? Select the correct answers that apply.

A) The security role is not properly assigned to the affected users.
B) The entity permissions are incorrectly set for the restricted data.
C) There is a misconfiguration in the field-level security settings.
D) The users belong to multiple security roles, with conflicting permissions.
E) The security role cache needs to be refreshed for the changes to take effect.

QUESTION 10

Your team needs to extend the user experience in a custom app by adding a REST API integration that retrieves detailed weather information. Write the JavaScript code to send a GET request to the API endpoint and handle the response asynchronously.

A) fetch('https://api.weatherapi.com/v1/current.json?key=YOUR_KEY&q=Location').then(response => response.json()).then(data => console.log(data));

B) XMLHttpRequest('GET', 'https://api.weatherapi.com/v1/current.json?key=YOUR_KEY&q=Location', true).send();

C) axios.get('https://api.weatherapi.com/v1/current.json?key=YOUR_KEY&q=Location').then(function(response) { console.log(response.data); });

D) new HTTPRequest('GET', 'https://api.weatherapi.com/v1/current.json?key=YOUR_KEY&q=Location').send().onload = (resp) => console.log(resp);

E) fetch('https://api.weatherapi.com/v1/current.json?key=YOUR_KEY&q=Location', { method: 'GET' }).then(res => res.text()).then(data -> console.log(data));

QUESTION 11

A healthcare organization is implementing a patient management system using Power Apps and Dataverse. They want to ensure efficient data validation and enforce certain restrictions on patient records. Which best practice should be followed for implementing business rules in this scenario?

A) Use complex JavaScript code for advanced rule logic
B) Apply business rules to a limited number of fields to avoid performance issues
C) Utilize server-side execution for better reliability and performance
D) Implement business rules within each individual form instead of globally
E) Avoid using business rules for data validation to prevent user experience degradation

QUESTION 12

You are tasked with developing a model-driven Power Apps app for a financial institution's loan processing system. The app requires dynamic adjustments to user interface elements based on loan application statuses and employee roles. How can you leverage business rules to meet these requirements effectively? Select the correct answers that apply.

A) Clear column values for approved loan applications.
B) Enable and disable columns for different user roles.
C) Show and hide tabs based on loan types.
D) Show and hide sections based on application statuses.

QUESTION 13

An organization is committed to following best practices for dependency resolution within Microsoft Power Platform to ensure optimal performance and reliability. What are the recommended best practices for resolving dependencies effectively? Select the correct answers that apply.

A) Prioritize resolving direct dependencies before transitive dependencies
B) Regularly review and update dependency configurations
C) Implement automated dependency resolution workflows
D) Establish a centralized repository for shared dependencies
E) Perform impact analysis before making dependency changes

QUESTION 14

Designing user interfaces for model-driven apps requires adherence to best practices to ensure a seamless and intuitive user experience. What are some recommended best practices for user interface design in model-driven apps? Select the correct answers that apply.

A) Limit the number of fields on a single form to improve readability
B) Utilize tabbed layouts to organize related fields and reduce clutter
C) Apply consistent styling and branding across all forms for visual coherence
D) Implement responsive design principles to ensure compatibility with various devices
E) Use dynamic layouts to adjust form elements based on user roles and permissions

QUESTION 15

You are designing a model-driven app for a nonprofit organization's donor management system. The app aims to streamline donor interactions and enhance fundraising efforts. What are two functionalities that you can achieve by using a business rule in this scenario? Select the correct answers that apply.

A) Access external data.
B) Enable or disable a column based on donor contribution level.
C) Show or hide a column based on user role.
D) Run the rule on demand.

QUESTION 16

A financial services company is developing a canvas app to access customer data from various sources, including Microsoft Dataverse and external APIs. What considerations should they keep in mind when integrating these data sources? Select the correct answers that apply.

A) Ensure secure authentication and authorization mechanisms for accessing data

B) Optimize data retrieval and processing to minimize latency and improve performance
C) Handle data synchronization and conflict resolution in scenarios involving multiple sources
D) Implement caching strategies to reduce the number of requests made to external APIs
E) Utilize API versioning and error handling mechanisms to maintain compatibility and reliability

QUESTION 17

A consulting firm is building a suite of custom components to be shared across multiple client projects. What strategies can they employ to ensure efficient sharing of components across different Power Apps instances? Select the correct answers that apply.

A) Leveraging solutions packaging to bundle and distribute components along with associated metadata
B) Implementing role-based access control to manage permissions for accessing and modifying shared components
C) Establishing a centralized component repository with versioning support for easy access and updates
D) Utilizing import/export capabilities to transfer components between development and production environments
E) Integrating automated deployment pipelines to streamline the deployment process for shared components

QUESTION 18

You are tasked with developing a model-driven app for an asset management system. The app requires executing custom code when a user selects a button on the ribbon, but this functionality should only be available to users with asset manager roles. What option should you select to meet this requirement?

A) Custom API
B) Custom process action
C) Classic workflow
D) Business rule

QUESTION 19

A company is integrating a third-party API into their Power Apps solution to access sensitive customer data. What security consideration should be prioritized during the API integration process? Select the correct answers that apply.

A) Use API keys for authentication to simplify the integration process
B) Encrypt all data transmitted between Power Apps and the API endpoints
C) Store API credentials directly in the app configuration for convenience
D) Implement OAuth 2.0 for secure authorization and token management
E) Disable all security measures to optimize performance

QUESTION 20

How can you use JavaScript to dynamically update the visibility of a button in a model-driven app based on a field value?

A) formContext.getControl("new_button").setVisible(formContext.getAttribute("status").getValue() ===

"active")

B) document.getElementById("new_button").style.display = formContext.data.entity.attributes.get("status").value === "active" ? "block" : "none"

C) Xrm.Page.ui.controls.get("new_button").setVisible(Xrm.Page.getAttribute("status").getValue() === "active")

D) formContext.ui.controls.get("new_button").setVisible(formContext.getAttribute("status").getValue() === "active")

E) $("#new_button").css('display', formContext.getAttribute("status").getValue() === "active" ? 'block' : 'none')

QUESTION 21

Your organization is implementing a customer relationship management (CRM) solution using Microsoft Dataverse. You need to integrate an external customer support system, which exposes a SOAP API, to provide seamless access to customer data within the CRM solution. Considering the integration requirements, which three options should you utilize to ensure a robust integration solution? Select the correct answers that apply.

A) Azure function
B) Custom connector
C) Custom API
D) HTTP request
E) Business rule

QUESTION 22

A Power Apps developer is troubleshooting an issue with event handling in a canvas app. Which of the following represents a recommended approach for troubleshooting event handling issues in Power Apps?

A) Reviewing the browser console for JavaScript errors
B) Enabling verbose logging in the canvas app settings
C) Inspecting network requests in the browser developer tools
D) Using the Power Apps formula bar to debug event handling logic
E) Analyzing user session data in Azure Monitor

QUESTION 23

A Power Apps developer is learning how to navigate the object model while developing canvas apps. Which of the following methods represents a valid approach to accessing attributes of an entity using the Client API object model?

A) Utilize the fetchXML query language to retrieve entity attributes dynamically.
B) Access entity attributes directly through JavaScript functions using dot notation.
C) Query entity metadata through RESTful Web API endpoints for attribute details.
D) Use SQL queries to retrieve entity attribute values from the underlying database.
E) Invoke client-side plugins to fetch entity attributes asynchronously for improved performance.

QUESTION 24

Your organization is developing a model-driven app for tracking project milestones. You need to create a custom control that visualizes project timelines and allows users to update milestone statuses directly from the control. The control should be reusable across multiple forms and support modern client frameworks like React and Fluent UI. Considering the requirements, which development option should you choose?

A) Power Apps custom control
B) Power Automate
C) Azure Functions
D) Power Virtual Agents

QUESTION 25

In setting up a PCF component, what is the best practice for manifest configuration to ensure proper handling of user context and resource access?

A) <resources><code path="index.ts" order="1"/><css path="styles.css" order="2"/></resources>
B) <accessibility><resource name="accessible" /></accessibility>
C) <namespace name="MyNamespace" />
D) <feature-usage><uses-feature name="UserContext" required="true" /></feature-usage>
E) <capabilities><capability name="contextualdata" /></capabilities>

QUESTION 26

How are PCF components consumed within Power Apps applications?

A) By directly embedding JavaScript code within app formulas.
B) Through the importation of compiled binary files.
C) Via custom controls added to app screens in the Power Apps Studio.
D) By executing SQL queries against component metadata tables.
E) Through RESTful API calls to the component endpoints.

QUESTION 27

Your organization is migrating data from a third-party cloud storage provider to Dataverse tables using an Azure Logic Apps integration. The integration process involves extracting data from the cloud storage provider's APIs and loading it into Dataverse tables. However, you encounter errors related to rate limiting imposed by the cloud storage provider's APIs, which restrict the number of requests per minute. What are two potential strategies to address the rate limiting errors and ensure the successful completion of the data migration? Select the correct answers that apply.

A) Implement throttling logic to dynamically adjust the request rate based on the rate limit imposed by the cloud storage provider's APIs.

B) Utilize Azure Functions to parallelize data extraction and loading operations, distributing the workload across multiple instances to stay within the rate limits.

C) Increase the Azure Logic Apps concurrency control settings to allow more concurrent requests, effectively bypassing the rate limits imposed by the cloud storage provider's APIs.

D) Modify the integration workflow to use a scheduled batch processing approach, spreading the data migration workload over longer time periods to avoid exceeding the rate limits.

QUESTION 28

A development team is experiencing issues with the integration of a PCF component with an external system, resulting in inconsistent data synchronization. What troubleshooting step should the team prioritize to identify and resolve integration issues effectively?

A) Review API request logs to identify failed or erroneous requests.
B) Implement additional error handling within the PCF component code.
C) Analyze network traffic to identify potential connectivity issues.
D) Monitor system resource utilization to identify performance bottlenecks.
E) Verify data mapping and transformation logic between systems for accuracy.

QUESTION 29

A Power Platform developer needs to access entity data within a plug-in for processing in their solution. Which method is commonly used to access entity data through the plug-in execution context?

A) Querying the database directly using SQL commands
B) Retrieving the target entity using early-bound classes
C) Accessing the organization service to retrieve entity records
D) Parsing JSON payloads received in HTTP requests
E) Invoking external RESTful APIs to fetch entity data

QUESTION 30

You are developing an integration between Microsoft Dataverse and an external system. The integration requires retrieving related records from a custom entity named "Tasks." When querying Tasks, you need to include the details of the associated "Contacts" records. Which attribute should you use to access the contact's details in your integration code? Select the correct answers that apply.

A) _contactid
B) _contact_value
C) _contactid_value
D) _contact_name

QUESTION 31

A team of Power Platform developers is discussing tools for performance profiling of plug-ins. Which tool is commonly used for profiling plug-in performance?

A) Visual Studio Debugger
B) Azure DevOps Pipelines
C) Power Platform Admin Center
D) Azure Application Insights
E) SQL Server Management Studio

QUESTION 32

A Power Platform developer is troubleshooting registration issues with custom assemblies. What is a recommended approach in this situation?

A) Manually editing the Dataverse solution XML file.
B) Restarting the Plug-in Registration service.
C) Deleting all existing plug-ins and re-registering them.
D) Reviewing the Plug-in Registration Tool logs for errors.
E) Disabling assembly verification for faster registration.

QUESTION 33

To implement a JavaScript Web API that submits user inputs from a custom form to initiate a process automation, which HTTP method is appropriate?

A) POST
B) GET
C) PUT
D) PATCH
E) TRACE

QUESTION 34

A Power Platform developer is tasked with implementing a policy template to enforce data validation rules for incoming requests through a connector. What is a crucial step in implementing policies at runtime using policy templates?

A) Manually updating the connector configuration in the Power Platform Admin Center.
B) Defining policy expressions based on specific conditions.
C) Creating separate connector instances for each policy.
D) Disabling connector caching to ensure policy changes take effect immediately.
E) Testing policy changes in a production environment without validation.

QUESTION 35

When integrating an Azure service via a custom connector in Power Apps, what is a common issue and its solution?

A) API rate limits exceeded, resolved by implementing a retry policy in the connector.
B) Data type mismatches, resolved by using explicit casts in the API.
C) Authentication errors, resolved by updating the Azure AD app registrations.
D) Timeout errors, resolved by increasing the timeout settings in Power Apps.
E) Cross-origin resource sharing (CORS) issues, resolved by modifying Azure API settings.

QUESTION 36

A retail company uses a Power Automate cloud flow to process customer orders through an external inventory API. How should the flow be configured to handle cases where the API does not respond? Select the correct answers that apply.

A) Implement a timeout and retry policy
B) Add a notification for successful API calls
C) Set actions to skip on failure
D) Use a "Configure run after" for error notifications
E) Increase the timeout duration for the API call

QUESTION 37

In the context of transaction handling with the Organization service API, what is a best practice for ensuring data consistency and integrity?

A) Using bulk delete operations for efficiency
B) Committing changes individually to reduce transaction scope
C) Implementing distributed transactions across multiple services
D) Rolling back transactions on error occurrence
E) Delaying transaction commits for performance optimization

QUESTION 38

When implementing batch operations in a Power Platform solution, what is a key consideration for ensuring efficient processing and resource utilization?

A) Minimizing batch sizes to reduce memory consumption
B) Using synchronous processing for immediate feedback
C) Performing batch operations within a single transaction
D) Leveraging parallel processing to maximize throughput
E) Applying exponential backoff for retrying failed batch requests

QUESTION 39

A Power Automate flow should trigger only if a SharePoint document's 'ReviewDate' is set to today's date or is overdue. What expressions would correctly configure this condition? Select the correct answers that apply.

A) @equals(triggerBody()?['ReviewDate'], utcNow())
B) @less(triggerBody()?['ReviewDate'], utcNow())
C) @greater(triggerBody()?['ReviewDate'], utcNow())
D) @not(empty(triggerBody()?['ReviewDate']))
E) @or(equals(triggerBody()?['ReviewDate'], utcNow()), less(triggerBody()?['ReviewDate'], utcNow()))

QUESTION 40

A software development company is building a Power Platform solution that integrates with various external APIs. They are exploring the use of managed identities for Azure services to streamline authentication processes. The team needs to understand the troubleshooting steps for authentication issues that may arise during the integration phase.

A) C#: var azureServiceTokenProvider = new AzureServiceTokenProvider();
B) PowerShell: Connect-AzureAD -ManagedIdentity

C) JavaScript: const msiTokenProvider = new ManagedIdentityCredential();
D) TypeScript: const credential = new DefaultAzureCredential();
E) SQL: CREATE USER [Identity] FROM EXTERNAL PROVIDER;

QUESTION 41

When configuring connector actions to interact with Dataverse data, what security consideration should developers prioritize?

A) Restricting access based on user roles and permissions
B) Enabling anonymous access for public data retrieval
C) Utilizing static API keys for authentication
D) Disabling encryption for faster data transfer
E) Allowing open access without authentication for seamless integration

QUESTION 42

You are developing a custom connector for Power Platform to fetch data from a third-party weather API. The API requires a client certificate for all requests. What type of authentication should be implemented?

A) API key
B) OAuth 2.0
C) Certificate based
D) Password based
E) Single sign-on

QUESTION 43

A financial institution is deploying a Power Platform solution for loan application processing. They need to ensure that their workflows comply with regulatory requirements and can recover from transient errors, such as network timeouts or service outages. What is a best practice for designing resilient flows in this scenario?

A) Using a single monolithic flow for all processing steps to simplify management
B) Implementing periodic manual backups of flow configurations to restore in case of errors
C) Splitting complex workflows into smaller, modular flows for better error isolation
D) Allowing unrestricted access to sensitive data within flows for faster processing
E) Using static error handling routines without retries or compensatory actions

QUESTION 44

A technology company is developing a Power Platform solution for secure document management. They need to ensure security best practices are followed when creating Dataverse plug-ins to handle sensitive document data. What is a security best practice in plug-in creation for this scenario?

A) Storing sensitive data directly within plug-in code for improved performance
B) Assigning least privileged security roles and permissions to plug-in assemblies
C) Embedding API keys and credentials within plug-in configurations for easy access

D) Allowing anonymous access to plug-in endpoints to facilitate external integration
E) Disabling encryption and data protection features to optimize plug-in performance

QUESTION 45

You want to delete a record in Microsoft Dataverse using the Web API. What HTTP method should you use to ensure the request is processed correctly?

A) DELETE
B) POST
C) GET
D) PATCH
E) PUT

QUESTION 46

A financial institution is developing a Power Platform solution to analyze customer transaction data and detect fraudulent activities. They are concerned about the potential performance impacts of event publishing using the Plug-in Registration Tool. What are some performance impacts to consider when using the Plug-in Registration Tool for event publishing? Select the correct answers that apply.

A) Increased latency and response times during event processing
B) Higher resource utilization and potential scalability issues
C) Impact on overall system throughput and transaction processing rates
D) Potential bottlenecks in event handling and processing pipelines
E) Compatibility issues with legacy systems and custom integrations

QUESTION 47

A financial institution is developing a Power Platform solution to monitor stock market fluctuations and execute trades based on predefined criteria. They are exploring tools and services that can assist in event listening and processing for their scenario. Which options align with their requirements? Select the correct answers that apply.

A) Azure Logic Apps for orchestrating event-driven workflows
B) Azure Functions with Service Bus triggers for processing high-throughput events
C) Power Automate for integrating Dataverse events with external systems
D) Azure Event Grid for routing and filtering Dataverse events to various endpoints
E) Custom-built event listeners using WebSocket protocols for real-time data streaming

QUESTION 48

A municipality uses Power Apps to schedule inspections. To manage periodic re-inspections, which Azure Durable Function method should be used to set up these recurring tasks in an orchestrator function?

A) createTimer() method
B) Task.Delay() method
C) setInterval() function
D) scheduleReinspection() method

E) setTimeout() function

QUESTION 49

A technology company is preparing data for upsert operations in Microsoft Dataverse to synchronize customer information from various sources. What steps should they take to prepare data for upsert operations effectively? Select the correct answers that apply.

A) Identify unique identifiers to determine whether records should be inserted or updated.
B) Cleanse and standardize data to ensure consistency and accuracy across systems.
C) Validate data against predefined business rules to prevent errors during upsert operations.
D) Map fields between source and target systems to facilitate data transformation during synchronization.
E) Optimize data structures and indexes in Dataverse to improve upsert performance.

QUESTION 50

A software development company is tasked with monitoring the health and performance of integrations between its project management system and Microsoft Dataverse. Which tool or technique would best support monitoring integration health in this scenario? Select the correct answers that apply.

A) Leveraging Azure Monitor to track performance metrics and detect issues in real-time.
B) Implementing custom logging and telemetry to capture integration activity and errors.
C) Using Microsoft Dataverse audit logs to monitor data changes and access patterns.
D) Employing synthetic transactions to simulate integration workflows and identify bottlenecks.
E) Configuring anomaly detection algorithms to automatically detect abnormal integration behavior.

PRACTICE TEST 8 - ANSWERS ONLY

QUESTION 1

Answer - [A) Guest access in Azure Active Directory (AAD)]

A) Guest access in Azure Active Directory (AAD) - AAD guest access allows external users to access resources securely with controlled permissions.

B) Sharing links with expiration dates - Sharing links may not provide sufficient control over access and permissions for external users.

C) Assigning user licenses - Assigning user licenses is important but does not directly address managing access for external users.

D) Creating separate environments for external users - Creating separate environments may be complex and may not be necessary for managing access.

E) Using service principals - Service principals are typically used for automation tasks and may not be suitable for managing access for external users.

QUESTION 2

Answer - [C) Logic Apps and Power Automate have similar performance characteristics, with slight variations depending on the complexity of the workflow]

A) Logic Apps offer higher performance due to their serverless architecture, while Power Automate may experience latency issues for complex workflows - While Logic Apps have a serverless architecture, the performance difference between Logic Apps and Power Automate depends on various factors and may not always favor Logic Apps.

B) Power Automate provides better performance for real-time event processing, while Logic Apps are more efficient for batch processing - The performance characteristics of Logic Apps and Power Automate can vary depending on the specific use case, and there is no blanket statement regarding their performance for real-time event processing versus batch processing.

C) Logic Apps and Power Automate have similar performance characteristics, with slight variations depending on the complexity of the workflow - Both Logic Apps and Power Automate can offer similar performance levels, with differences based on factors such as workflow complexity, resource allocation, and optimization.

D) Power Automate is more scalable than Logic Apps, making it a better choice for handling large volumes of data - While Power Automate may have certain scalability advantages, Logic Apps also offer scalability features and can handle large volumes of data effectively.

E) Logic Apps have lower operational costs compared to Power Automate, but Power Automate offers better performance optimization features - Performance optimization features may vary between Logic Apps and Power Automate, but their operational costs and performance are influenced by multiple factors beyond optimization features alone.

QUESTION 3

Answer - A) 0 6 1 1,4,7,10

A) Correct. This cron triggers at 6:00 AM on the first day of January, April, July, and October.
B) Incorrect. The hour and minute fields are reversed.
C) Incorrect. This pattern is not valid for specifying specific months.
D) Incorrect. Azure cron does not recognize month names.
E) Incorrect. The pattern incorrectly sets the hour and uses an invalid format for specifying months.

QUESTION 4

Answer - A, B, and E) Implement OAuth authentication to securely authenticate users and authorize access to external resources. Ensure compliance with OpenAPI specifications to standardize the interface and improve interoperability with other systems. Design connectors to handle transient faults gracefully and implement retry policies for robustness.

A) - Correct. Implementing OAuth authentication helps securely authenticate users and authorize access to external resources, enhancing the security of custom connectors.

B) - Correct. Ensuring compliance with OpenAPI specifications standardizes the interface of custom connectors and improves interoperability with other systems, promoting seamless integration.

C) - Incorrect. Using proprietary protocols for data exchange may limit compatibility and interoperability with other systems, contrary to the goal of integration.

D) - Incorrect. Embedding API keys directly into the connector code poses security risks and compromises access control, making the connectors vulnerable to unauthorized access.

E) - Correct. Designing connectors to handle transient faults gracefully and implementing retry policies improves their robustness and reliability, ensuring consistent performance even in challenging network conditions.

QUESTION 5

Answer - E

Option A - Incorrect. PATCH is correct but lacks Prefer header to get updated entity back.

Option B - Incorrect. PUT method might replace the entire entity which is not typically desirable.

Option C - Incorrect. PUT method is used; should be PATCH for partial updates.

Option D - Incorrect. POST is not correct for updates, it's used for creation.

Option E - Correct. Uses PATCH method with Prefer header for optimal handling of partial updates and retrieving updated data.

QUESTION 6

Answer - A) Filter('Products', StockLevel < 5)

A) Correct. Appropriately filters products with stock levels below 5.
B) Incorrect. This expression includes all products.

C) Incorrect. Collect is not needed for this operation and is used incorrectly.

D) Incorrect. Lookup is for finding single records, not for filtering.

E) Incorrect. Misuses quotes around 'StockLevel', indicating it is not used as a field.

QUESTION 7

Answer - A, B, and C) Increased latency and response times due to additional security checks and access validation for each data query. Higher resource utilization and storage overhead resulting from the maintenance of access control lists (ACLs) for individual columns. Reduced throughput and data processing speed due to the enforcement of fine-grained access controls for each data access operation.

A) - Correct. Implementing column-level security may result in increased latency and response times as additional security checks and access validation processes are performed for each data query, affecting system performance.

B) - Correct. Maintaining access control lists (ACLs) for individual columns incurs higher resource utilization and storage overhead, as additional metadata is required to manage column-level security settings, impacting system performance.

C) - Correct. Enforcing fine-grained access controls at the column level may lead to reduced throughput and data processing speed, especially in scenarios with complex security configurations, affecting overall system performance.

D) - Incorrect. While caching mechanisms and query optimizations can enhance performance, they are not directly related to the implementation of column-level security in Dataverse.

E) - Incorrect. Data integrity and reliability measures such as backups and failover mechanisms are important for system resilience but are not directly impacted by the implementation of column-level security.

QUESTION 8

Answer - A, B, and C) Implement role-based access control (RBAC) to assign granular permissions and privileges to team members based on their roles and responsibilities within the organization. Regularly review and update team memberships and permissions to reflect changes in organizational structure, personnel, or access requirements. Utilize team-based security roles and privileges to control access to sensitive data and resources.

A) - Correct. Implementing RBAC allows for granular control over permissions, ensuring that team members have appropriate access based on their roles and responsibilities.

B) - Correct. Regularly reviewing and updating team memberships and permissions helps maintain data security and compliance by reflecting changes in organizational structure or access requirements.

C) - Correct. Utilizing team-based security roles and privileges enables controlled access to sensitive data and resources, reducing the risk of unauthorized access or data breaches within Microsoft Dataverse.

D) - Incorrect. While MFA and SSO are important security measures, they are not specifically related to managing team security within Microsoft Dataverse but rather focus on user authentication and identity management.

E) - Incorrect. While monitoring team activities is essential for security, it is not specifically a best practice for managing team security within Microsoft Dataverse, which focuses more on access control and permissions management.

QUESTION 9

Answer - [B], [C], and [D].

A) Incorrect assignment would result in no access, not partial access.

E) Security role cache refresh is unlikely to selectively affect data access.

B) Incorrect entity permissions would allow unauthorized access.

C) Misconfigured field-level security would bypass data restrictions.

D) Conflicting permissions from multiple roles could lead to unexpected access.

QUESTION 10

Answer - A

Option A - Correct: Proper use of the fetch API to make an asynchronous GET request and handle JSON data.

Option B - Incorrect: Incorrect usage and syntax of XMLHttpRequest.

Option C - Correct: Proper use of axios for making an asynchronous GET request.

Option D - Incorrect: HTTPRequest is not a standard API.

Option E - Incorrect: Improper handling of the response, should parse JSON not text for detailed data.

QUESTION 11

Answer - [B] Apply business rules to a limited number of fields to avoid performance issues

Option B is correct as applying business rules to a limited number of fields helps avoid performance degradation, especially in scenarios with a large number of records or complex rule logic.

Option A is incorrect as complex JavaScript code is not necessary for implementing business rules, which can be configured using a point-and-click interface.

Option C is incorrect as business rules in Microsoft Dataverse execute client-side and do not involve server-side execution.

Option D is incorrect as implementing business rules globally ensures consistency across all forms and reduces maintenance efforts.

Option E is incorrect as business rules are commonly used for data validation within Power Apps to enhance user experience.

QUESTION 12

Answer - [B] Enable and disable columns for different user roles.

A) Business rules cannot directly clear column values based on specific application statuses, which might require more complex logic or integration with other components.

C) Business rules cannot directly control tab visibility based on loan types, which might require additional customization or use of other features.

D) Business rules cannot directly control section visibility based on dynamic application statuses, which might require more advanced logic or use of other features.

B) Business rules can enable or disable columns dynamically based on user roles, providing a secure and efficient data entry experience tailored to different users' responsibilities.

QUESTION 13

Answer - [A, B, D, E] Prioritize resolving direct dependencies before transitive dependencies, Regularly review and update dependency configurations, Establish a centralized repository for shared dependencies, Perform impact analysis before making dependency changes

Options A, B, D, and E are correct as they represent recommended best practices for resolving dependencies effectively within Microsoft Power Platform, focusing on prioritization, review, repository management, and impact analysis.

Option C, while potentially beneficial, may not always be feasible or necessary for all organizations.

QUESTION 14

Answer - [A, B, C, D] Limit the number of fields on a single form to improve readability, Utilize tabbed layouts to organize related fields and reduce clutter, Apply consistent styling and branding across all forms for visual coherence, Implement responsive design principles to ensure compatibility with various devices

Options A, B, C, and D are correct as they represent recommended best practices for user interface design in model-driven apps, including readability improvement, organization, visual coherence, and responsiveness.

Option E, while potentially beneficial, is not a common practice for user interface design in model-driven apps.

QUESTION 15

Answer - [B] and [C].

A) Business rules cannot directly access external data.

B) Business rules can enable or disable a column dynamically based on donor contribution level, facilitating effective donor management and targeted fundraising efforts.

C) Business rules can show or hide a column based on user role, ensuring that staff members have access to relevant donor information for their roles, thereby improving user experience and fundraising efficiency.

QUESTION 16

Answer - [A, B, C, D, E] Ensure secure authentication and authorization mechanisms for accessing data, Optimize data retrieval and processing to minimize latency and improve performance, Handle data synchronization and conflict resolution in scenarios involving multiple sources, Implement caching strategies to reduce the number of requests made to external APIs, Utilize API versioning and error handling mechanisms to maintain compatibility and reliability

Options A, B, C, D, and E are correct as they represent considerations for integrating data sources in a canvas app, including security, performance optimization, data synchronization, caching, and error handling.

QUESTION 17

Answer - [A, C, D, E] Leveraging solutions packaging to bundle and distribute components along with associated metadata, Establishing a centralized component repository with versioning support for easy access and updates, Utilizing import/export capabilities to transfer components between development and production environments, Integrating automated deployment pipelines to streamline the deployment process for shared components

Options A, C, D, and E represent effective strategies for sharing components across different Power Apps instances, including solutions packaging, centralized repositories, import/export capabilities, and automated deployment pipelines.

Option B, while relevant, focuses more on access control rather than sharing mechanisms.

QUESTION 18

Answer - [B] Custom process action.

A) Custom APIs are typically used for integrating external systems or services with the Power Platform but do not provide user-specific execution control.

B) Custom process actions allow developers to define custom actions that can be executed by specific users, making them suitable for restricting code execution to users with asset manager roles. This ensures that only authorized personnel, such as asset managers, can execute the custom code, maintaining data security and accuracy within the asset management system.

C) Classic workflows are automation processes but do not offer the capability to control code execution based on user roles or privileges.

D) Business rules are used for implementing simple business logic within the app's user interface but do not involve executing custom code on the ribbon.

QUESTION 19

Answer - [B, D] Encrypt all data transmitted between Power Apps and the API endpoints, Implement OAuth 2.0 for secure authorization and token management

A) Use API keys for authentication to simplify the integration process - API keys may provide basic authentication but lack the security features offered by OAuth 2.0.

B) Encrypt all data transmitted between Power Apps and the API endpoints - Encrypting data transmission helps protect sensitive information from unauthorized access during transit.

C) Store API credentials directly in the app configuration for convenience - Storing API credentials directly in the app configuration poses a security risk, as they may be compromised if the app is accessed or intercepted.

D) Implement OAuth 2.0 for secure authorization and token management - OAuth 2.0 provides robust security features for API authentication and authorization, including secure token management.

E) Disable all security measures to optimize performance - Disabling security measures introduces vulnerabilities and compromises data integrity, making it an unsuitable option for sensitive customer data.

QUESTION 20

Answer - D

Option A - Incorrect: Syntax issues with getControl and setVisible.

Option B - Incorrect: Direct DOM manipulation not recommended.

Option C - Incorrect: Uses deprecated API.

Option D - Correct: Proper usage of the current client API.

Option E - Incorrect: jQuery is not standard in model-driven apps.

QUESTION 21

Answer - [B] Custom connector
[C] Custom API
[D] HTTP request.

B) Custom connectors enable easy and streamlined integration between Microsoft Dataverse and external systems like the customer support system's SOAP API, ensuring seamless access to customer data within the CRM solution.

C) Custom APIs offer tailored integration solutions, allowing direct communication between Microsoft Dataverse and the SOAP API of the external customer support system, ensuring data consistency and reliability in the CRM solution.

D) HTTP requests can facilitate data exchange and communication between the CRM solution in Microsoft Dataverse and the SOAP API of the external customer support system, supporting seamless integration and access to customer data.

QUESTION 22

Answer - [A] Reviewing the browser console for JavaScript errors

A) Reviewing the browser console for JavaScript errors - This is a standard practice for identifying JavaScript errors, making it the correct answer.

B) Enabling verbose logging in the canvas app settings - While verbose logging may provide additional information, it's not typically used for troubleshooting event handling issues specifically.

C) Inspecting network requests in the browser developer tools - Network requests are unrelated to event handling, so this approach is not applicable for troubleshooting event handling issues.

D) Using the Power Apps formula bar to debug event handling logic - The formula bar is primarily used for Power Apps formulas, not JavaScript event handling code.

E) Analyzing user session data in Azure Monitor - While Azure Monitor can provide insights into app performance, it's not specifically geared toward troubleshooting JavaScript event handling issues within Power Apps.

QUESTION 23

Answer - [B] Access entity attributes directly through JavaScript functions using dot notation.

A) Utilize the fetchXML query language to retrieve entity attributes dynamically - While fetchXML can be used for querying data, it's not directly related to accessing entity attributes through the Client API object model.

B) Access entity attributes directly through JavaScript functions using dot notation - This is a valid method to access entity attributes within the Client API object model.

C) Query entity metadata through RESTful Web API endpoints for attribute details - While RESTful Web APIs can provide metadata, they are not typically used for direct attribute access within the Client API object model.

D) Use SQL queries to retrieve entity attribute values from the underlying database - Direct SQL queries are not supported in the Client API object model for Power Apps development.

E) Invoke client-side plugins to fetch entity attributes asynchronously for improved performance - Client-side plugins are not typically used for attribute retrieval within the Client API object model and may introduce unnecessary complexity.

QUESTION 24

Answer - [A] Power Apps custom control.

A) Power Apps custom controls offer the flexibility to create interactive controls for visualizing data and supporting user interaction within model-driven apps. They support modern client frameworks like React and Fluent UI, making them ideal for visualizing project timelines and updating milestone statuses directly from the control.

Option B) Power Automate: Power Automate is used for workflow automation and integration but is not suitable for creating custom controls for user interaction within model-driven apps.

Option C) Azure Functions: Azure Functions are serverless compute services used for executing code in response to events but are not meant for creating custom controls in Power Apps.

Option D) Power Virtual Agents: Power Virtual Agents are used for creating chatbots and conversational interfaces but are not suitable for creating custom controls in model-driven apps.

QUESTION 25

Answer - D

Option A - Incorrect: Specifies resources but not context handling.

Option B - Incorrect: Accessibility tag does not control context or resource access.

Option C - Incorrect: Namespace is for organizing but doesn't address context or resource access.

Option D - Correct: Declaring use of 'UserContext' ensures the component can handle user-specific data securely.

Option E - Incorrect: 'contextualdata' capability does not specifically ensure proper user context handling.

QUESTION 26

Answer - [C] Via custom controls added to app screens in the Power Apps Studio.

A) By directly embedding JavaScript code within app formulas - While JavaScript may be used for customization, PCF components are typically consumed as custom controls within Power Apps Studio.

B) Through the importation of compiled binary files - This option does not align with the standard method of consuming PCF components within Power Apps applications.

C) Via custom controls added to app screens in the Power Apps Studio - PCF components are added to app screens as custom controls, allowing for their integration into app designs.

D) By executing SQL queries against component metadata tables - SQL queries are not used to consume PCF components within Power Apps applications.

E) Through RESTful API calls to the component endpoints - PCF components are not typically consumed via RESTful API calls.

QUESTION 27

Answer - [A] Implement throttling logic to dynamically adjust the request rate based on the rate limit imposed by the cloud storage provider's APIs.
Answer - [B] Utilize Azure Functions to parallelize data extraction and loading operations, distributing the workload across multiple instances to stay within the rate limits.

A) Implementing throttling logic allows the integration to dynamically adjust the request rate based on the rate limit imposed by the cloud storage provider's APIs. By monitoring response headers and adjusting the request frequency accordingly, the application can avoid exceeding the rate limits and ensure the successful completion of the data migration.

B) Utilizing Azure Functions to parallelize data extraction and loading operations enables the workload to be distributed across multiple instances, preventing any single instance from exceeding the rate limits imposed by the cloud storage provider's APIs. This approach allows the migration to stay within the rate limits and complete successfully.

Option C) Increase the Azure Logic Apps concurrency control settings: While increasing concurrency may allow more requests to be processed concurrently, it does not address the underlying rate limits imposed by the cloud storage provider's APIs and may lead to continued rate limiting errors.

Option D) Modify the integration workflow to use batch processing: While batch processing may spread the workload over longer periods, it may not be sufficient to stay within the rate limits imposed by the cloud storage provider's APIs and may prolong the data migration process unnecessarily.

QUESTION 28

Answer - [A] Review API request logs to identify failed or erroneous requests.

A) Review API request logs to identify failed or erroneous requests - Analyzing logs helps identify specific integration issues, such as failed requests or unexpected errors.

B) Implement additional error handling within the PCF component code - While error handling is important, reviewing logs provides more targeted insights into integration issues.

C) Analyze network traffic to identify potential connectivity issues - Network analysis is useful but may not directly pinpoint integration issues within the PCF component.

D) Monitor system resource utilization to identify performance bottlenecks - Resource monitoring is valuable but may not address data synchronization issues directly.

E) Verify data mapping and transformation logic between systems for accuracy - Data mapping verification is important but may not reveal underlying integration issues causing inconsistency.

QUESTION 29

Answer - [C] Accessing the organization service to retrieve entity records

A) Querying the database directly using SQL commands - This bypasses the platform security and is not recommended.

B) Retrieving the target entity using early-bound classes - Early-bound classes are not directly related to the plug-in execution context.

C) Accessing the organization service to retrieve entity records - Correct, the organization service is commonly used to interact with entity data in plug-ins.

D) Parsing JSON payloads received in HTTP requests - This is more relevant to web API integration, not plug-in context.

E) Invoking external RESTful APIs to fetch entity data - External APIs are not part of the plug-in execution context.

QUESTION 30

Answer - [B] _contact_value

B) In this context, the _contact_value attribute provides access to the details of the associated contact record. When querying related records in an integration, you should use the _contact_value attribute to access and include the contact's details effectively.

Option A) _contactid - Incorrect: This attribute may contain the GUID of the associated contact record, but it does not provide access to the contact's details.

Option C) _contactid_value - Incorrect: This attribute combination does not exist and would not provide access to the contact's details.

Option D) _contact_name - Incorrect: This attribute contains the display name of the contact record, not its details.

QUESTION 31

Answer - [D] Azure Application Insights

A) Visual Studio Debugger - While useful for debugging, it is not specifically designed for profiling plug-in performance.

B) Azure DevOps Pipelines - Primarily used for CI/CD processes, not performance profiling of plug-ins.

C) Power Platform Admin Center - Provides administration tools but not specific to plug-in performance profiling.

D) Azure Application Insights - Correct, Azure Application Insights offers comprehensive performance monitoring and profiling capabilities for various Azure services, including plug-ins.

E) SQL Server Management Studio - Used for managing SQL Server databases, not for plug-in performance profiling.

QUESTION 32

Answer - [D] Reviewing the Plug-in Registration Tool logs for errors.

A) Manually editing the Dataverse solution XML file - Direct XML manipulation is error-prone and can lead to data corruption or system instability.

B) Restarting the Plug-in Registration service - Restarting services may not address underlying registration issues and can disrupt ongoing operations.

C) Deleting all existing plug-ins and re-registering them - Drastic measures like deleting plug-ins should be avoided without proper investigation.

D) Reviewing the Plug-in Registration Tool logs for errors - Correct, examining logs helps identify specific issues encountered during registration for targeted troubleshooting.

E) Disabling assembly verification for faster registration - Disabling verification compromises system integrity and security, making it an unsuitable solution.

QUESTION 33

Answer - A) POST

A) POST - Correct. Appropriate for sending data to server to create/update resources.
B) GET - Incorrect. Only retrieves data, does not send.

C) PUT - Incorrect. Replaces all current representations of the target resource.
D) PATCH - Incorrect. Partial modification.
E) TRACE - Incorrect. Echoes the received request.

QUESTION 34

Answer - [B] Defining policy expressions based on specific conditions.

A) Manually updating the connector configuration in the Power Platform Admin Center - Manual updates may introduce human error and maintenance overhead and are not suitable for runtime modification.

B) Defining policy expressions based on specific conditions - Correct, defining policy expressions allows for specifying conditions under which policy templates modify connector behavior at runtime, ensuring flexibility and customization.

C) Creating separate connector instances for each policy - Creating separate instances increases complexity and management overhead, especially for scenarios requiring frequent changes.

D) Disabling connector caching to ensure policy changes take effect immediately - Disabling caching may impact performance and is not necessary for policy changes to take effect.

E) Testing policy changes in a production environment without validation - Testing policy changes in a production environment without validation introduces risks and should be avoided.

QUESTION 35

Answer - A

Option A - Correct: API rate limits are a common issue; implementing a retry policy helps handle this elegantly.

Option B - Incorrect: While possible, type mismatches are less common and typically caught during development.

Option C - Incorrect: Common but involves a different approach involving the Azure portal, not just app registration updates.

Option D - Incorrect: Increasing timeout may help but doesn't address the root cause of timeouts.

Option E - Incorrect: CORS is generally not an issue with server-to-server communications like those in custom connectors.

QUESTION 36

Answer - A) and D)

A) Correct. Ensures the flow attempts to reconnect, critical for maintaining order processing continuity.

B) Incorrect. We need to handle failures, not successes.

C) Incorrect. Skipping failures does not resolve or notify about them.

D) Correct. Ensures stakeholders are informed of non-responses, which is vital for customer service.

E) Incorrect. Increasing timeout may not be effective without a retry strategy.

QUESTION 37

Answer - [D] Rolling back transactions on error occurrence

A) Using bulk delete operations for efficiency - Bulk delete operations may be efficient but are not suitable for ensuring data consistency in transactional scenarios.

B) Committing changes individually to reduce transaction scope - Committing changes individually may increase the risk of partial commits and data inconsistency.

C) Implementing distributed transactions across multiple services - Distributed transactions can introduce complexity and performance overhead and may not be supported by all services.

D) Rolling back transactions on error occurrence - Correct, rolling back transactions on error ensures that changes are not committed if an error occurs, maintaining data integrity.

E) Delaying transaction commits for performance optimization - Delaying commits may introduce latency but does not address data consistency directly.

QUESTION 38

Answer - [D] Leveraging parallel processing to maximize throughput

A) Minimizing batch sizes to reduce memory consumption - While smaller batches may reduce memory usage, they can also increase overhead and decrease processing efficiency.

B) Using synchronous processing for immediate feedback - Synchronous processing may introduce latency and block other operations, reducing throughput.

C) Performing batch operations within a single transaction - Batch operations within a single transaction may increase contention and hinder parallel processing.

D) Leveraging parallel processing to maximize throughput - Correct, parallel processing allows multiple batch operations to execute simultaneously, optimizing resource utilization and throughput.

E) Applying exponential backoff for retrying failed batch requests - Exponential backoff is more suitable for retrying individual requests, not batch operations.

QUESTION 39

Answer - A) and E)

A) Correct. Checks if the 'ReviewDate' is exactly today.

B) Incorrect. Only checks if the date is less than today, not equal.

C) Incorrect. Checks for dates in the future.

D) Incorrect. Only ensures the date is not empty, does not compare it to today.

E) Correct. Covers both conditions when the date is today or earlier.

QUESTION 40

Answer - A)

A) Correct - This C# code initializes an AzureServiceTokenProvider for managed identity authentication, suitable for Power Platform scenarios.

B) Incorrect - PowerShell cmdlet is not specific to troubleshooting authentication issues with managed identities in Power Platform solutions.

C) Incorrect - JavaScript snippet is for initializing managed identity credential, but it lacks troubleshooting context.

D) Incorrect - TypeScript snippet is for default Azure credentials, not troubleshooting managed identity authentication issues.

E) Incorrect - SQL statement is unrelated to troubleshooting managed identity authentication issues in Power Platform solutions.

QUESTION 41

Answer - [A] Restricting access based on user roles and permissions

A) Restricting access based on user roles and permissions - Correct, restricting access ensures that only authorized users can interact with Dataverse data based on their assigned roles and permissions.

B) Enabling anonymous access for public data retrieval - Enabling anonymous access may compromise data security and violate privacy regulations.

C) Utilizing static API keys for authentication - Static API keys may pose security risks if exposed and are not recommended for authentication.

D) Disabling encryption for faster data transfer - Disabling encryption may compromise data security, especially for sensitive information.

E) Allowing open access without authentication for seamless integration - Open access without authentication is risky and exposes data to unauthorized access and manipulation.

QUESTION 42

Answer - C) Certificate based

A) Incorrect. API key is not suitable for secure environments requiring certificates.
B) Incorrect. OAuth 2.0 is for user-specific access control.
C) Correct. Required for secure certificate-based communications.
D) Incorrect. Password-based is less secure and not suitable.
E) Incorrect. SSO is for user credentials, not APIs.

QUESTION 43

Answer - [C] Splitting complex workflows into smaller, modular flows for better error isolation

A) Using a single monolithic flow for all processing steps to simplify management - Monolithic flows can be difficult to manage and may increase the risk of errors impacting the entire process.

B) Implementing periodic manual backups of flow configurations to restore in case of errors - Manual backups introduce delays and may not address the need for real-time error recovery.

C) Splitting complex workflows into smaller, modular flows for better error isolation - Correct, modular flows allow for better error isolation, making it easier to identify and address issues without impacting the entire process.

D) Allowing unrestricted access to sensitive data within flows for faster processing - Allowing unrestricted access to sensitive data violates security best practices and may lead to compliance issues.

E) Using static error handling routines without retries or compensatory actions - Static error handling routines may not adequately address transient errors or provide options for automatic recovery.

QUESTION 44

Answer - [B] Assigning least privileged security roles and permissions to plug-in assemblies

A) Storing sensitive data directly within plug-in code for improved performance - Storing sensitive data directly within code is a security risk and not a best practice.

B) Assigning least privileged security roles and permissions to plug-in assemblies - Correct, assigning the least privileged roles and permissions helps limit potential security vulnerabilities and access to sensitive data.

C) Embedding API keys and credentials within plug-in configurations for easy access - Embedding credentials within configurations is risky and can lead to unauthorized access.

D) Allowing anonymous access to plug-in endpoints to facilitate external integration - Allowing anonymous access can compromise security and is not a best practice.

E) Disabling encryption and data protection features to optimize plug-in performance - Disabling encryption and data protection features reduces security and is not recommended.

QUESTION 45

Answer - A) DELETE

A) Correct. DELETE is the appropriate HTTP method for removing a record.
B) Incorrect. POST is used for creating new records.
C) Incorrect. GET is used for retrieving data.
D) Incorrect. PATCH is used for updating existing records.
E) Incorrect. PUT is used for replacing an existing record entirely.

QUESTION 46

Answer - [A, B, C, D] Increased latency and response times during event processing, Higher resource utilization and potential scalability issues, Impact on overall system throughput and transaction processing rates, Potential bottlenecks in event handling and processing pipelines

A) Increased latency and response times during event processing - Event processing overhead can introduce latency and impact system responsiveness.

B) Higher resource utilization and potential scalability issues - Increased resource consumption may lead to scalability challenges, especially under high event volumes.

C) Impact on overall system throughput and transaction processing rates - Event processing can affect overall system throughput and transaction processing rates.

D) Potential bottlenecks in event handling and processing pipelines - Inefficient event handling pipelines can become bottlenecks in the system architecture.

E) Compatibility issues with legacy systems and custom integrations - While important, compatibility issues are not directly related to performance impacts of event publishing using the Plug-in Registration Tool.

QUESTION 47

Answer - [A, B, C, D] Azure Logic Apps for orchestrating event-driven workflows, Azure Functions with Service Bus triggers for processing high-throughput events, Power Automate for integrating Dataverse events with external systems, Azure Event Grid for routing and filtering Dataverse events to various endpoints

A) Azure Logic Apps for orchestrating event-driven workflows - Logic Apps provide a visual designer for creating automated workflows triggered by events.

B) Azure Functions with Service Bus triggers for processing high-throughput events - Azure Functions offer serverless computing for processing events at scale, with Service Bus triggers supporting reliable message delivery.

C) Power Automate for integrating Dataverse events with external systems - Power Automate enables easy integration with Dataverse events for automated actions and notifications.

D) Azure Event Grid for routing and filtering Dataverse events to various endpoints - Event Grid simplifies event handling by routing events to specific endpoints based on defined filters and subscriptions.

E) Custom-built event listeners using WebSocket protocols for real-time data streaming - While WebSocket protocols offer real-time data streaming capabilities, they may require more development effort compared to managed services like Azure Logic Apps or Event Grid.

QUESTION 48

Answer - A) createTimer() method

A) Correct. createTimer() method allows for setting up timers that can manage recurring tasks in an orchestrator function.
B) Incorrect. Task.Delay() is for simple, non-recurring delays.
C) Incorrect. setInterval() is for JavaScript and not for durable functions.
D) Incorrect. scheduleReinspection() does not exist as a method.
E) Incorrect. setTimeout() is not suitable for recurring tasks.

QUESTION 49

Answer - [A, B, C, D] Identify unique identifiers to determine whether records should be inserted or updated, Cleanse and standardize data to ensure consistency and accuracy across systems, Validate data against predefined business rules to prevent errors during upsert operations, Map fields between source and target systems to facilitate data transformation during synchronization.

A) Identify unique identifiers to determine whether records should be inserted or updated. - Understanding unique identifiers helps determine whether incoming data should result in new record creation or existing record update during upsert operations.

B) Cleanse and standardize data to ensure consistency and accuracy across systems. - Data cleansing improves data quality and ensures that upsert operations are based on reliable and standardized data.

C) Validate data against predefined business rules to prevent errors during upsert operations. - Data validation helps identify and rectify errors before performing upsert operations, reducing the likelihood of data inconsistencies.

D) Map fields between source and target systems to facilitate data transformation during synchronization. - Field mapping ensures that data from different sources is correctly mapped to corresponding fields in Dataverse, enabling seamless data transformation during synchronization.

E) Optimize data structures and indexes in Dataverse to improve upsert performance. - While data optimization can enhance overall system performance, it's not directly related to preparing data for upsert operations.

QUESTION 50

Answer - [A, B] Leveraging Azure Monitor to track performance metrics and detect issues in real-time, Implementing custom logging and telemetry to capture integration activity and errors.

A) Leveraging Azure Monitor to track performance metrics and detect issues in real-time. - Azure Monitor provides comprehensive monitoring capabilities, including real-time tracking of performance metrics and the ability to detect issues promptly, making it suitable for monitoring integration health.

B) Implementing custom logging and telemetry to capture integration activity and errors. - Custom logging and telemetry allow for detailed tracking of integration activity and errors, providing insights into integration health and performance.

C) Using Microsoft Dataverse audit logs to monitor data changes and access patterns. - While Dataverse audit logs are useful for tracking data changes, they may not provide the real-time monitoring capabilities required for integration health monitoring.

D) Employing synthetic transactions to simulate integration workflows and identify bottlenecks. - Synthetic transactions are useful for performance testing but may not directly support real-time monitoring of integration health.

E) Configuring anomaly detection algorithms to automatically detect abnormal integration behavior. - While anomaly detection algorithms can help identify abnormal behavior, they may not provide the detailed insights required for comprehensive integration health monitoring.

PRACTICE TEST 9 - QUESTIONS ONLY

QUESTION 1

A company is designing its authentication strategy for a Power Platform solution that integrates with Azure services. They need to ensure seamless user authentication and single sign-on (SSO) across different applications. Which feature of Azure Active Directory (Azure AD) is essential for achieving this objective?

A) Conditional Access policies
B) Identity Protection
C) Seamless Single Sign-On (SSSO)
D) Role-based access control (RBAC)
E) Multi-factor Authentication (MFA)

QUESTION 2

A financial institution is assessing the cost differences between Logic Apps and Power Automate for their transaction processing system. They need to analyze the cost implications of each tool to make an informed decision. Which statement accurately describes the cost differences between Logic Apps and Power Automate?

A) Logic Apps have a pay-per-execution pricing model, while Power Automate offers a subscription-based pricing model.

B) Power Automate has lower upfront costs compared to Logic Apps, but Logic Apps offer more cost-effective scaling options for high-volume workflows.

C) Logic Apps are more cost-effective for long-running workflows, while Power Automate is suitable for short-lived workflows with frequent executions.

D) Power Automate has a usage-based pricing model, while Logic Apps provide fixed pricing tiers based on resource consumption.

E) Logic Apps require additional licensing for integration with external services, whereas Power Automate includes built-in connectors for popular SaaS applications at no extra cost.

QUESTION 3

To ensure timely updates, a timer-triggered Azure Function must run every half-hour between 9 AM and 5 PM on weekdays for a task in Microsoft Dataverse. What cron expression should you use?

A) */30 9-17 * * 1-5
B) 0,30 9-17 * * 1-5
C) 0 */30 9-17 * * 1-5
D) 0/30 9-17 * * 1-5
E) 0,30 9-17 * * MON-FRI

QUESTION 4

A financial services firm is creating Dataverse code components such as plug-ins and Custom APIs to extend the functionality of their Power Platform solution. They need to ensure that the code components are efficient, maintainable, and compliant with industry standards for development.
Which best practices should they follow when creating Dataverse code components? Select THREE.

A) Implement asynchronous processing for long-running operations to prevent blocking user interactions.

B) Use synchronous plug-ins for real-time data validation and enforce immediate business rules.

C) Minimize the use of external dependencies to reduce the risk of compatibility issues and version conflicts.

D) Include error handling and logging mechanisms to facilitate troubleshooting and debugging of code components.

E) Utilize inline code execution within workflows to simplify development and deployment processes.

QUESTION 5

Construct a PowerFx formula to calculate the total price of items stored in a collection with quantity and unit price. Which formula correctly performs this calculation?

A) TotalPrice = Sum(Products, Product.Quantity * Product.UnitPrice)
B) TotalPrice = Collect(Products, Sum(Product.Quantity * Product.UnitPrice))
C) TotalPrice = Sum(Products, Quantity * UnitPrice)
D) TotalPrice = ForAll(Products, Sum(Quantity * UnitPrice))
E) TotalPrice = Sum(Products, Product => Product.Quantity * Product.UnitPrice)

QUESTION 6

In a canvas app used for tracking project tasks, you need to show only tasks that are due within the next week. The app is linked to Microsoft Dataverse. What is the appropriate PowerFx expression for the Items property of the task list?

A) Filter('Tasks', DueDate <= DateAdd(Today(), 7, Days))
B) 'Tasks'
C) Filter('Tasks', DateAdd(DueDate, 7, Days) <= Today())
D) Filter('Tasks', DueDate <= DateAdd(Today(), -7, Days))
E) Collect('UpcomingTasks', Filter(Tasks, DueDate <= DateAdd(Today(), 7, Days)))

QUESTION 7

A consultancy firm specializing in Microsoft Power Platform solutions is advising clients on best practices for configuring column-level security in Dataverse. They need to provide clear guidance on recommended configuration approaches to ensure effective access control and data protection.
What are considered best practices for configuring column-level security in Dataverse? Select THREE.

A) Implement role-based access control (RBAC) to assign access permissions to columns based on users' job roles or responsibilities.

B) Use security roles and privileges to manage access at both the entity and column levels, ensuring consistency and scalability.

C) Minimize the number of security roles and profiles to simplify administration and reduce overhead in managing access controls.

D) Regularly review and update column-level security configurations to align with evolving business requirements and compliance standards.

E) Leverage automated testing and validation procedures to ensure the effectiveness of column-level security controls and identify potential vulnerabilities.

QUESTION 8

A multinational corporation with diverse business units and departments is considering the use of teams within Microsoft Dataverse to improve collaboration and streamline business processes. They need to evaluate the suitability of teams for their organization's size and complexity.
How do teams perform in large organizations with diverse business units compared to smaller organizations? Select THREE.

A) Teams may face scalability challenges in large organizations with numerous departments and business units, leading to increased administrative overhead and complexity in managing team memberships and permissions.

B) Large organizations may benefit from teams' ability to facilitate cross-departmental collaboration and data sharing, enhancing organizational agility and efficiency in project management and decision-making.

C) Teams in large organizations often require additional customization and configuration to align with complex organizational structures and reporting hierarchies, potentially delaying implementation and adoption.

D) Smaller organizations may find teams more suitable due to their simplicity and ease of setup, requiring minimal administrative effort and resources to manage team memberships and permissions effectively.

E) Large organizations may experience performance issues with teams, such as slower load times and increased latency, especially when handling large volumes of data or complex business processes.

QUESTION 9

You are designing a model-driven app in Microsoft Dataverse that includes a custom entity for tracking project tasks. However, users report that they cannot find the custom entity when navigating through the app. What could be potential reasons for this issue? Select the correct answers that apply.

A) The entity is not included in any app navigation menu.
B) The users' security roles do not have privileges to access the custom entity.
C) The entity is marked as "Inactive" in the solution settings.
D) The entity's display name is different from what users expect.
E) The app's metadata cache needs to be refreshed for the entity to appear.

QUESTION 10

A requirement in your project involves creating a custom process automation that triggers upon changes in a Dataverse table. Write a JavaScript function using the Web API to listen for changes on the 'Orders' table and execute a callback function.

A) Xrm.WebApi.online.retrieveMultipleRecords('Orders').then(changes => { callback(changes); });
B) Xrm.WebApi.onChange('Orders', function(update) { callback(update); });
C) document.addEventListener('OrdersOnChange', function(e) { callback(e.detail); });
D) Xrm.WebApi.monitorChanges('Orders', callback);
E) Xrm.WebApi.registerOnChange('Orders', callback);

QUESTION 11

A financial institution is developing a loan approval system using Power Apps and Dataverse. They need to ensure that when a loan application is rejected, certain fields related to the application status are updated accordingly, and an email notification is sent to the applicant. What is the impact of implementing business rules on user experience and data integrity in this scenario?

A) Improved user experience due to real-time validation and feedback
B) Decreased data integrity as business rules may override manual changes
C) Enhanced data integrity by enforcing consistent data entry and validation rules
D) Increased user experience degradation due to server-side processing delays
E) No impact on user experience or data integrity since business rules are optional

QUESTION 12

You are designing a model-driven Power Apps app for a manufacturing company's production tracking system. The app needs to adjust user interface elements based on production stages and employee roles to optimize data entry and management. Which two functionalities can you implement using business rules to address these requirements effectively? Select the correct answers that apply.

A) Automatically clear column values for completed production orders.
B) Enable and disable columns for different user roles.
C) Show and hide tabs based on product categories.
D) Show and hide sections based on production stages.

QUESTION 13

A development team is concerned about the implications of unresolved dependencies within Microsoft Power Platform solutions. What are the potential implications of unresolved dependencies? Select the correct answers that apply.

A) Deployment failures due to missing components
B) Runtime errors and application crashes
C) Data corruption or loss
D) Performance degradation and system instability
E) Security vulnerabilities and unauthorized access

QUESTION 14

Performance optimization is crucial for ensuring responsive and efficient model-driven apps. Which techniques can help optimize performance when configuring forms in model-driven apps? Select the correct answers that apply.

A) Minimize the use of calculated fields and rollup attributes
B) Enable form caching to reduce load times for frequently accessed forms
C) Break complex forms into multiple smaller forms to reduce rendering time
D) Avoid excessive use of subgrids and embedded Power BI components
E) Optimize data retrieval by limiting the number of records displayed on forms

QUESTION 15

You are customizing a form in a model-driven app for a legal firm's case management system. The app aims to streamline case documentation and improve legal workflow efficiency. What are two primary actions that you can perform by using a business rule in this context? Select the correct answers that apply.

A) Access external data.
B) Enable or disable a column based on case status.
C) Show or hide a column based on user role.
D) Run the rule on demand.

QUESTION 16

When configuring security for a canvas app, developers must adhere to best practices to protect sensitive data and ensure compliance with regulations. What are some security best practices to implement in a canvas app? Select the correct answers that apply.

A) Role-based access control (RBAC) to restrict app functionality based on user roles
B) Encryption of data at rest and in transit to prevent unauthorized access
C) Implementation of data loss prevention (DLP) policies to prevent leakage of sensitive information
D) Regular security audits and penetration testing to identify vulnerabilities
E) Use of single sign-on (SSO) to streamline user authentication across multiple apps

QUESTION 17

A technology startup is developing a component library to support rapid prototyping and iterative development of their Power Apps projects. How can they manage version control and updates effectively to ensure seamless integration with evolving app requirements? Select the correct answers that apply.

A) Implementing semantic versioning to communicate the significance of changes and updates to developers

B) Establishing release management processes to review and approve changes before deployment

C) Utilizing dependency management tools to track relationships between components and their dependencies

D) Setting up automated testing and validation pipelines to verify component functionality and compatibility

E) Enabling rollback mechanisms to revert to previous versions in case of compatibility issues or regressions

QUESTION 18

You are developing a model-driven app for an expense tracking system. The app needs to execute custom code when a user interacts with a button on the ribbon. However, only finance managers should have access to this functionality. Which option should you choose to implement this requirement?

A) Custom API
B) Custom process action
C) Classic workflow
D) Business rule

QUESTION 19

A development team is experiencing slow performance when retrieving data from an external database using a custom connector in Power Apps. What approach should they take to optimize the performance of the connector? Select the correct answers that apply.

A) Increase the timeout duration for connector operations
B) Reduce the volume of data retrieved in each request
C) Decrease the number of concurrent requests to the database
D) Implement caching mechanisms to store frequently accessed data locally
E) Upgrade the database server hardware for better performance

QUESTION 20

For performance monitoring in a Canvas app, which tool provides the most detailed insights?

A) App checker in Power Apps Studio
B) Performance Monitor under App settings
C) Use of Console.log in browser developer tools
D) Power Apps Monitor tool
E) Azure Application Insights integration

QUESTION 21

Your organization is deploying a procurement management solution using Microsoft Dataverse. You are tasked with integrating an external procurement system, which exposes a SOAP API, to facilitate procurement workflows within the solution. Considering the integration requirements, which three options should you leverage to create an effective integration solution? Select the correct answers that apply.

A) Azure function
B) Custom connector
C) Custom API

D) HTTP request
E) Business rule

QUESTION 22

A Power Apps developer is tasked with registering event handlers for a canvas app that requires strict adherence to security standards. Which of the following security considerations should the developer keep in mind when registering event handlers?

A) Validate user input within event handlers to prevent injection attacks
B) Restrict event handling logic to trusted domains to mitigate cross-site scripting (XSS) risks
C) Encrypt event handling logic to protect against eavesdropping during transmission
D) Utilize OAuth for authentication when registering event handlers with external services
E) Implement role-based access control (RBAC) for event handling functions to enforce least privilege

QUESTION 23

A Power Apps developer is cautioned about common pitfalls in using the Client API. Which of the following pitfalls should the developer be aware of when working with the Client API object model?

A) Overuse of synchronous operations leading to poor app responsiveness.
B) Dependency on external libraries for core functionality, risking compatibility issues.
C) Relying on undocumented features that may change without notice in future updates.
D) Ignoring data validation and sanitization, exposing apps to security vulnerabilities.
E) Neglecting to optimize queries and data retrieval operations for performance.

QUESTION 24

Your organization is developing a model-driven app for managing sales leads. You need to create a custom control that displays lead conversion metrics and allows users to perform lead qualification actions directly from the control. The control should be reusable across multiple forms and support modern client frameworks like React and Fluent UI. Considering the requirements, which development option should you choose?

A) Power Apps custom control
B) Power BI
C) Power Automate Desktop
D) Power Virtual Agents

QUESTION 25

What should be included in the PCF manifest to handle large data sets efficiently, minimizing load times and improving component responsiveness?

A) <data-set name="largeDataSet" fetch-xml="true" />
B) <paging enabled="true" pageSize="50" />
C) <data-set usage="input" lazy-load="true" />
D) <data-options fetch-xml="true" paging="true" />
E) <data-fetch mode="lazy" />

QUESTION 26

What is a key aspect of monitoring and maintaining deployed PCF components?

A) Monitoring browser cache utilization for component performance.
B) Regularly updating component metadata in the Common Data Service.
C) Analyzing usage telemetry and error logs in Azure Monitor.
D) Optimizing network bandwidth for component data transfer.
E) Encrypting component configuration settings for enhanced security.

QUESTION 27

Your organization is migrating data from a legacy on-premises database to Dataverse tables using a Python script. During the migration process, you encounter errors related to data transformation and mapping discrepancies between the legacy database schema and Dataverse table structure. These errors result in failed data inserts and impact the overall migration progress. What are two possible strategies to address the data transformation and mapping discrepancies and ensure the successful completion of the data migration? Select the correct answers that apply.

A) Implement data validation checks to identify and correct mapping discrepancies before executing data inserts into Dataverse tables.

B) Utilize Python libraries for data manipulation and transformation to reconcile differences between the legacy database schema and Dataverse table structure.

C) Convert the legacy database schema to match the structure of Dataverse tables, ensuring seamless data migration without mapping discrepancies.

D) Parallelize data transformation and loading operations using multithreading or multiprocessing techniques to expedite the migration process and reduce the likelihood of errors.

QUESTION 28

When integrating a PCF component with a legacy ERP system, what best practice should the development team follow to ensure long-term compatibility and maintainability?

A) Implement version control for the PCF component codebase using Git.
B) Document integration requirements and dependencies for future reference.
C) Utilize standardized data formats and protocols for interoperability.
D) Design the integration with backward compatibility for legacy ERP versions.
E) Perform regular code reviews and refactoring to optimize integration performance.

QUESTION 29

A development team is considering the role of the plug-in execution context in logging and debugging within their Power Platform solution. What is a significant role of the context in logging and debugging?

A) It provides detailed error messages in case of exceptions during plug-in execution.
B) The context stores log entries generated by plug-ins for later analysis.
C) It enables real-time monitoring of plug-in execution through Azure Monitor.
D) The context facilitates tracing of plug-in execution steps for debugging purposes.

E) It automatically generates performance metrics for each plug-in invocation.

QUESTION 30

You are configuring a business process flow (BPF) in Microsoft Power Automate for managing sales orders. The BPF involves a custom entity named "Opportunities" with a lookup field to the "Accounts" entity. During the opportunity management process, users need to view the name of the associated account. Which attribute should you reference in the BPF to display the account's name?

A) _accountid
B) _account_value
C) _account_name
D) _accountid_value

QUESTION 31

A Power Platform developer is considering the impact of asynchronous operations on plug-in performance. What is an important consideration regarding asynchronous operations?

A) Asynchronous operations always execute faster than synchronous operations.
B) Asynchronous operations can improve system responsiveness by running in the background.
C) Asynchronous operations do not affect the order of execution compared to synchronous operations.
D) Asynchronous operations are not suitable for long-running tasks.
E) Asynchronous operations guarantee immediate execution upon trigger.

QUESTION 32

When registering custom assemblies using the Plug-in Registration Tool, what is a security consideration?

A) Granting unrestricted access to all plug-ins.
B) Using unencrypted communication channels for registration.
C) Storing sensitive data within assembly metadata.
D) Limiting access to authorized users for registration tasks.
E) Sharing registration credentials openly within the development team.

QUESTION 33

In a scenario where partial updates to an existing entity in Power Platform are needed through JavaScript, which HTTP method should be used?

A) PATCH
B) PUT
C) POST
D) GET
E) DELETE

QUESTION 34

A Power Platform solution requires testing and validation of policy changes made to modify connector behavior. What is a recommended approach for testing and validation in this scenario?

A) Implementing policy changes directly in a production environment.
B) Using a staging environment to test policy changes before deployment.
C) Skipping testing and relying on rollback options if issues arise.
D) Conducting manual validation without testing in a sandbox environment.
E) Reviewing policy changes without testing in a development environment.

QUESTION 35

What is the best practice for maintaining version control of Azure API definitions used in Power Platform custom connectors?

A) Store the API definitions in a GitHub repository and set up automated sync with Power Apps.
B) Keep a manual log of changes and update the custom connector as needed.
C) Use Azure DevOps pipelines to automate deployment of updates to Power Apps.
D) Store definitions directly in Azure Blob Storage and reference them in Power Apps.
E) Version control is unnecessary for API definitions in production environments.

QUESTION 36

For a logistics company integrating real-time shipment tracking via Power Automate, how can you ensure that failures in API communication do not go unnoticed? Select the correct answers that apply.

A) Set up alerts for every API call
B) Implement a retry logic with exponential backoff
C) Add conditional branches based on API response status
D) Log all API responses for audit purposes
E) Set "Configure run after" settings for failure notifications

QUESTION 37

What is a limitation of the Organization service API that developers should consider when designing Power Platform solutions?

A) Inability to perform complex data queries
B) Limited support for asynchronous processing
C) Dependency on server-side code execution
D) Restricted access to certain system metadata
E) Lack of integration with external authentication providers

QUESTION 38

In a Power Platform solution, developers need to analyze performance metrics to identify bottlenecks and optimize system performance. Which tool or service is most appropriate for conducting performance analysis in this scenario?

A) Azure Monitor
B) Power BI
C) Azure Application Insights

D) Azure Data Explorer
E) Log Analytics

QUESTION 39

In a legal firm, a Power Automate flow needs to be triggered when any document in the SharePoint 'Contracts' library is flagged for renewal. Which expressions should be used? Select the correct answers that apply.

A) @equals(triggerBody()?['Flagged'], true)
B) @not(equals(triggerBody()?['LibraryName'], 'Contracts'))
C) @equals(triggerBody()?['ContentType'], 'Contract')
D) @contains(triggerBody()?['Title'], 'Renewal')
E) @and(equals(triggerBody()?['LibraryName'], 'Contracts'), equals(triggerBody()?['Flagged'], true))

QUESTION 40

A manufacturing company is developing a Power Platform solution to monitor and manage its production processes. They want to utilize managed identities for Azure services to ensure secure authentication for data access. The team needs to understand the benefits and limitations of managed identities in the context of Power Platform development and system integrations.

A) TypeScript: const tokenCredential = new ManagedIdentityCredential(clientId);
B) JSON: { "identity": { "type": "UserAssigned" } }
C) PowerShell: az identity create -g MyResourceGroup -n MyIdentity
D) C#: var azureServiceTokenProvider = new AzureServiceTokenProvider();
E) HTML: <input type="button" onclick="createManagedIdentity()" value="Create Managed Identity">

QUESTION 41

In a Power Platform solution, developers are tasked with optimizing flow performance for real-time data processing in Dataverse. What strategy can help achieve this goal effectively?

A) Increasing batch sizes for bulk data processing
B) Utilizing synchronous API calls for immediate response
C) Minimizing connector actions and dependencies
D) Enabling verbose logging for detailed performance analysis
E) Adding additional layers of data validation for accuracy

QUESTION 42

A custom connector in Power Platform needs to access a social media API that uses OAuth 2.0 for authentication. Which authentication type should you select to meet this requirement?

A) API key
B) OAuth 2.0
C) Single sign-on
D) Client certificate
E) Password based

QUESTION 43

A healthcare organization is implementing a Power Platform solution for patient appointment scheduling. They need to ensure that their workflows can handle unexpected errors and recover without manual intervention to avoid disruptions in healthcare services. What technique should they use for error detection and handling in cloud flows?

A) Configuring custom exception handling routines using SQL queries
B) Utilizing built-in error handling capabilities of Power Automate to catch and process errors
C) Redirecting errors to a centralized error reporting database for analysis
D) Disabling error handling to minimize workflow complexity
E) Manually monitoring flow executions for errors and manual intervention

QUESTION 44

A manufacturing company is deploying a Power Platform solution for inventory management. They need to deploy and update plug-ins in production environments efficiently while minimizing downtime. What is a recommended approach for deploying and updating plug-ins in this scenario?

A) Performing live updates to plug-in assemblies without testing in a production-like environment
B) Using Microsoft Dynamics 365 Package Deployer for automated plug-in deployment
C) Manually copying plug-in assemblies directly to production servers for rapid deployment
D) Implementing version control and release management processes for plug-in assemblies
E) Deploying plug-ins during peak business hours to minimize impact on operations

QUESTION 45

How should you handle a scenario where you need to update multiple records in Microsoft Dataverse with a single Web API call to improve performance?

A) Use a batch operation
B) Send multiple PATCH requests concurrently
C) Utilize the ExecuteMultiple request
D) Apply a global PATCH
E) Use the $batch query option

QUESTION 46

An e-commerce company is developing a Power Platform solution to manage product inventory and order fulfillment processes. They encounter common issues when using the Plug-in Registration Tool for event publishing and need to troubleshoot them effectively. What are some common issues to troubleshoot when using the Plug-in Registration Tool for event publishing? Select the correct answers that apply.

A) Configuration errors in event subscriptions and webhook endpoints
B) Plugin registration failures due to invalid assembly references or missing dependencies
C) Runtime exceptions and errors in plugin code execution
D) Event delivery failures or message processing errors
E) Connectivity issues with external systems or services

QUESTION 47

A retail chain is developing a Power Platform solution to manage inventory across multiple stores. They anticipate a high volume of events generated from inventory updates and sales transactions. How can they scale event listeners effectively to handle this volume? Select the correct answers that apply.

A) Implementing auto-scaling mechanisms based on CPU utilization metrics
B) Utilizing serverless architectures such as Azure Functions for event processing
C) Deploying event listeners across multiple geographical regions for load balancing
D) Using Azure Event Hubs partitions to distribute event processing across multiple consumers
E) Implementing message batching and parallel processing techniques for efficiency

QUESTION 48

For a Power Apps application tracking equipment maintenance, you must send a notification three days before scheduled maintenance. Which Azure Durable Function method should you call in the orchestrator function?

A) setTimeout() function
B) createTimer() method
C) Task.Delay() method
D) remindMaintenance() function
E) setInterval() function

QUESTION 49

A logistics company is encountering conflicts during upsert operations in Microsoft Dataverse when multiple systems attempt to update the same records simultaneously. How should they handle conflicts effectively? Select the correct answers that apply.

A) Implement a conflict resolution strategy to prioritize updates based on predefined rules or timestamps.
B) Roll back transactions and retry upsert operations after resolving conflicts manually.
C) Use transaction isolation levels to prevent concurrent updates from interfering with each other.
D) Apply locking mechanisms to prevent other systems from accessing records being updated.
E) Increase the frequency of upsert operations to minimize the likelihood of conflicts.

QUESTION 50

A rapidly growing startup is scaling its integrations to accommodate increasing data volumes and user demands. Which best practice should the company prioritize to ensure scalable integrations? Select the correct answers that apply.

A) Implementing horizontal scaling by adding more resources or instances to handle increased workload.
B) Utilizing asynchronous processing to decouple components and improve scalability.
C) Implementing caching mechanisms to reduce redundant data retrieval and processing.
D) Partitioning data into smaller segments to distribute processing across multiple nodes or instances.
E) Using serverless architectures to automatically scale resources based on demand.

PRACTICE TEST 9 - ANSWERS ONLY

QUESTION 1

Answer - [C) Seamless Single Sign-On (SSSO)]

A) Conditional Access policies - Conditional Access policies provide granular control over access but do not specifically address seamless SSO.

B) Identity Protection - Identity Protection helps detect and mitigate identity-related risks but does not directly enable seamless SSO.

C) Seamless Single Sign-On (SSSO) - SSSO allows users to authenticate once and access multiple applications without re-entering credentials, facilitating seamless SSO.

D) Role-based access control (RBAC) - RBAC controls access based on roles and permissions but does not provide seamless SSO.

E) Multi-factor Authentication (MFA) - MFA adds an extra layer of security but does not directly enable seamless SSO.

QUESTION 2

Answer - [B) Power Automate has lower upfront costs compared to Logic Apps, but Logic Apps offer more cost-effective scaling options for high-volume workflows]

A) Logic Apps have a pay-per-execution pricing model, while Power Automate offers a subscription-based pricing model - Both Logic Apps and Power Automate offer different pricing models, but the choice between them should consider factors beyond just the pricing model, such as workflow complexity and execution frequency.

B) Power Automate has lower upfront costs compared to Logic Apps, but Logic Apps offer more cost-effective scaling options for high-volume workflows - While Power Automate may have lower upfront costs, Logic Apps can be more cost-effective for high-volume workflows due to their scaling options and resource utilization efficiency.

C) Logic Apps are more cost-effective for long-running workflows, while Power Automate is suitable for short-lived workflows with frequent executions - The cost-effectiveness of Logic Apps and Power Automate depends on various factors beyond just the workflow duration, such as execution frequency and resource consumption.

D) Power Automate has a usage-based pricing model, while Logic Apps provide fixed pricing tiers based on resource consumption - Both Logic Apps and Power Automate offer pricing models based on resource consumption, but the specific details of the pricing models may vary.

E) Logic Apps require additional licensing for integration with external services, whereas Power Automate includes built-in connectors for popular SaaS applications at no extra cost - While Logic Apps may require additional licensing for certain integrations, the cost considerations for Logic Apps and Power Automate should include factors beyond just the availability of built-in connectors.

QUESTION 3

Answer - B) 0,30 9-17 * * 1-5

A) Incorrect. This pattern is not valid for Azure cron syntax.
B) Correct. Runs at the start and 30 minutes past each hour from 9 AM to 5 PM on weekdays.
C) Incorrect. This pattern misuses the interval notation.
D) Incorrect. The interval syntax used is incorrect for Azure Functions.
E) Incorrect. Azure cron expressions do not recognize day names like 'MON-FRI'.

QUESTION 4

Answer - A, B, and D) Implement asynchronous processing for long-running operations to prevent blocking user interactions. Use synchronous plug-ins for real-time data validation and enforce immediate business rules. Include error handling and logging mechanisms to facilitate troubleshooting and debugging of code components.

A) - Correct. Implementing asynchronous processing for long-running operations prevents blocking user interactions and enhances the responsiveness of the Power Platform solution.

B) - Correct. Using synchronous plug-ins for real-time data validation ensures immediate enforcement of business rules, maintaining data integrity and consistency.

C) - Incorrect. Minimizing the use of external dependencies may limit functionality and hinder integration with external systems, reducing the flexibility of code components.

D) - Correct. Including error handling and logging mechanisms facilitates troubleshooting and debugging of code components, improving maintainability and reliability.

E) - Incorrect. Utilizing inline code execution within workflows may lead to code duplication and hinder code reuse, complicating maintenance and deployment processes.

QUESTION 5

Answer - E

Option A - Incorrect. Syntax is not correct for PowerFx.

Option B - Incorrect. Collect is not used for summing values.

Option C - Incorrect. Lacks proper reference to Product in the formula.

Option D - Incorrect. ForAll does not perform aggregation.

Option E - Correct. Correctly uses the Sum function with a lambda expression to calculate total price, properly iterating over each product in the collection.

QUESTION 6

Answer - A) Filter('Tasks', DueDate <= DateAdd(Today(), 7, Days))

A) Correct. Filters tasks to show those due within the next 7 days from today.
B) Incorrect. Includes all tasks, not just those due within a week.
C) Incorrect. This expression is backward, and would incorrectly calculate due dates.

D) Incorrect. This sets the condition for tasks due more than a week ago.

E) Incorrect. Collect is not necessary and misapplied in this use case.

QUESTION 7

Answer - A, B, and D) Implement role-based access control (RBAC) to assign access permissions to columns based on users' job roles or responsibilities. Use security roles and privileges to manage access at both the entity and column levels, ensuring consistency and scalability. Regularly review and update column-level security configurations to align with evolving business requirements and compliance standards.

A) - Correct. Implementing role-based access control (RBAC) allows for the assignment of access permissions to columns based on users' job roles or responsibilities, ensuring granular control over data access.

B) - Correct. Using security roles and privileges to manage access at both the entity and column levels ensures consistency and scalability in access control, enabling efficient management of permissions across the organization.

C) - Incorrect. While minimizing the number of security roles may simplify administration, it may not always be feasible or advisable, as different departments or teams may require distinct access permissions.

D) - Correct. Regularly reviewing and updating column-level security configurations helps ensure that access controls remain effective and aligned with evolving business requirements and compliance standards, enhancing data protection and regulatory compliance.

E) - Incorrect. While automated testing can help validate security controls, it may not specifically address column-level security or identify vulnerabilities in access controls.

QUESTION 8

Answer - A, B, and C) Teams may face scalability challenges in large organizations with numerous departments and business units, leading to increased administrative overhead and complexity in managing team memberships and permissions. Large organizations may benefit from teams' ability to facilitate cross-departmental collaboration and data sharing. Teams in large organizations often require additional customization and configuration to align with complex organizational structures and reporting hierarchies.

A) - Correct. Teams may face scalability challenges in large organizations due to the complexity of managing memberships and permissions across numerous departments and business units, potentially leading to increased administrative overhead and operational complexity.

B) - Correct. Despite scalability challenges, large organizations may benefit from teams' ability to facilitate cross-departmental collaboration and data sharing, enhancing organizational agility and efficiency in project management and decision-making.

C) - Correct. Teams in large organizations often require additional customization and configuration to align with complex organizational structures and reporting hierarchies, which may involve more time and resources compared to smaller organizations.

D) - Incorrect. While smaller organizations may find teams easier to manage, this option does not specifically address the challenges or benefits of using teams in large organizations compared to smaller ones.

E) - Incorrect. While performance issues may arise with teams in large organizations, such as slower load times, this option does not fully capture the scalability and customization challenges faced by teams in such environments.

QUESTION 9

Answer - [A], [B], and [D].

C) Inactive status would hide the entity entirely, not just from navigation.

E) Metadata cache refresh would not selectively affect entity visibility.

A) Absence from navigation menus would make the entity inaccessible.

B) Lack of privileges would prevent users from accessing the entity.

D) Discrepancies in display names can confuse users searching for the entity.

QUESTION 10

Answer - A

Option A - Correct: Correct method for retrieving records and potentially handling changes through polling.

Option B - Incorrect: onChange is not a method available in the Xrm.WebApi.

Option C - Incorrect: 'OrdersOnChange' is not a standard event in the Web API.

Option D - Incorrect: monitorChanges is not a recognized method in the Xrm.WebApi.

Option E - Incorrect: registerOnChange is not a method in the Xrm.WebApi.

QUESTION 11

Answer - [C] Enhanced data integrity by enforcing consistent data entry and validation rules

Option C is correct as implementing business rules ensures consistent data entry and validation rules, thereby enhancing data integrity within the loan approval system.

Option A, B, D, and E are incorrect as they do not accurately represent the impact of implementing business rules in this scenario. Business rules generally contribute to improved user experience and data integrity when applied effectively.

QUESTION 12

Answer - [A] and [B].

C) Business rules cannot directly control tab visibility based on product categories, which might require additional customization or integration with other components.

D) Business rules cannot directly control section visibility based on dynamic production stages, which might require more advanced logic or use of other features.

A) Business rules can automatically clear column values for completed production orders, ensuring accurate production tracking and management.

B) Business rules can enable or disable columns based on user roles, providing a secure and efficient data entry experience tailored to different users' responsibilities.

QUESTION 13

Answer - [A, B, C, D] Deployment failures due to missing components, Runtime errors and application crashes, Data corruption or loss, Performance degradation and system instability

Options A, B, C, and D are correct as they represent potential consequences of unresolved dependencies within Microsoft Power Platform solutions, including deployment failures, runtime errors, data issues, and performance problems.

Option E, while a valid concern, is less directly related to unresolved dependencies.

QUESTION 14

Answer - [A, B, D, E] Minimize the use of calculated fields and rollup attributes, Enable form caching to reduce load times for frequently accessed forms, Avoid excessive use of subgrids and embedded Power BI components, Optimize data retrieval by limiting the number of records displayed on forms

Options A, B, D, and E are correct as they represent techniques for optimizing performance when configuring forms in model-driven apps, including minimizing calculations, enabling caching, reducing component usage, and optimizing data retrieval.

Option C is incorrect because breaking forms into smaller forms may not necessarily reduce rendering time and could introduce complexity.

QUESTION 15

Answer - [B] and [C].

A) Business rules cannot directly access external data.

B) Business rules can enable or disable a column dynamically based on case status, facilitating efficient case documentation and ensuring accurate legal records.

C) Business rules can show or hide a column based on user role, ensuring that legal professionals have access to relevant case information for their roles, thereby improving user experience and workflow efficiency.

QUESTION 16

Answer - [A, B, C, D] Role-based access control (RBAC) to restrict app functionality based on user roles, Encryption of data at rest and in transit to prevent unauthorized access, Implementation of data loss prevention (DLP) policies to prevent leakage of sensitive information, Regular security audits and penetration testing to identify vulnerabilities

Options A, B, C, and D are correct as they represent security best practices for configuring a canvas app, including RBAC, encryption, DLP policies, and security audits.

Option E, while useful, is not specifically related to security practices within the canvas app itself.

QUESTION 17

Answer - [A, B, C, D, E] Implementing semantic versioning to communicate the significance of changes and updates to developers, Establishing release management processes to review and approve changes before deployment, Utilizing dependency management tools to track relationships between components and their dependencies, Setting up automated testing and validation pipelines to verify component functionality and compatibility, Enabling rollback mechanisms to revert to previous versions in case of compatibility issues or regressions

Options A, B, C, D, and E outline effective practices for managing version control and updates of component libraries, including semantic versioning, release management, dependency tracking, testing, and rollback mechanisms.

QUESTION 18

Answer - [B] Custom process action.

A) Custom APIs are typically used for integrating external systems or services with the Power Platform but do not provide user-specific execution control.

B) Custom process actions enable developers to define custom actions that can be executed by specific users, making them suitable for restricting code execution to finance managers. This ensures that only authorized personnel, such as finance managers, have access to execute the custom code, maintaining data confidentiality and integrity within the expense tracking system.

C) Classic workflows are automation processes but do not offer the capability to control code execution based on user roles or privileges.

D) Business rules are used for implementing simple business logic within the app's user interface but do not involve executing custom code on the ribbon.

QUESTION 19

Answer - [B, D] Reduce the volume of data retrieved in each request, Implement caching mechanisms to store frequently accessed data locally

A) Increase the timeout duration for connector operations - Increasing the timeout duration may address latency issues but does not directly optimize data retrieval performance.

B) Reduce the volume of data retrieved in each request - Limiting the amount of data retrieved in each request reduces network overhead and improves performance.

C) Decrease the number of concurrent requests to the database - Decreasing concurrent requests may alleviate database load but could lead to slower response times for users.

D) Implement caching mechanisms to store frequently accessed data locally - Caching frequently accessed data locally reduces the need for repeated database queries, improving performance.

E) Upgrade the database server hardware for better performance - While upgrading hardware may provide performance gains, it is not always the most cost-effective solution and may not address underlying inefficiencies in data retrieval.

QUESTION 20

Answer - D

Option A - Incorrect: Good for formula errors, not performance.

Option B - Incorrect: Does not exist as described.

Option C - Incorrect: Useful for debugging, not performance monitoring.

Option D - Correct: Provides real-time performance data.

Option E - Incorrect: Overkill for specific app performance monitoring.

QUESTION 21

Answer - [A] Azure function
[B] Custom connector
[C] Custom API.

A) Azure functions can be utilized to implement custom logic and workflows, facilitating seamless integration between Microsoft Dataverse and the SOAP API of the external procurement system for procurement workflows.

B) Custom connectors provide a standardized and efficient way to connect Microsoft Dataverse with external systems like the procurement system's SOAP API, enabling smooth data exchange and integration for procurement management.

C) Custom APIs offer tailored integration solutions, facilitating direct communication between Microsoft Dataverse and the SOAP API of the external procurement system, ensuring data consistency and reliability for procurement workflows within the solution.

QUESTION 22

Answer - [B] Restrict event handling logic to trusted domains to mitigate cross-site scripting (XSS) risks

A) Validate user input within event handlers to prevent injection attacks - While input validation is important, it's not directly related to security risks associated with event handling logic.

B) Restrict event handling logic to trusted domains to mitigate cross-site scripting (XSS) risks - This is a recommended security practice to prevent malicious code execution in the context of a canvas app, making it the correct answer.

C) Encrypt event handling logic to protect against eavesdropping during transmission - Encryption is important for securing data in transit, but it's not typically applied to event handling logic itself.

D) Utilize OAuth for authentication when registering event handlers with external services - OAuth is more relevant for authentication mechanisms rather than securing event handling logic within a canvas app.

E) Implement role-based access control (RBAC) for event handling functions to enforce least privilege - RBAC is important for access control but may not directly address security risks associated with event handling logic.

QUESTION 23

Answer - [C] Relying on undocumented features that may change without notice in future updates.

A) Overuse of synchronous operations leading to poor app responsiveness - While this can be a concern, it's not specific to the Client API object model and relates more broadly to app design considerations.

B) Dependency on external libraries for core functionality, risking compatibility issues - While external dependencies can introduce risks, it's not a common pitfall specifically associated with the Client API object model.

C) Relying on undocumented features that may change without notice in future updates - This is a common pitfall as undocumented features may not be officially supported and could change unexpectedly, leading to app issues.

D) Ignoring data validation and sanitization, exposing apps to security vulnerabilities - Data validation is important for security but is not inherently tied to the Client API object model.

E) Neglecting to optimize queries and data retrieval operations for performance - While performance optimization is crucial, it's not specific to the Client API object model and applies to various aspects of app development.

QUESTION 24

Answer - [B] Power BI.

B) Power BI is a powerful business analytics tool used for creating interactive visualizations and reports, making it suitable for displaying lead conversion metrics within a custom control. It supports modern client frameworks like React and Fluent UI and can be embedded within model-driven apps for seamless integration.

Option A) Power Apps custom control: While custom controls can provide interactive displays, Power BI offers more advanced analytics capabilities for lead conversion metrics.

Option C) Power Automate Desktop: Power Automate Desktop is a robotic process automation tool used for desktop automation, which is not suitable for displaying lead conversion metrics within a custom control.

Option D) Power Virtual Agents: Power Virtual Agents are used for creating chatbots and conversational interfaces but are not suitable for displaying lead conversion metrics within model-driven apps.

QUESTION 25

Answer - C

Option A - Incorrect: 'fetch-xml' is not an attribute for data-set.

Option B - Incorrect: Paging should be specified within the data-set tag.

Option C - Correct: Enabling lazy-load in the data-set tag optimizes data loading.

Option D - Incorrect: There is no 'data-options' tag in PCF manifest.

Option E - Incorrect: 'data-fetch' and 'mode' are not recognized attributes or tags in PCF manifest.

QUESTION 26

Answer - [C] Analyzing usage telemetry and error logs in Azure Monitor.

A) Monitoring browser cache utilization for component performance - While browser cache utilization may impact performance, it is not specific to monitoring and maintaining PCF components.

B) Regularly updating component metadata in the Common Data Service - Updating metadata is important but not the primary aspect of monitoring and maintaining deployed PCF components.

C) Analyzing usage telemetry and error logs in Azure Monitor - Azure Monitor provides insights into component usage, performance, and errors, facilitating effective monitoring and maintenance.

D) Optimizing network bandwidth for component data transfer - Bandwidth optimization is important but not directly related to monitoring and maintaining PCF components.

E) Encrypting component configuration settings for enhanced security - Encryption enhances security but is not the primary aspect of monitoring and maintaining deployed PCF components.

QUESTION 27

Answer - [A] Implement data validation checks to identify and correct mapping discrepancies before executing data inserts into Dataverse tables.
Answer - [B] Utilize Python libraries for data manipulation and transformation to reconcile differences between the legacy database schema and Dataverse table structure.

A) Implementing data validation checks allows you to identify and correct mapping discrepancies between the legacy database schema and Dataverse table structure before executing data inserts. By validating data against predefined rules and correcting discrepancies, the application can ensure the integrity of migrated data and prevent errors during insertion.

B) Utilizing Python libraries for data manipulation and transformation provides flexible tools to reconcile differences between the legacy database schema and Dataverse table structure. By leveraging built-in functions and libraries, the application can transform data on-the-fly to match the target schema, reducing mapping discrepancies and ensuring successful data migration.

Option C) Convert the legacy database schema: While converting the schema may address mapping discrepancies, it may not be feasible or practical due to potential data loss or complexity.

Option D) Parallelize data transformation: While parallelization may expedite the migration process, it does not inherently address mapping discrepancies and may introduce additional complexity and risk of errors.

QUESTION 28

Answer - [C] Utilize standardized data formats and protocols for interoperability.

A) Implement version control for the PCF component codebase using Git - While version control is important, it focuses on code management rather than compatibility with external systems.

B) Document integration requirements and dependencies for future reference - Documentation is valuable but may not directly impact long-term compatibility.

C) Utilize standardized data formats and protocols for interoperability - Standardization ensures compatibility and reduces the risk of integration issues with legacy systems over time.

D) Design the integration with backward compatibility for legacy ERP versions - Backward compatibility is beneficial but may not address changes in data formats or protocols.

E) Perform regular code reviews and refactoring to optimize integration performance - Code reviews and refactoring are important for maintainability but may not directly address compatibility with legacy systems.

QUESTION 29

Answer - [D] The context facilitates tracing of plug-in execution steps for debugging purposes.

A) It provides detailed error messages in case of exceptions during plug-in execution - While error messages may be part of the context, this is not its primary role in logging and debugging.

B) The context stores log entries generated by plug-ins for later analysis - The context itself does not store log entries; it provides information for logging.

C) It enables real-time monitoring of plug-in execution through Azure Monitor - Azure Monitor is a separate service for monitoring.

D) The context facilitates tracing of plug-in execution steps for debugging purposes - Correct, the context provides information for tracing and debugging plug-in execution.

E) It automatically generates performance metrics for each plug-in invocation - Performance metrics are not directly generated by the plug-in execution context.

QUESTION 30

Answer - [C] _account_name

C) In the context of business process flows (BPFs) and related entities, the _account_name attribute contains the display name of the associated account record. When configuring a BPF to display related information, you should reference the _account_name attribute to ensure that the account's name is displayed correctly.

Option A) _accountid - Incorrect: This attribute may contain the GUID of the associated account record, not the account's name.
Option B) _account_value - Incorrect: This attribute is not typically used to display the name of related records.
Option D) _accountid_value - Incorrect: This attribute combination does not exist and would not represent the account's name.

QUESTION 31

Answer - [B] Asynchronous operations can improve system responsiveness by running in the background.

A) Asynchronous operations always execute faster than synchronous operations - Asynchronous execution may be faster in some scenarios but not always guaranteed.

B) Asynchronous operations can improve system responsiveness by running in the background - Correct, asynchronous operations allow other tasks to proceed while long-running operations are processed in the background, enhancing system responsiveness.

C) Asynchronous operations do not affect the order of execution compared to synchronous operations - Asynchronous operations may execute out of order depending on system resources and workload.

D) Asynchronous operations are not suitable for long-running tasks - Asynchronous operations are suitable for long-running tasks but require careful implementation to avoid performance issues.

E) Asynchronous operations guarantee immediate execution upon trigger - Asynchronous execution may not happen immediately depending on system load and resources.

QUESTION 32

Answer - [D] Limiting access to authorized users for registration tasks.

A) Granting unrestricted access to all plug-ins - Least privilege principles dictate limiting access to only necessary operations.

B) Using unencrypted communication channels for registration - Registration tasks should be conducted over secure channels to prevent data interception or tampering.

C) Storing sensitive data within assembly metadata - Storing sensitive data within metadata exposes it to potential leaks or unauthorized access.

D) Limiting access to authorized users for registration tasks - Correct, restricting access ensures that only authorized personnel can perform assembly registration, reducing the risk of unauthorized modifications.

E) Sharing registration credentials openly within the development team - Credential sharing compromises security and accountability, increasing the risk of unauthorized actions.

QUESTION 33

Answer - A) PATCH

A) PATCH - Correct. Suitable for partial updates to a resource.
B) PUT - Incorrect. Used for full replacements.
C) POST - Incorrect. Generally used to create new entries.
D) GET - Incorrect. Used for retrieving data.
E) DELETE - Incorrect. Used for removing data.

QUESTION 34

Answer - [B] Using a staging environment to test policy changes before deployment.

A) Implementing policy changes directly in a production environment - Implementing changes directly in production increases the risk of downtime and unexpected behavior, violating best practices.

B) Using a staging environment to test policy changes before deployment - Correct, using a staging environment allows for thorough testing and validation of policy changes before deploying them to production, minimizing risks and ensuring smooth deployment.

C) Skipping testing and relying on rollback options if issues arise - Skipping testing increases the likelihood of issues and requires unnecessary reliance on rollback options, which may not always be feasible.

D) Conducting manual validation without testing in a sandbox environment - Manual validation without proper testing increases the risk of overlooking potential issues and may lead to production errors.

E) Reviewing policy changes without testing in a development environment - Reviewing changes without testing does not provide assurance of functionality and may result in unforeseen consequences in production.

QUESTION 35

Answer - C

Option A - Incorrect: Power Apps does not support automated sync with GitHub for API definitions.

Option B - Incorrect: Manual logs are error-prone and not scalable.

Option C - Correct: Azure DevOps provides a robust method for automating and managing deployments and updates.

Option D - Incorrect: While Azure Blob Storage is useful for storage, it does not provide version control capabilities.

Option E - Incorrect: Version control is critical for maintaining consistency and rollback capabilities in production environments.

QUESTION 36

Answer - B) and E)

A) Incorrect. Inefficient to alert every call rather than failures.

B) Correct. Provides a methodical approach to handling API downtime, crucial for logistics operations.

C) Incorrect. Conditional branches help with logic flow but do not ensure notification of failures.

D) Incorrect. Logging is good for audits but doesn't alert to failures.

E) Correct. Specifically addresses the need to inform stakeholders about API failures.

QUESTION 37

Answer - [B] Limited support for asynchronous processing

A) Inability to perform complex data queries - The Organization service API supports complex queries using FetchXML.

B) Limited support for asynchronous processing - Correct, the Organization service API has limited support for asynchronous operations compared to other Power Platform components like Power Automate.

C) Dependency on server-side code execution - The Organization service API allows both client-side and server-side code execution.

D) Restricted access to certain system metadata - Developers typically have access to system metadata needed for customization and development tasks.

E) Lack of integration with external authentication providers - The Organization service API supports various authentication mechanisms, including OAuth.

QUESTION 38

Answer - [C] Azure Application Insights

A) Azure Monitor - While Azure Monitor provides monitoring capabilities, Azure Application Insights offers more detailed performance analysis features.

B) Power BI - Power BI is a business analytics tool and may not provide the level of performance analysis required for system optimization.

C) Azure Application Insights - Correct, Azure Application Insights offers rich performance telemetry and analytics to identify performance bottlenecks and optimize system performance.

D) Azure Data Explorer - Azure Data Explorer is designed for real-time analytics on large volumes of data and may not be the best fit for performance analysis in this scenario.

E) Log Analytics - While Log Analytics can collect and analyze log data, Azure Application Insights offers specialized features for performance analysis.

QUESTION 39

Answer - A) and E)

A) Correct. Checks if the 'Flagged' field is set to true.

B) Incorrect. Checks if it's not in the 'Contracts' library.

C) Incorrect. Checks content type but not the specific flag.

D) Incorrect. Looks for 'Renewal' in the title, not the flag.

E) Correct. Ensures the document is in the 'Contracts' library and flagged for renewal.

QUESTION 40

Answer - A)

A) Correct - TypeScript snippet correctly initializes a managed identity credential, aligning with Power Platform development requirements.

B) Incorrect - JSON represents a user-assigned identity but lacks context on benefits and limitations.

C) Incorrect - PowerShell command is for creating managed identities but does not explain benefits and limitations.

D) Incorrect - C# code initializes AzureServiceTokenProvider, which is not specific to managed identities' benefits and limitations.

E) Incorrect - HTML button click cannot be used to create managed identities and lacks context on benefits and limitations.

QUESTION 41

Answer - [C] Minimizing connector actions and dependencies

A) Increasing batch sizes for bulk data processing - Increasing batch sizes may improve efficiency for bulk processing but may not directly address real-time data processing needs.

B) Utilizing synchronous API calls for immediate response - Synchronous calls may introduce delays and reduce scalability for real-time processing.

C) Minimizing connector actions and dependencies - Correct, reducing the number of connector actions and dependencies helps streamline flow execution and improve performance, especially for real-time processing.

D) Enabling verbose logging for detailed performance analysis - Verbose logging may provide insights but does not directly impact flow performance.

E) Adding additional layers of data validation for accuracy - Data validation is important but may not directly address performance optimization concerns.

QUESTION 42

Answer - B) OAuth 2.0

A) Incorrect. API key does not support OAuth protocols.
B) Correct. OAuth 2.0 is specifically designed for services like social media.
C) Incorrect. Single sign-on is not used directly with OAuth for APIs.
D) Incorrect. Certificates are for machine-based authentication.
E) Incorrect. Password based is not used for social media APIs.

QUESTION 43

Answer - [B] Utilizing built-in error handling capabilities of Power Automate to catch and process errors

A) Configuring custom exception handling routines using SQL queries - Configuring custom exception handling using SQL queries may not be supported or practical within Power Automate.

B) Utilizing built-in error handling capabilities of Power Automate to catch and process errors - Correct, Power Automate provides built-in error handling actions to catch and process errors, allowing for automated recovery and notification processes.

C) Redirecting errors to a centralized error reporting database for analysis - While centralized error reporting can be useful for analysis, it may not provide immediate error recovery capabilities.

D) Disabling error handling to minimize workflow complexity - Disabling error handling increases the risk of disruptions and may lead to manual intervention for error recovery.

E) Manually monitoring flow executions for errors and manual intervention - Manual monitoring introduces delays and may not be scalable for large-scale deployments.

QUESTION 44

Answer - [D] Implementing version control and release management processes for plug-in assemblies

A) Performing live updates to plug-in assemblies without testing in a production-like environment - Performing live updates without testing can lead to unforeseen issues and downtime.

B) Using Microsoft Dynamics 365 Package Deployer for automated plug-in deployment - While the Package Deployer can be used, it may not be the only consideration for deployment.

C) Manually copying plug-in assemblies directly to production servers for rapid deployment - Manual copying can introduce errors and is not recommended for production deployments.

D) Implementing version control and release management processes for plug-in assemblies - Correct, implementing version control and release management ensures controlled deployments and minimizes downtime in production environments.

E) Deploying plug-ins during peak business hours to minimize impact on operations - Deploying during peak hours can increase risk and disrupt operations if issues arise.

QUESTION 45

Answer - A) Use a batch operation

A) Correct. Batch operations allow multiple CRUD operations in a single HTTP request, improving performance.
B) Incorrect. Sending multiple PATCH requests concurrently isn't supported as a single call solution.
C) Incorrect. ExecuteMultiple is a specific operation in some APIs but not standard in Web API.
D) Incorrect. There's no concept of a global PATCH in Dataverse Web API.
E) Incorrect. $batch is used correctly in the context but with the wrong terminology.

QUESTION 46

Answer - [A, B, C, D, E] Configuration errors in event subscriptions and webhook endpoints, Plugin registration failures due to invalid assembly references or missing dependencies, Runtime exceptions and errors in plugin code execution, Event delivery failures or message processing errors, Connectivity issues with external systems or services

A) Configuration errors in event subscriptions and webhook endpoints - Incorrect configuration settings can lead to event subscription failures.

B) Plugin registration failures due to invalid assembly references or missing dependencies - Missing or invalid references can cause registration failures for plugin assemblies.

C) Runtime exceptions and errors in plugin code execution - Bugs or errors in plugin logic can result in runtime exceptions and failures.

D) Event delivery failures or message processing errors - Issues with event delivery or message processing can disrupt event publishing.

E) Connectivity issues with external systems or services - Connectivity problems can prevent communication with external systems or services, impacting event publishing.

QUESTION 47

Answer - [B, C, D, E] Utilizing serverless architectures such as Azure Functions for event processing, Deploying event listeners across multiple geographical regions for load balancing, Using Azure Event Hubs partitions to distribute event processing across multiple consumers, Implementing message batching and parallel processing techniques for efficiency

A) Implementing auto-scaling mechanisms based on CPU utilization metrics - While auto-scaling can help adjust resources dynamically, it may not be as effective for handling sudden spikes in event volume.

B) Utilizing serverless architectures such as Azure Functions for event processing - Serverless architectures offer scalability and cost-effectiveness for processing events, automatically scaling based on demand.

C) Deploying event listeners across multiple geographical regions for load balancing - Distributing event listeners geographically helps distribute the load and reduce latency for consumers.

D) Using Azure Event Hubs partitions to distribute event processing across multiple consumers - Event Hubs partitions allow for parallel processing of events by multiple consumers, improving scalability and throughput.

E) Implementing message batching and parallel processing techniques for efficiency - Message batching and parallel processing help optimize resource utilization and improve overall efficiency when handling high volumes of events.

QUESTION 48

Answer - B) createTimer() method

A) Incorrect. setTimeout() is used for a single delay.
B) Correct. createTimer() can be set to trigger events at specific times, suitable for maintenance reminders.
C) Incorrect. Task.Delay() provides a simple delay mechanism, not scheduled reminders.
D) Incorrect. remindMaintenance() function does not exist.
E) Incorrect. setInterval() is for repeated intervals, not a single reminder.

QUESTION 49

Answer - [A, C] Implement a conflict resolution strategy to prioritize updates based on predefined rules or timestamps, Use transaction isolation levels to prevent concurrent updates from interfering with each other.

A) Implement a conflict resolution strategy to prioritize updates based on predefined rules or timestamps. - Defining rules or timestamps helps prioritize updates and resolve conflicts automatically, reducing manual intervention and ensuring consistency.

B) Roll back transactions and retry upsert operations after resolving conflicts manually. - While manual resolution is an option, it's not efficient for handling conflicts in real-time scenarios and may result in data inconsistencies or delays.

C) Use transaction isolation levels to prevent concurrent updates from interfering with each other. - Transaction isolation levels ensure that concurrent updates do not interfere with each other, reducing the likelihood of conflicts during upsert operations.

D) Apply locking mechanisms to prevent other systems from accessing records being updated. - Locking mechanisms may introduce performance overhead and hinder system scalability, making them less suitable for handling conflicts during upsert operations.

E) Increase the frequency of upsert operations to minimize the likelihood of conflicts. - Increasing the frequency of operations does not address the root cause of conflicts and may exacerbate concurrency issues, leading to more conflicts.

QUESTION 50

Answer - [A, B, D, E] Implementing horizontal scaling by adding more resources or instances to handle increased workload, Utilizing asynchronous processing to decouple components and improve scalability, Partitioning data into smaller segments to distribute processing across multiple nodes or instances, Using serverless architectures to automatically scale resources based on demand.

A) Implementing horizontal scaling by adding more resources or instances to handle increased workload. - Horizontal scaling allows for adding more resources or instances to handle increased workload, ensuring scalability and accommodating growing data volumes and user demands.

B) Utilizing asynchronous processing to decouple components and improve scalability. - Asynchronous processing decouples components and improves scalability by allowing tasks to execute independently, reducing bottlenecks and enhancing scalability.

C) Implementing caching mechanisms to reduce redundant data retrieval and processing. - While caching improves performance, it may not directly address scalability concerns related to handling increasing data volumes and user demands.

D) Partitioning data into smaller segments to distribute processing across multiple nodes or instances. - Data partitioning enables distributed processing across multiple nodes or instances, improving scalability by distributing the workload effectively.

E) Using serverless architectures to automatically scale resources based on demand. - Serverless architectures automatically scale resources based on demand, making them well-suited for accommodating fluctuating workloads and ensuring scalability in dynamic environments.

PRACTICE TEST 10 - QUESTIONS ONLY

QUESTION 1

A financial institution is implementing multi-factor authentication (MFA) as part of its security measures for accessing Power Platform resources. They need to ensure a smooth implementation without compromising user experience. Which consideration is important for the successful implementation of MFA in this scenario?

A) Minimize user authentication frequency
B) Use biometric authentication methods
C) Implement strict lockout policies
D) Require frequent password changes
E) Enable SMS-based authentication

QUESTION 2

A consulting firm is evaluating decision factors for choosing between Logic Apps and Power Automate for their client's workflow automation needs. They need to outline the decision factors based on scenario complexity to make an informed recommendation. Which factor should be considered when assessing the complexity of the scenario to determine whether to use Logic Apps or Power Automate?

A) The availability of pre-built connectors for integrating with third-party services
B) The level of customization required to meet unique business requirements
C) The familiarity of the development team with each tool's interface and capabilities
D) The frequency of workflow updates and the ease of making changes
E) The need for real-time monitoring and alerting capabilities to track workflow performance

QUESTION 3

You need a timer-triggered Azure Function to run at the start of every business hour Monday through Friday for an application in Microsoft Dataverse. What is the appropriate cron expression?

A) 0 * 9-17 * * 1-5
B) 0 0-59 9-17 * * 1-5
C) 0 0 9-17 * * 1-5
D) 0 0 * * 1-5 9-17
E) 0 0 9-17 * * MON-FRI

QUESTION 4

A healthcare organization is outlining the design of automations using cloud flows and real-time workflows to optimize patient care processes and streamline administrative tasks. They need to ensure that the design of automations aligns with industry best practices and regulatory requirements for data privacy and security.
 Which considerations should they take into account when outlining the design of automations using cloud flows and real-time workflows? Select FOUR.

A) Implement data loss prevention (DLP) policies to prevent unauthorized access and leakage of sensitive

patient information.
B) Encrypt data in transit and at rest to safeguard patient confidentiality and comply with privacy regulations.
C) Configure role-based access controls (RBAC) to restrict access to patient records based on user roles and permissions.
D) Monitor workflow execution metrics to identify performance bottlenecks and optimize automation efficiency.
E) Integrate with external services securely using OAuth authentication and encrypted connections to ensure data integrity during transmission.

QUESTION 5

Implement a function to authenticate and retrieve a token for a custom connector in C# that interfaces with Dataverse. Identify the correct implementation.

A) public async Task<string> GetToken() { var client = new HttpClient(); var result = await client.PostAsync(tokenUrl, new StringContent("{\"grant_type\":\"client_credentials\"}", Encoding.UTF8, "application/json")); return await result.Content.ReadAsStringAsync(); }

B) public async Task<string> GetToken() { using (var client = new HttpClient()) { var content = new FormUrlEncodedContent(new Dictionary<string, string> { { "grant_type", "client_credentials" } }); var result = await client.PostAsync(tokenUrl, content); return await result.Content.ReadAsStringAsync(); } }

C) public string GetToken() { WebClient client = new WebClient(); return client.UploadString(tokenUrl, "grant_type=client_credentials"); }

D) public async Task<string> GetToken() { var client = new HttpClient(); var content = new StringContent("{\"client_id\":\"your_client_id\",\"client_secret\":\"your_secret\",\"grant_type\":\"client_credentials\"}", Encoding.UTF8, "application/json"); var result = await client.PostAsync(tokenUrl, content); return await result.Content.ReadAsStringAsync(); }

E) public async Task<string> GetToken() { var client = new HttpClient(); var content = new FormUrlEncodedContent(new Dictionary<string, string> { { "client_id", "your_client_id" }, { "client_secret", "your_secret" }, { "grant_type", "client_credentials" } }); var result = await client.PostAsync(tokenUrl, content); return await result.Content.ReadAsStringAsync(); }

QUESTION 6

To enhance user experience in a service request management canvas app, you need to display only those service requests that have been completed. The app utilizes Microsoft Dataverse. Which PowerFx expression is best for the Items property of a list?

A) Filter('ServiceRequests', Status = 'Completed')
B) 'ServiceRequests'
C) Lookup('ServiceRequests', Status = 'Completed')
D) Collect('CompletedRequests', Filter(ServiceRequests, Status = 'Completed'))
E) Filter('ServiceRequests', Completed = true)

QUESTION 7

A financial services company is evaluating the limitations and benefits of implementing column-level security in their Dataverse environment. They need to assess the trade-offs and advantages of this approach to make informed decisions regarding their data protection strategy.
What are the limitations and benefits associated with implementing column-level security in Dataverse? Select THREE.

A) Limitation: Increased complexity and administration overhead. Benefit: Enhanced data protection and access control granularity.

B) Limitation: Potential impact on system performance and response times. Benefit: Improved regulatory compliance and data governance.

C) Limitation: Restricted flexibility in data access and sharing. Benefit: Minimized data exposure and risk of unauthorized access.

D) Limitation: Limited scalability and support for complex security models. Benefit: Streamlined access management and auditability.

E) Limitation: Dependency on user roles and permissions for access control. Benefit: Increased transparency and accountability in data handling.

QUESTION 8

An organization has encountered common issues with team setups within Microsoft Dataverse, impacting collaboration and data management. They need to troubleshoot these issues effectively to restore normal functionality and optimize team performance.
What are common issues encountered with team setups in Microsoft Dataverse, and how can they be addressed? Select correct answers that apply.

A) Inconsistent team membership and permissions may lead to data access issues and security breaches, requiring regular reviews and updates to ensure accuracy and compliance.

B) Lack of clear communication and guidelines for team usage may result in confusion and misuse of team resources, necessitating comprehensive training and documentation for team members.

C) Performance degradation and slow response times may occur with large teams or excessive data sharing, requiring optimization of team configurations and data access controls.

D) Integration challenges with external systems or applications may disrupt data flow and interoperability, necessitating adjustments to integration settings and authentication mechanisms.

E) Data duplication and inconsistency may arise from improper data sharing practices within teams, necessitating data cleanup and validation processes to maintain data integrity and accuracy.

QUESTION 9

You are creating a canvas app in Power Apps that integrates with Microsoft Dataverse to display employee records. However, users report that the app is slow to load and often freezes during usage. What could be potential reasons for this issue? Select the correct answers that apply.

A) The app retrieves too much data at once, causing performance issues.

B) The Dataverse environment is experiencing high server load.
C) There is inefficient use of formula expressions in the app.
D) The app's connection to Dataverse is unstable or slow.
E) Users' devices do not meet the minimum requirements for running the app.

QUESTION 10

To improve data quality and integrity in your Power Apps application, you need to enforce data validation in Dataverse columns using PowerFx. Write a code snippet that ensures the 'Email' column in the 'Contacts' table only accepts valid email addresses.

A) If(IsMatch(TextInput1.Text, "\b[A-Z0-9._%+-]+@[A-Z0-9.-]+\.[A-Z]{2,}\b", IgnoreCase), Patch(Contacts, Defaults(Contacts), {Email: TextInput1.Text}), Notify('Invalid email format', NotificationType.Error))

B) ValidateColumn(Contacts.Email, "\b[A-Z0-9._%+-]+@[A-Z0-9.-]+\.[A-Z]{2,}\b")

C) Contacts.OnValidate('Email', If(IsMatch(TextInput1.Text, '^[A-Z0-9._%+-]+@[A-Z0-9.-]+\.[A-Z]{2,}$', IgnoreCase), Success, Notify('Invalid email format', NotificationType.Error)));

D) SetColumnValidation(Contacts, 'Email', Regex.Match(Email, '^[A-Z0-9._%+-]+@[A-Z0-9.-]+\.[A-Z]{2,}$'))

E) If(!IsMatch(Contacts.Email, "\b[A-Z0-9._%+-]+@[A-Z0-9.-]+\.[A-Z]{2,}\b", IgnoreCase), Notify('Invalid email', NotificationType.Error), Patch(Contacts, Defaults(Contacts), {Email: Contacts.Email}))

QUESTION 11

An insurance company is developing a claims management system using Power Apps and Dataverse. They encounter issues where business rules are not triggering as expected, leading to data inconsistencies. What common issue should the development team investigate when troubleshooting business rule implementation?

A) Incorrect field types configured in business rules
B) Server-side execution disabled for business rules
C) Dependencies on external APIs impacting rule execution
D) Conflicts between multiple business rules applied to the same fields
E) Insufficient user permissions to trigger business rules

QUESTION 12

You are developing a model-driven Power Apps app for a real estate agency's property management system. The app needs to adjust user interface elements dynamically based on property statuses and employee roles to optimize data entry and management. What are two key functionalities that you can implement using business rules to address these requirements effectively? Select the correct answers that apply.

A) Automatically clear column values for sold properties.
B) Enable and disable columns for different user roles.
C) Show and hide tabs based on property types.
D) Show and hide sections based on property statuses.

QUESTION 13

A company is experiencing issues with dependency resolution in their Microsoft Power Platform solutions and needs to troubleshoot common dependency issues effectively. What strategies can be employed to troubleshoot dependency issues within the platform? Select the correct answers that apply.

A) Utilize dependency analysis tools to identify missing dependencies
B) Review solution import logs for error messages related to dependencies
C) Check for circular dependencies between solution components
D) Verify solution metadata to ensure accurate dependency definitions
E) Perform rollback of recent changes to isolate dependency-related issues

QUESTION 14

During the development of a model-driven app, developers may encounter errors or unexpected behavior in forms that require troubleshooting. What are some common issues that developers may need to troubleshoot when dealing with forms in model-driven apps? Select the correct answers that apply.

A) Form layout inconsistencies across different screen resolutions
B) Data validation failures due to misconfigured business rules
C) Performance degradation caused by inefficient JavaScript functions
D) Integration errors with external data sources connected through Power Automate
E) Security vulnerabilities resulting from incorrect entity permissions

QUESTION 15

You are enhancing the user experience of a model-driven app for a consulting company's project management system. The app aims to streamline project tracking and improve team collaboration. What are two key functionalities that you can achieve using a business rule in this scenario? Select the correct answers that apply.

A) Access external data.
B) Enable or disable a column based on project status.
C) Show or hide a column based on user role.
D) Run the rule on demand.

QUESTION 16

During the development of a canvas app, developers may encounter common errors that require troubleshooting to resolve. What are some common errors that developers may encounter, and how can they troubleshoot them effectively? Select the correct answers that apply.

A) Data source connectivity issues due to misconfigured credentials or permissions
B) Formula errors resulting from incorrect syntax or referencing non-existent fields
C) Performance degradation caused by inefficient data retrieval or processing
D) User interface inconsistencies due to improper layout or control placement
E) Authentication failures when accessing external APIs or services

QUESTION 17

A government agency is developing a set of accessibility-focused components for their public-facing Power Apps projects. What compliance considerations should they address when sharing these components across different departments and agencies? Select the correct answers that apply.

A) Ensuring adherence to accessibility standards and guidelines such as WCAG (Web Content Accessibility Guidelines)

B) Incorporating user feedback mechanisms to gather insights on component usability and accessibility

C) Conducting regular accessibility audits and evaluations to identify and address potential issues

D) Providing documentation and training materials to educate developers on accessible design principles and practices

E) Implementing role-based access controls to restrict access to sensitive components and data

QUESTION 18

You are designing a model-driven app for an event management system. The app requires executing specialized code when a user clicks on a button in the app's ribbon. However, this functionality should only be accessible to event coordinators. What option should you select to fulfill this requirement?

A) Custom API
B) Custom process action
C) Classic workflow
D) Business rule

QUESTION 19

A development team is tasked with diagnosing connectivity issues between Power Apps and an external API. Which tool or technique would be most effective for identifying and troubleshooting these connectivity issues?

A) Network packet analysis
B) Application log analysis
C) API performance profiling
D) Endpoint load testing
E) User feedback collection

QUESTION 20

To enhance performance in a model-driven app, you are adding asynchronous JavaScript to defer non-critical operations. Which implementation is correct?

A) setTimeout(() => { Xrm.WebApi.retrieveMultipleRecords("contact") }, 2000)

B) Xrm.Page.data.save().then(() => { Xrm.WebApi.retrieveMultipleRecords("contact") })

C) document.addEventListener('DOMContentLoaded', function() { Xrm.WebApi.retrieveMultipleRecords("contact") })

D) window.onload = async () => { await Xrm.WebApi.retrieveMultipleRecords("contact") }

E) Xrm.Page.data.refresh(true).then(() => { Xrm.WebApi.retrieveMultipleRecords("contact") })

QUESTION 21

Your organization is developing a sales forecasting solution using Microsoft Dataverse. You need to integrate an external sales analytics system, which exposes a SOAP API, to provide advanced analytics capabilities within the solution. Considering the integration requirements, which three options should you employ to ensure a seamless integration solution? Select the correct answers that apply.

A) Azure function
B) Custom connector
C) Custom API
D) HTTP request
E) Business rule

QUESTION 22

A Power Apps developer is considering different methods for registering event handlers in canvas apps. Which of the following represents a potential performance impact associated with certain event handler registration options?

A) Inline event handlers in HTML elements can lead to increased app load times
B) Using addEventListener method can result in memory leaks if not managed properly
C) Defining event handlers within the app's manifest file can introduce compatibility issues with older browsers
D) Attaching event handlers via jQuery can cause conflicts with built-in Power Apps functionality
E) Embedding event handling logic directly in Power Apps controls can limit flexibility for future updates

QUESTION 23

A Power Apps developer is reviewing case studies of complex uses of the Client API object model. Which of the following scenarios best exemplifies a complex use case of the Client API?

A) Implementing a basic form validation logic for mandatory fields in a data entry app.
B) Dynamically generating custom charts based on user-selected data filters in a reporting dashboard.
C) Retrieving static data from an external RESTful API and displaying it in a read-only gallery.
D) Adding simple conditional formatting to highlight overdue tasks in a task management app.
E) Creating a navigation menu with static links to various app sections for improved user experience.

QUESTION 24

Your organization is developing a model-driven app for managing employee onboarding. You need to create a custom control that displays onboarding progress and allows users to complete onboarding tasks directly from the control. The control should be reusable across multiple forms and support modern client frameworks like React and Fluent UI. Considering the requirements, which development option should you choose?

A) Power Apps custom control

B) Azure Logic Apps
C) Power Automate
D) Power Virtual Agents

QUESTION 25

When troubleshooting a PCF component that fails to render correctly, which manifest element is critical to verify first for syntax errors or misconfigurations?

A) <control version="1.0.0" constructor="MyComponent" namespace="MyNamespace" />
B) <manifest id="com.example.mycomponent" version="1.0" />
C) <resources><resource path="index.ts" type="JavaScript" loadBehavior="lazy" /></resources>
D) <properties><property name="text" type="SingleLine.Text" /></properties>
E) <control-resources><resource path="index.js" loadBehavior="preload" /></control-resources>

QUESTION 26

What are best practices for version control when managing PCF component deployments?

A) Storing component code in a local file system without versioning.
B) Using Git or other source control systems to manage code changes.
C) Sharing component deployment packages via email for collaboration.
D) Publishing component updates directly from development environments.
E) Maintaining a single deployment branch for all component versions.

QUESTION 27

Your organization is implementing a data migration strategy to move data from an existing Salesforce instance to Microsoft Dataverse. During the migration process, you encounter errors related to data validation failures, such as missing required fields and invalid data types. These errors prevent certain records from being migrated successfully. What are two possible approaches to address the data validation failures and ensure the successful completion of the migration? Select the correct answers that apply.

A) Configure data transformation rules to automatically map Salesforce fields to corresponding Dataverse fields.

B) Utilize data profiling tools to analyze source data and identify discrepancies before initiating the migration.

C) Implement custom validation logic to verify data integrity and enforce compliance with Dataverse schema requirements.

D) Leverage third-party data migration software with built-in error handling capabilities to automatically handle validation failures.

QUESTION 28

A development team is tasked with integrating a PCF component with a third-party SaaS application to enable real-time data exchange. What security measure should the team prioritize to protect sensitive data during integration?

A) Implement OAuth 2.0 for secure authentication and authorization.
B) Utilize data encryption for sensitive fields transmitted between systems.
C) Apply IP whitelisting to restrict access to authorized IP addresses only.
D) Implement multi-factor authentication (MFA) for user access to the PCF component.
E) Utilize role-based access controls (RBAC) to manage data access within the SaaS application.

QUESTION 29

A security team is reviewing the use of the plug-in execution context in a Power Platform solution to ensure compliance and minimize risks. What is a critical security consideration when using the context?

A) Ensuring that sensitive data is encrypted before passing it through the context.
B) Limiting the privileges assigned to the plug-in user account to prevent unauthorized access.
C) Implementing role-based access control (RBAC) to restrict access to certain entities and fields.
D) Validating input parameters passed through the context to prevent injection attacks.
E) Using OAuth authentication for secure access to external services accessed through the context.

QUESTION 30

You are developing a custom connector in Microsoft Power Apps to integrate with an external API. The connector interacts with a custom entity named "Tickets" in Microsoft Dataverse. When retrieving ticket records, you need to include the name of the associated "Customers." What attribute should you include in your custom connector to retrieve the customer's name along with the ticket details?

A) _customer_name
B) _customerid
C) _customer_value
D) _customerid_name

QUESTION 31

A Power Platform developer wants to optimize data access and processing in plug-ins for improved performance. What is a recommended approach for optimizing data access?

A) Retrieving all data at once to minimize database calls.
B) Implementing pagination for large datasets.
C) Increasing the batch size for data retrieval operations.
D) Utilizing complex join operations for data aggregation.
E) Avoiding caching mechanisms to reduce overhead.

QUESTION 32

A Power Platform development team is considering registering custom assemblies using the Plug-in Registration Tool. What is a potential challenge they might face during this process?

A) Lack of documentation for the assembly's functionality.
B) Incompatibility with legacy plug-ins.
C) Dependency on external libraries not supported by Dataverse.

D) Complexity in configuring assembly deployment settings.
E) Insufficient permissions to access the Plug-in Registration Tool.

QUESTION 33

For a JavaScript function that interacts with an external system to fetch updated data settings without modifying them, which HTTP method is most suitable for the Web API call?

A) GET
B) POST
C) PUT
D) DELETE
E) HEAD

QUESTION 34

A Power Platform development team is tasked with managing policy templates for modifying connector behavior efficiently. What is a best practice for policy management and versioning in this scenario?

A) Sharing policy templates without version control.
B) Creating separate policy templates for each connector instance.
C) Implementing version control for policy templates using source control systems.
D) Modifying policy templates directly in a production environment.
E) Using a single policy template for all connectors without customization.

QUESTION 35

How should you test and validate a newly created custom connector for Azure services in Power Platform?

A) Conduct unit testing within the Azure portal before deploying to Power Apps.
B) Use the Test operation feature in Power Apps to simulate API calls and check responses.
C) Deploy directly to production and monitor with Azure Monitor for issues.
D) Validate only the authentication method without testing actual API calls.
E) Run automated scripts from Power Automate to ensure connector functionality.

QUESTION 36

In an e-commerce platform's order fulfillment flow, if an external payment gateway API fails during transaction processing, how should the flow respond to mitigate customer service issues? Select the correct answers that apply.

A) Retry the transaction automatically
B) Notify customer service of the failure
C) Redirect customers to an alternative payment method
D) Log the failure for later review
E) Set a conditional path that triggers on API failure

QUESTION 37

What optimization technique can developers employ to enhance the performance of data retrieval operations using the Organization service API?

A) Increasing batch size for fetch requests
B) Enabling client-side caching of retrieved data
C) Using server-side paging for large result sets
D) Implementing parallel execution of data queries
E) Limiting the number of attributes retrieved per record

QUESTION 38

Consider an enterprise application built on the Power Platform that requires optimization for performance and concurrency to handle a large volume of transactions. Which approach is most likely to achieve these optimization goals while maintaining data integrity?

A) Implementing row-level locking to ensure data consistency
B) Using asynchronous processing for non-blocking operations
C) Employing long-running transactions for comprehensive data processing
D) Applying synchronous API calls for immediate response
E) Implementing distributed transactions with two-phase commit

QUESTION 39

For a document approval process in a SharePoint site, a Power Automate flow must trigger when a document's 'Confidential' field is marked as true, and it's stored in the 'HR Documents' folder. Which expressions are suitable? Select the correct answers that apply.

A) @equals(triggerBody()?['Confidential'], true)
B) @contains(triggerBody()?['Path'], 'HR Documents')
C) @and(equals(triggerBody()?['Confidential'], true), contains(triggerBody()?['Path'], 'HR Documents'))
D) @not(empty(triggerBody()?['Confidential']))
E) @startsWith(triggerBody()?['Name'], 'Confidential')

QUESTION 40

A retail chain is deploying a Power Platform solution to streamline inventory management across its stores. They want to implement managed identities for Azure services to enhance security and simplify authentication processes. The team needs to understand the use cases and practical applications of managed identities within the context of Power Platform scenarios.

A) C#: ManagedIdentityCredential credential = new ManagedIdentityCredential(clientId);
B) PowerShell: Connect-AzAccount -Identity
C) JavaScript: const msiTokenProvider = new ManagedIdentityCredential();
D) TypeScript: const credential = new DefaultAzureCredential();
E) SQL: CREATE USER [Identity] FROM EXTERNAL PROVIDER;

QUESTION 41

When troubleshooting connectivity and flow issues related to Dataverse connector actions, what initial step should developers take?

A) Reviewing connector configuration settings for errors
B) Disabling antivirus software to test network connectivity
C) Increasing flow concurrency limits for faster execution
D) Restarting the Power Platform environment for a fresh start
E) Deleting and recreating the flow for a clean slate

QUESTION 42

To integrate a custom connector with a cloud storage service using Power Platform, the service requires both an API key for the application and user-specific access tokens via OAuth 2.0. What type of authentication should you configure?

A) API key and OAuth 2.0
B) API key
C) OAuth 2.0
D) Single sign-on and API key
E) Certificate based and OAuth 2.0

QUESTION 43

A manufacturing company is designing a Power Platform solution for production line monitoring. They need to ensure that their workflows incorporate effective flow control actions to manage exceptions and unexpected conditions during operation. What case studies can demonstrate effective flow control in this scenario?

A) Case study showcasing the use of parallel branches for concurrent processing and error handling

B) Case study demonstrating the implementation of exponential backoff retries for resilient error recovery

C) Case study illustrating the integration of Azure Monitor with Power Automate for real-time error detection

D) Case study highlighting the use of conditional branching for dynamic workflow routing based on runtime conditions

E) Case study featuring the implementation of compensatory actions for error recovery and data integrity

QUESTION 44

A retail company is experiencing performance issues with plug-ins in their customer relationship management system. They need to measure and optimize plug-in performance to ensure efficient system operation. What is a recommended approach for measuring and optimizing plug-in performance in this scenario?

A) Analyzing plug-in execution logs in real-time using Azure Monitor

B) Implementing caching mechanisms to reduce database queries and improve plug-in performance
C) Configuring SQL Profiler to monitor database interactions and identify performance bottlenecks
D) Utilizing performance testing tools to simulate load and measure plug-in response times
E) Monitoring plug-in CPU and memory usage using Azure Application Insights

QUESTION 45

To ensure no duplicate records are created when updating data in Microsoft Dataverse, what should you include in your Web API request?

A) Set MSCRM.SuppressDuplicateDetection to true in the PATCH request
B) Use If-Match: * header
C) Pass the CalculateMatchCodeSynchronously parameter
D) Set MSCRM.SuppressDuplicateDetection to false
E) Use the DuplicateDetection parameter

QUESTION 46

A logistics company is developing a Power Platform solution to track shipment status and optimize delivery routes. They need to integrate with third-party logistics providers and other external services when publishing events using the Plug-in Registration Tool. How can the Plug-in Registration Tool be integrated with other services for event publishing? Select the correct answers that apply.

A) Implementing custom HTTP endpoints and webhooks to receive event notifications
B) Leveraging Azure Event Grid for event routing and delivery
C) Using Azure Service Bus queues for reliable event buffering and processing
D) Configuring Azure Functions to process event data asynchronously
E) Integrating with Azure Logic Apps for event-driven workflows and automation

QUESTION 47

An online gaming platform is developing a Power Platform solution to manage user accounts, game sessions, and virtual currency transactions. They prioritize data consistency and reliability to ensure a seamless user experience. What practices can they adopt to ensure data consistency and reliability in event-driven architectures? Select the correct answers that apply.

A) Implementing idempotent event processing to handle duplicate events
B) Using distributed transactions across multiple data sources for atomicity
C) Leveraging message queues with at-least-once delivery guarantees
D) Employing event sourcing patterns to capture and replay state changes
E) Implementing compensating transactions to rollback incomplete operations

QUESTION 48

If you are automating a weekly status update for a Power Apps project management application using Azure Durable Functions, which method is best for setting a timer to run every week in the orchestrator function?

A) createWeeklyTimer() method

B) createTimer() method
C) Task.WeeklyDelay() method
D) setInterval() function
E) setTimeout() function

QUESTION 49

A financial institution is evaluating the performance and scalability considerations of using UpsertRequest for data synchronization between its core banking system and Microsoft Dataverse. What factors should they consider in this evaluation? Select the correct answers that apply.

A) Volume of data to be synchronized and frequency of upsert operations.
B) Network latency and bandwidth availability for transmitting data between systems.
C) Complexity of data transformation and mapping requirements during upsert operations.
D) Availability of resources for monitoring and troubleshooting upsert performance issues.
E) Compatibility of Dataverse environment with external systems for seamless integration.

QUESTION 50

A financial institution aims to reduce costs associated with data integrations while maintaining reliability and performance. Which approach would best help the institution manage and reduce integration costs? Select the correct answers that apply.

A) Implementing data archiving and purging strategies to manage storage costs effectively.
B) Optimizing data transformation processes to minimize resource usage and processing time.
C) Utilizing resource tagging and cost allocation to track and optimize integration-related expenses.
D) Consolidating integration workflows to reduce the number of components and simplify management.
E) Implementing serverless computing to pay only for the resources consumed during integration tasks.

PRACTICE TEST 10 - ANSWERS ONLY

QUESTION 1

Answer - [B) Use biometric authentication methods]

A) Minimize user authentication frequency - While reducing authentication frequency may improve user experience, it may also compromise security.

B) Use biometric authentication methods - Biometric authentication methods provide a balance between security and user experience by offering strong authentication without the need for additional passwords or tokens.

C) Implement strict lockout policies - Strict lockout policies may frustrate users and lead to support issues without significantly enhancing security.

D) Require frequent password changes - Frequent password changes may increase user frustration and decrease security by encouraging weak passwords.

E) Enable SMS-based authentication - SMS-based authentication methods may be susceptible to phishing attacks and may not provide the desired level of security.

QUESTION 2

Answer - [B) The level of customization required to meet unique business requirements]

A) The availability of pre-built connectors for integrating with third-party services - Both Logic Apps and Power Automate offer pre-built connectors, but the decision between them should consider factors beyond just the availability of connectors, such as workflow complexity and scalability.

B) The level of customization required to meet unique business requirements - The complexity of customization needed to meet unique business requirements can be a significant factor in choosing between Logic Apps and Power Automate, as Logic Apps offer more extensive customization options compared to Power Automate.

C) The familiarity of the development team with each tool's interface and capabilities - While team familiarity is important, it should not be the sole factor in choosing between Logic Apps and Power Automate, as other considerations such as workflow complexity and integration capabilities are also crucial.

D) The frequency of workflow updates and the ease of making changes - Both Logic Apps and Power Automate offer capabilities for workflow updates and changes, but the decision between them should consider factors such as ease of maintenance and update frequency.

E) The need for real-time monitoring and alerting capabilities to track workflow performance - Real-time monitoring and alerting capabilities are essential for tracking workflow performance, but both Logic Apps and Power Automate offer similar capabilities in this regard, so this factor alone may not heavily influence the decision between the two tools.

QUESTION 3

Answer - C) 0 0 9-17 * * 1-5

A) Incorrect. This would run every minute of every hour within the range.
B) Incorrect. This expression tries to specify minutes incorrectly.
C) Correct. This triggers the function at the start of every hour from 9 AM to 5 PM, Monday through Friday.
D) Incorrect. This pattern misplaces the time and weekday fields.
E) Incorrect. Azure Functions cron doesn't accept day names like 'MON-FRI'.

QUESTION 4

Answer - A, B, C, and D) Implement data loss prevention (DLP) policies to prevent unauthorized access and leakage of sensitive patient information. Encrypt data in transit and at rest to safeguard patient confidentiality and comply with privacy regulations. Configure role-based access controls (RBAC) to restrict access to patient records based on user roles and permissions. Monitor workflow execution metrics to identify performance bottlenecks and optimize automation efficiency.

A) - Correct. Implementing data loss prevention (DLP) policies helps prevent unauthorized access and leakage of sensitive patient information, enhancing data privacy and security.

B) - Correct. Encrypting data in transit and at rest safeguards patient confidentiality and ensures compliance with privacy regulations such as HIPAA.

C) - Correct. Configuring role-based access controls (RBAC) restricts access to patient records based on user roles and permissions, ensuring data confidentiality and compliance with regulatory requirements.

D) - Correct. Monitoring workflow execution metrics enables the identification of performance bottlenecks and optimization of automation efficiency, enhancing overall workflow performance.

E) - Incorrect. While integrating with external services securely is important, it is not directly related to the design of automations using cloud flows and real-time workflows within the Power Platform.

QUESTION 5

Answer - E

Option A - Incorrect. Lacks client credentials which are necessary for client_credentials grant type.

Option B - Incorrect. Uses form URL encoded content but incomplete without client_id and client_secret.

Option C - Incorrect. WebClient is outdated and method incorrectly formats data.

Option D - Incorrect. JSON content is not typically supported for OAuth token requests which expect URL-encoded form data.

Option E - Correct. Properly includes client_id and client_secret in a URL-encoded form, aligned with OAuth specifications for retrieving a token.

QUESTION 6

Answer - A) Filter('ServiceRequests', Status = 'Completed')

A) Correct. Filters service requests to include only those with a status of 'Completed'.
B) Incorrect. Includes all service requests.
C) Incorrect. Lookup is intended for single records, not for filtering lists.
D) Incorrect. Collect is unnecessary for this purpose.
E) Incorrect. Assumes a 'Completed' boolean field, which is not specified and differs from the provided correct field 'Status'.

QUESTION 7

Answer - A, B, and C) Limitation: Increased complexity and administration overhead. Benefit: Enhanced data protection and access control granularity. Potential impact on system performance and response times. Improved regulatory compliance and data governance. Restricted flexibility in data access and sharing. Minimized data exposure and risk of unauthorized access.

A) - Correct. Implementing column-level security may lead to increased complexity and administration overhead, but it also offers enhanced data protection and access control granularity, providing finer control over who can access specific data columns.

B) - Correct. While column-level security may impact system performance and response times, it can also improve regulatory compliance and data governance by ensuring that sensitive data is adequately protected and access is restricted to authorized users.

C) - Correct. Column-level security may restrict flexibility in data access and sharing, but it also minimizes data exposure and the risk of unauthorized access, enhancing data security and confidentiality.

D) - Incorrect. While scalability may be a concern in some cases, column-level security can still support complex security models, and it can streamline access management and auditability rather than limiting them.

E) - Incorrect. Dependency on user roles and permissions is inherent in access control mechanisms, but it does not necessarily represent a limitation of column-level security, and it may increase transparency and accountability in data handling.

QUESTION 8

Answer - A, B, C, D, and E) Inconsistent team membership and permissions may lead to data access issues and security breaches, requiring regular reviews and updates to ensure accuracy and compliance. Lack of clear communication and guidelines for team usage may result in confusion and misuse of team resources, necessitating comprehensive training and documentation for team members. Performance degradation and slow response times may occur with large teams or excessive data sharing, requiring optimization of team configurations and data access controls.

Integration challenges with external systems or applications may disrupt data flow and interoperability, necessitating adjustments to integration settings and authentication mechanisms. Data duplication and inconsistency may arise from improper data sharing practices within teams, necessitating data cleanup and validation processes to maintain data integrity and accuracy.

A) - Correct. Inconsistent team membership and permissions can lead to data access issues and security breaches, highlighting the importance of regular reviews and updates to ensure accuracy and compliance.

B) - Correct. Lack of clear communication and guidelines for team usage can result in confusion and misuse of resources, emphasizing the need for comprehensive training and documentation to guide team members effectively.

C) - Correct. Performance degradation may occur with large teams or excessive data sharing, underscoring the importance of optimizing team configurations and access controls to improve responsiveness and efficiency.

D) - Correct. Integration challenges with external systems may disrupt data flow, necessitating adjustments to integration settings and authentication mechanisms to ensure seamless interoperability.

E) - Correct. Data duplication and inconsistency can arise from improper data sharing practices, highlighting the need for data cleanup and validation processes to maintain data integrity and accuracy within teams.

QUESTION 9

Answer - [A], [C], and [D].

B) Server load would affect all operations, not just app performance.

E) Device requirements affect usability but not app performance.

A) Overloading with data retrieval impacts app performance.

C) Inefficient formulas can slow down app execution.

D) Slow or unstable connections hinder data fetching, leading to app freezes.

QUESTION 10

Answer - A

Option A - Correct: Correct use of PowerFx for validating an email format before patching the data into the Dataverse.

Option B - Incorrect: ValidateColumn is not a real PowerFx function.

Option C - Incorrect: OnValidate method does not exist in PowerFx.

Option D - Incorrect: SetColumnValidation is not a function in PowerFx.

Option E - Incorrect: Misuse of IsMatch function, should validate before data entry, not after.

QUESTION 11

Answer - [D] Conflicts between multiple business rules applied to the same fields

Option D is correct as conflicts between multiple business rules applied to the same fields can lead to unexpected behavior and data inconsistencies, requiring investigation and resolution.

Option A, B, C, and E may also contribute to issues with business rule execution but are less likely to cause conflicts between rules applied to the same fields. Therefore, Option D is the most common issue to investigate in this scenario.

QUESTION 12

Answer - [A] and [B].

C) Business rules cannot directly control tab visibility based on property types, which might require additional customization or integration with other components.

D) Business rules cannot directly control section visibility based on dynamic property statuses, which might require more advanced logic or use of other features.

A) Business rules can automatically clear column values for sold properties, ensuring accurate property management and tracking.

B) Business rules can enable or disable columns based on user roles, providing a secure and efficient data entry experience tailored to different users' responsibilities.

QUESTION 13

Answer - [A, B, C, D] Utilize dependency analysis tools to identify missing dependencies, Review solution import logs for error messages related to dependencies, Check for circular dependencies between solution components, Verify solution metadata to ensure accurate dependency definitions

Options A, B, C, and D are correct as they represent effective strategies for troubleshooting dependency issues within Microsoft Power Platform, including analysis, log review, circular dependency checks, and metadata verification.

Option E, while a potential troubleshooting step, may not always be practical or necessary for resolving dependency issues.

QUESTION 14

Answer - [A, B, C, D] Form layout inconsistencies across different screen resolutions, Data validation failures due to misconfigured business rules, Performance degradation caused by inefficient JavaScript functions, Integration errors with external data sources connected through Power Automate

Options A, B, C, and D are correct as they represent common issues that developers may encounter when dealing with forms in model-driven apps, including layout inconsistencies, data validation failures, performance issues, and integration errors.

Option E is incorrect because entity permissions are typically managed at a broader level and are less likely to cause form-specific issues.

QUESTION 15

Answer - [B] and [C].

A) Business rules cannot directly access external data.

B) Business rules can enable or disable a column dynamically based on project status, facilitating efficient project tracking and ensuring accurate project information.

C) Business rules can show or hide a column based on user role, ensuring that team members have access to relevant project details for their roles, thereby improving user experience and collaboration efficiency.

QUESTION 16

Answer - [A, B, C, E] Data source connectivity issues due to misconfigured credentials or permissions, Formula errors resulting from incorrect syntax or referencing non-existent fields, Performance degradation caused by inefficient data retrieval or processing, Authentication failures when accessing external APIs or services

Options A, B, C, and E are correct as they represent common errors encountered during canvas app development, including data source connectivity issues, formula errors, performance degradation, and authentication failures.

Option D, while a potential issue, is not commonly associated with errors requiring troubleshooting in canvas apps.

QUESTION 17

Answer - [A, C, D] Ensuring adherence to accessibility standards and guidelines such as WCAG (Web Content Accessibility Guidelines), Conducting regular accessibility audits and evaluations to identify and address potential issues, Providing documentation and training materials to educate developers on accessible design principles and practices

Options A, C, and D highlight compliance considerations related to accessibility when sharing components across different departments and agencies, including adherence to standards, audits, and education.

Options B and E, while relevant, focus more on usability and security aspects rather than accessibility compliance.

QUESTION 18

Answer - [B] Custom process action.

A) Custom APIs are typically used for integrating external systems or services with the Power Platform but do not provide user-specific execution control.

B) Custom process actions enable developers to define custom actions that can be executed by specific users, making them suitable for restricting code execution to event coordinators. This ensures that only authorized personnel, such as event coordinators, have access to execute the specialized code, maintaining data confidentiality and integrity within the event management system.

C) Classic workflows are automation processes but do not offer the capability to control code execution based on user roles or privileges.

D) Business rules are used for implementing simple business logic within the app's user interface but do not involve executing custom code on the ribbon.

QUESTION 19

Answer - [A] Network packet analysis

A) Network packet analysis - Network packet analysis allows developers to inspect network traffic between Power Apps and external API endpoints, making it an effective tool for identifying connectivity issues.

B) Application log analysis - While application log analysis may provide insights into app behavior, it may not specifically pinpoint connectivity issues between Power Apps and external APIs.

C) API performance profiling - API performance profiling focuses on analyzing API performance metrics rather than diagnosing connectivity issues.

D) Endpoint load testing - Endpoint load testing assesses the capacity and performance of API endpoints but does not directly diagnose connectivity issues between Power Apps and APIs.

E) User feedback collection - User feedback collection gathers user opinions and experiences but may not provide technical insights into connectivity issues.

QUESTION 20

Answer - A

Option A - Correct: Uses setTimeout to defer loading.

Option B - Incorrect: save().then() is not for deferring initial loads.

Option C - Incorrect: DOMContentLoaded is not typically used in model-driven apps.

Option D - Incorrect: window.onload with async/await is overly complex for this scenario.

Option E - Incorrect: Uses refresh inappropriately for deferring data retrieval.

QUESTION 21

Answer - [B] Custom connector
[C] Custom API
[D] HTTP request.

B) Custom connectors offer a streamlined integration approach, enabling seamless connectivity between Microsoft Dataverse and the SOAP API of the external sales analytics system for advanced analytics capabilities within the sales forecasting solution.

C) Custom APIs provide tailored integration solutions, facilitating direct communication between Microsoft Dataverse and the SOAP API of the external sales analytics system, ensuring data consistency and reliability for advanced analytics in the sales forecasting solution.

D) HTTP requests can facilitate data exchange and communication between the sales forecasting solution in Microsoft Dataverse and the SOAP API of the external sales analytics system, supporting seamless integration and access to advanced analytics capabilities.

QUESTION 22

Answer - [B] Using addEventListener method can result in memory leaks if not managed properly

A) Inline event handlers in HTML elements can lead to increased app load times - While inline event handlers can impact performance, they are not specifically associated with memory leaks.

B) Using addEventListener method can result in memory leaks if not managed properly - Improper management of event listeners can lead to memory leaks, making this the correct answer.

C) Defining event handlers within the app's manifest file can introduce compatibility issues with older browsers - The app's manifest file typically doesn't contain event handling logic, so this option is not relevant to performance impacts.

D) Attaching event handlers via jQuery can cause conflicts with built-in Power Apps functionality - jQuery usage may introduce dependencies but is not directly linked to memory leaks.

E) Embedding event handling logic directly in Power Apps controls can limit flexibility for future updates - While this option may impact maintainability, it's not specifically related to performance impacts such as memory leaks.

QUESTION 23

Answer - [B] Dynamically generating custom charts based on user-selected data filters in a reporting dashboard.

A) Implementing a basic form validation logic for mandatory fields in a data entry app - While important, basic form validation does not represent a complex use case of the Client API object model.

B) Dynamically generating custom charts based on user-selected data filters in a reporting dashboard - This scenario involves dynamic data manipulation and visualization, showcasing a complex use case of the Client API object model.

C) Retrieving static data from an external RESTful API and displaying it in a read-only gallery - This scenario involves simple data retrieval and display, which is not particularly complex in terms of Client API usage.

D) Adding simple conditional formatting to highlight overdue tasks in a task management app - Conditional formatting is a common feature and does not represent a complex use case of the Client API object model.

E) Creating a navigation menu with static links to various app sections for improved user experience - Static navigation menus are relatively straightforward to implement and do not require complex interactions with the Client API object model.

QUESTION 24

Answer - [A] Power Apps custom control.

A) Power Apps custom controls offer the flexibility to create interactive controls for visualizing data and supporting user interaction within model-driven apps. They support modern client frameworks like React and Fluent UI, making them ideal for displaying onboarding progress and allowing users to complete tasks directly from the control.

Option B) Azure Logic Apps: Azure Logic Apps are used for workflow automation and integration but are not suitable for creating custom controls for user interaction within model-driven apps.

Option C) Power Automate: Power Automate is used for workflow automation and integration but is not suitable for creating custom controls for user interaction within model-driven apps.

Option D) Power Virtual Agents: Power Virtual Agents are used for creating chatbots and conversational interfaces but are not suitable for creating custom controls in model-driven apps.

QUESTION 25

Answer - A

Option A - Correct: Control element is foundational and must be checked for correct attributes like version and constructor.

Option B - Incorrect: While important, the manifest ID and version are less likely to cause render issues.

Option C - Incorrect: Resource loading issues typically cause functionality errors, not render failures.

Option D - Incorrect: Property definitions are crucial but typically don't prevent rendering.

Option E - Incorrect: Resource path and loading behavior impact load time, not necessarily rendering.

QUESTION 26

Answer - [B] Using Git or other source control systems to manage code changes.

A) Storing component code in a local file system without versioning - This approach lacks version control and may lead to confusion and errors during deployments.

B) Using Git or other source control systems to manage code changes - Source control systems like Git enable versioning, branching, and collaboration, making them ideal for managing PCF component deployments.

C) Sharing component deployment packages via email for collaboration - Email collaboration lacks version control and auditability, posing risks to deployment integrity.

D) Publishing component updates directly from development environments - Direct publishing may bypass necessary testing and validation processes, leading to deployment issues.

E) Maintaining a single deployment branch for all component versions - A single deployment branch may hinder parallel development efforts and complicate version management.

QUESTION 27

Answer - [B] Utilize data profiling tools to analyze source data and identify discrepancies before initiating the migration.
Answer - [C] Implement custom validation logic to verify data integrity and enforce compliance with Dataverse schema requirements.

B) Utilizing data profiling tools allows you to analyze source data comprehensively and identify discrepancies or inconsistencies before initiating the migration process. By understanding the data quality issues upfront, you can take corrective actions to address them and ensure a smoother migration experience.

C) Implementing custom validation logic enables you to verify the integrity of data and enforce compliance with Dataverse schema requirements before inserting records. By incorporating validation checks into the migration workflow, you can prevent invalid data from being migrated and ensure the successful completion of the migration.

Option A) Configure data transformation rules: While configuring transformation rules may help map fields, it does not directly address data validation failures or ensure compliance with Dataverse schema requirements.

Option D) Leverage third-party migration software: While third-party software may offer error handling capabilities, relying solely on such tools may not provide the flexibility needed to address specific data validation issues or customize validation logic as required.

QUESTION 28

Answer - [B] Utilize data encryption for sensitive fields transmitted between systems.

A) Implement OAuth 2.0 for secure authentication and authorization - OAuth addresses authentication but may not directly protect data during transmission.

B) Utilize data encryption for sensitive fields transmitted between systems - Data encryption ensures confidentiality during transmission, crucial for protecting sensitive data exchanged between systems.

C) Apply IP whitelisting to restrict access to authorized IP addresses only - While IP whitelisting controls access, it may not directly address data security during transmission.

D) Implement multi-factor authentication (MFA) for user access to the PCF component - MFA enhances authentication but is not directly related to data transmission security.

E) Utilize role-based access controls (RBAC) to manage data access within the SaaS application - RBAC focuses on access control within the application but may not directly address data transmission security.

QUESTION 29

Answer - [B] Limiting the privileges assigned to the plug-in user account to prevent unauthorized access.

A) Ensuring that sensitive data is encrypted before passing it through the context - Encryption is important but not directly related to the plug-in user account privileges.

B) Limiting the privileges assigned to the plug-in user account to prevent unauthorized access - Correct, restricting privileges helps minimize the risk of unauthorized access to sensitive data or system resources.

C) Implementing role-based access control (RBAC) to restrict access to certain entities and fields - RBAC is important but does not directly address the privileges of the plug-in user account.

D) Validating input parameters passed through the context to prevent injection attacks - Input validation is important but not directly related to the plug-in user account privileges.

E) Using OAuth authentication for secure access to external services accessed through the context - OAuth is more about authentication for external services rather than plug-in user account privileges.

QUESTION 30

Answer - [A] _customer_name

A) When retrieving records using a custom connector and interacting with related entities, the _customer_name attribute contains the display name of the associated customer record. You should include the _customer_name attribute in your custom connector to ensure that the customer's name is retrieved along with the ticket details.

Option B) _customerid - Incorrect: This attribute may contain the GUID of the associated customer record, not the customer's name.
Option C) _customer_value - Incorrect: This attribute is not typically used to retrieve the name of related records.
Option D) _customerid_name - Incorrect: This attribute combination does not exist and would not represent the customer's name.

QUESTION 31

Answer - [B] Implementing pagination for large datasets.

A) Retrieving all data at once to minimize database calls - Retrieving all data at once can overload system resources and degrade performance.

B) Implementing pagination for large datasets - Correct, pagination allows for retrieving data in smaller chunks, reducing the load on the system and improving performance.

C) Increasing the batch size for data retrieval operations - Increasing batch size can lead to increased resource consumption and may not optimize performance.

D) Utilizing complex join operations for data aggregation - Complex join operations can increase processing time and may not always be necessary for performance optimization.

E) Avoiding caching mechanisms to reduce overhead - Caching mechanisms can actually improve performance by reducing data retrieval overhead.

QUESTION 32

Answer - [C] Dependency on external libraries not supported by Dataverse.

A) Lack of documentation for the assembly's functionality - While a challenge, it does not directly affect the registration process itself.

B) Incompatibility with legacy plug-ins - Compatibility issues may arise but are not inherent to the registration process.

C) Dependency on external libraries not supported by Dataverse - Correct, reliance on unsupported libraries can hinder assembly registration and functionality within Dataverse.

D) Complexity in configuring assembly deployment settings - Configuration complexity is manageable with proper understanding and documentation.

E) Insufficient permissions to access the Plug-in Registration Tool - Permissions issues can be resolved through proper access management.

QUESTION 33

Answer - A) GET

A) GET - Correct. Best suited for retrieving data without modifying it.
B) POST - Incorrect. Used for sending data that may change state.
C) PUT - Incorrect. Used for updating resources.
D) DELETE - Incorrect. Used for deletion.
E) HEAD - Incorrect. Retrieves headers only, similar to GET but does not fetch body.

QUESTION 34

Answer - [C] Implementing version control for policy templates using source control systems.

A) Sharing policy templates without version control - Sharing templates without version control makes it challenging to track changes and manage updates effectively.

B) Creating separate policy templates for each connector instance - Creating separate templates for each instance increases complexity and management overhead, especially for scenarios requiring policy updates across multiple connectors.

C) Implementing version control for policy templates using source control systems - Correct, implementing version control allows for tracking changes, managing revisions, and collaborating effectively on policy template modifications, ensuring consistency and reliability.

D) Modifying policy templates directly in a production environment - Modifying templates directly in production increases the risk of downtime and unintended consequences, violating best practices.

E) Using a single policy template for all connectors without customization - Using a single template may not accommodate specific connector requirements and lacks flexibility for customization.

QUESTION 35

Answer - B

Option A - Incorrect: Testing within Azure portal does not apply to Power Apps connectors.

Option B - Correct: Power Apps provides a 'Test operation' feature specifically for this purpose, allowing developers to simulate API calls and verify responses directly within the platform.

Option C - Incorrect: Deploying directly to production without testing is highly risky.

Option D - Incorrect: Authentication is important but testing actual API functionality is crucial.

Option E - Incorrect: While automated scripts can help, the primary testing should be done through the Power Apps test feature.

QUESTION 36

Answer - A), B), and E)

A) Correct. Reduces the chance of transaction failure impacting customer experience.

B) Correct. Ensures timely intervention by customer service, critical for maintaining customer satisfaction.

C) Incorrect. Useful, but not directly related to handling API failures within the flow.

D) Incorrect. Logging is important but does not address immediate customer issues.

E) Correct. Automates response mechanisms, essential for managing

QUESTION 37

Answer - [C] Using server-side paging for large result sets

A) Increasing batch size for fetch requests - Increasing batch size may improve efficiency but may not address performance issues related to large result sets.

B) Enabling client-side caching of retrieved data - Client-side caching can improve responsiveness but may not directly enhance server-side performance.

C) Using server-side paging for large result sets - Correct, server-side paging helps manage large result sets efficiently by retrieving data in smaller chunks, reducing memory consumption and improving performance.

D) Implementing parallel execution of data queries - While parallel execution can improve throughput, it may also increase server load and contention.

E) Limiting the number of attributes retrieved per record - Limiting attributes may reduce data transfer overhead but may not directly address performance issues with large result sets.

QUESTION 38

Answer - [B] Using asynchronous processing for non-blocking operations

A) Implementing row-level locking to ensure data consistency - Row-level locking may lead to contention and reduced concurrency, impacting system performance.

B) Using asynchronous processing for non-blocking operations - Correct, asynchronous processing allows concurrent execution of operations without blocking, improving performance and concurrency.

C) Employing long-running transactions for comprehensive data processing - Long-running transactions may increase the risk of deadlock and hinder concurrency.

D) Applying synchronous API calls for immediate response - Synchronous calls may introduce latency and block other operations, impacting performance and concurrency.

E) Implementing distributed transactions with two-phase commit - Distributed transactions can be complex to implement and may introduce latency and coordination overhead, potentially affecting performance and concurrency.

QUESTION 39

Answer - A) and C)

A) Correct. Directly checks if the 'Confidential' field is true.

B) Incorrect. Checks path but does not combine it with the 'Confidential' field.

C) Correct. Ensures both conditions are met: the document is marked as confidential and in the 'HR Documents' folder.

D) Incorrect. Only checks if the field is not empty.

E) Incorrect. Checks document name prefix, irrelevant to the field value.

QUESTION 40

Answer - A)

A) Correct - This C# code initializes a managed identity credential, relevant for Power Platform development.

B) Incorrect - PowerShell cmdlet is for connecting to Azure accounts, not specific to managed identities in Power Platform scenarios.

C) Incorrect - JavaScript snippet initializes managed identity credential but lacks context on practical applications within Power Platform solutions.

D) Incorrect - TypeScript snippet initializes default Azure credentials, not specific to managed identities in Power Platform scenarios.

E) Incorrect - SQL statement is unrelated to managed identities' practical applications within Power Platform scenarios.

QUESTION 41

Answer - [A] Reviewing connector configuration settings for errors

A) Reviewing connector configuration settings for errors - Correct, reviewing configuration settings helps identify misconfigurations or errors that may cause connectivity issues.

B) Disabling antivirus software to test network connectivity - Disabling antivirus software is unnecessary and may pose security risks.

C) Increasing flow concurrency limits for faster execution - Increasing concurrency limits may not directly resolve connectivity issues and could exacerbate performance problems.

D) Restarting the Power Platform environment for a fresh start - Restarting the environment is a drastic measure and may not be necessary for troubleshooting connectivity issues.

E) Deleting and recreating the flow for a clean slate - Deleting and recreating the flow should be a last resort and may result in data loss or disruption of services.

QUESTION 42

Answer - A) API key and OAuth 2.0

A) Correct. Both authentication methods are required for secure application and user access.
B) Incorrect. API key alone does not handle user-specific access.
C) Incorrect. OAuth 2.0 alone does not authenticate the application.
D) Incorrect. SSO is not required here.
E) Incorrect. Certificates are not specified by the cloud service.

QUESTION 43

Answer - [D] Case study highlighting the use of conditional branching for dynamic workflow routing based on runtime conditions

A) Case study showcasing the use of parallel branches for concurrent processing and error handling - While parallel branches can be useful, they may not directly address the need for dynamic workflow routing based on runtime conditions.

B) Case study demonstrating the implementation of exponential backoff retries for resilient error recovery - While retries are important, the case study focuses on conditional branching for workflow routing.

C) Case study illustrating the integration of Azure Monitor with Power Automate for real-time error detection - While Azure Monitor integration is valuable, it may not demonstrate flow control actions directly.

D) Case study highlighting the use of conditional branching for dynamic workflow routing based on runtime conditions - Correct, conditional branching allows for dynamic workflow routing based on runtime conditions, enabling effective flow control and error handling.

E) Case study featuring the implementation of compensatory actions for error recovery and data integrity - While compensatory actions are important, the case study focuses on conditional branching for workflow routing.

QUESTION 44

Answer - [D] Utilizing performance testing tools to simulate load and measure plug-in response times

A) Analyzing plug-in execution logs in real-time using Azure Monitor - While Azure Monitor provides insights, it may not directly measure plug-in performance under load.

B) Implementing caching mechanisms to reduce database queries and improve plug-in performance - Caching can improve performance but may not address all performance issues.

C) Configuring SQL Profiler to monitor database interactions and identify performance bottlenecks - SQL Profiler is useful for database monitoring but may not capture all plug-in performance metrics.

D) Utilizing performance testing tools to simulate load and measure plug-in response times - Correct, performance testing tools can simulate real-world scenarios and measure plug-in response times under load conditions.

E) Monitoring plug-in CPU and memory usage using Azure Application Insights - While monitoring CPU and memory usage is important, it may not provide direct insights into plug-in performance bottlenecks.

QUESTION 45

Answer - A) Set MSCRM.SuppressDuplicateDetection to true in the PATCH request

A) Correct. Setting this header to true helps prevent the creation of duplicates during update operations.
B) Incorrect. The If-Match: * header is used for concurrency control, not duplicate prevention.
C) Incorrect. CalculateMatchCodeSynchronously doesn't relate to duplicate detection.
D) Incorrect. Setting this to false would not suppress duplicate detection.

E) Incorrect. No such parameter exists for this purpose.

QUESTION 46

Answer - [A, B, C, D, E] Implementing custom HTTP endpoints and webhooks to receive event notifications, Leveraging Azure Event Grid for event routing and delivery, Using Azure Service Bus queues for reliable event buffering and processing, Configuring Azure Functions to process event data asynchronously, Integrating with Azure Logic Apps for event-driven workflows and automation

A) Implementing custom HTTP endpoints and webhooks to receive event notifications - Custom endpoints can receive event notifications from the Plug-in Registration Tool.

B) Leveraging Azure Event Grid for event routing and delivery - Event Grid provides scalable event routing and delivery capabilities.

C) Using Azure Service Bus queues for reliable event buffering and processing - Service Bus queues offer reliable message buffering and processing for events.

D) Configuring Azure Functions to process event data asynchronously - Azure Functions can process event data asynchronously for scalability and efficiency.

E) Integrating with Azure Logic Apps for event-driven workflows and automation - Logic Apps enable the creation of event-driven workflows and automation scenarios.

QUESTION 47

Answer - [A, C, D] Implementing idempotent event processing to handle duplicate events, Leveraging message queues with at-least-once delivery guarantees, Employing event sourcing patterns to capture and replay state changes

A) Implementing idempotent event processing to handle duplicate events - Idempotent processing ensures that duplicate events do not result in unintended side effects, maintaining data consistency.

B) Using distributed transactions across multiple data sources for atomicity - Distributed transactions may introduce complexity and performance overhead, and they are not always feasible in distributed systems.

C) Leveraging message queues with at-least-once delivery guarantees - Message queues with at-least-once delivery ensure that events are processed reliably, even in the event of failures or retries.

D) Employing event sourcing patterns to capture and replay state changes - Event sourcing allows for the reconstruction of system state by replaying events, ensuring data consistency and reliability.

E) Implementing compensating transactions to rollback incomplete operations - Compensating transactions are more commonly used in traditional transactional systems and may not align well with event-driven architectures.

QUESTION 48

Answer - B) createTimer() method

A) Incorrect. createWeeklyTimer() method does not exist.
B) Correct. createTimer() method can be configured to fire at weekly intervals, appropriate for weekly

updates.

C) Incorrect. Task.WeeklyDelay() method does not exist.
D) Incorrect. setInterval() is used in JavaScript environments.
E) Incorrect. setTimeout() is for a single time delay setup.

QUESTION 49

Answer - [A, B, C, D] Volume of data to be synchronized and frequency of upsert operations, Network latency and bandwidth availability for transmitting data between systems, Complexity of data transformation and mapping requirements during upsert operations, Availability of resources for monitoring and troubleshooting upsert performance issues.

A) Volume of data to be synchronized and frequency of upsert operations. - The volume and frequency of data synchronization impact performance and scalability, influencing resource allocation and optimization strategies.

B) Network latency and bandwidth availability for transmitting data between systems. - Network performance affects data transmission speed and reliability, influencing overall synchronization efficiency and scalability.

C) Complexity of data transformation and mapping requirements during upsert operations. - Complex data transformation and mapping processes may increase processing overhead and impact upsert performance, requiring optimization and resource allocation.

D) Availability of resources for monitoring and troubleshooting upsert performance issues. - Adequate resources and tools for monitoring and troubleshooting are essential for identifying performance bottlenecks and optimizing upsert operations to ensure scalability.

E) Compatibility of Dataverse environment with external systems for seamless integration. - While compatibility is important for integration, it's not directly related to performance and scalability considerations specific to upsert operations.

QUESTION 50

Answer - [A, C, E] Implementing data archiving and purging strategies to manage storage costs effectively, Utilizing resource tagging and cost allocation to track and optimize integration-related expenses, Implementing serverless computing to pay only for the resources consumed during integration tasks.

A) Implementing data archiving and purging strategies to manage storage costs effectively. - Data archiving and purging help manage storage costs by removing obsolete data and optimizing storage usage, reducing overall integration costs.

B) Optimizing data transformation processes to minimize resource usage and processing time. - While optimizing data transformation processes is important for performance, it may not directly address cost reduction concerns related to integration expenses.

C) Utilizing resource tagging and cost allocation to track and optimize integration-related expenses. - Resource tagging and cost allocation provide visibility into integration-related expenses, allowing for optimization and reduction of costs associated with data integrations.

D) Consolidating integration workflows to reduce the number of components and simplify management.
- While consolidation may simplify management, it may not directly reduce integration costs unless it leads to more efficient resource utilization or licensing optimization.

E) Implementing serverless computing to pay only for the resources consumed during integration tasks.
- Serverless computing allows institutions to pay only for the resources consumed during integration tasks, minimizing costs associated with idle resources and providing cost-efficient scalability.

ABOUT THE AUTHOR

Step into the world of Anand, and you're in for a journey beyond just tech and algorithms. While his accolades in the tech realm are numerous, including penning various tech-centric and personal improvement ebooks, there's so much more to this multi-faceted author.

At the heart of Anand lies an AI enthusiast and investor, always on the hunt for the next big thing in artificial intelligence. But turn the page, and you might find him engrossed in a gripping cricket match or passionately cheering for his favorite football team. His weekends? They might be spent experimenting with a new recipe in the kitchen, penning down his latest musings, or crafting a unique design that blends creativity with functionality.

While his professional journey as a Solution Architect and AI Consultant, boasting over a decade of AI/ML expertise, is impressive, it's the fusion of this expertise with his diverse hobbies that makes Anand's writings truly distinctive.

So, as you navigate through his works, expect more than just information. Prepare for stories interwoven with passion, experiences peppered with life's many spices, and wisdom that transcends beyond the tech realm. Dive in and discover Anand, the author, the enthusiast, the chef, the sports lover, and above all, the storyteller.

Printed in Great Britain
by Amazon